Postdisciplinary Studies in Discourse

Series Editors

Johannes Angermuller
University of Warwick
Coventry, United Kingdom

Judith Baxter
Halescombe House
Minehead, United Kingdom

AF070636

Postdisciplinary Studies in Discourse engages in the exchange between discourse theory and analysis while putting emphasis on the intellectual challenges in discourse research. Moving beyond disciplinary divisions in today's social sciences, the contributions deal with critical issues at the intersections between language and society.

More information about this series at
http://www.springer.com/series/14534

Benno Herzog

Discourse Analysis as Social Critique

Discursive and Non-Discursive Realities
in Critical Social Research

Benno Herzog
Dept of Sociology & Social Anthropology
University of Valencia
Spain

ISBN 978-1-137-56907-3 (hardcover) ISBN 978-1-137-56908-0 (eBook)
ISBN 978-1-349-84930-7 (softcover)
DOI 10.1057/978-1-137-56908-0

Library of Congress Control Number: 2016953470

© The Editor(s) (if applicable) and The Author(s) 2016, First softcover printing 2018
The author(s) has/have asserted their right(s) to be identified as the author(s) of this work in accordance with the Copyright, Design and Patents Act 1988.
This work is subject to copyright. All rights are solely and exclusively licensed by the Publisher, whether the whole or part of the material is concerned, specifically the rights of translation, reprinting, reuse of illustrations, recitation, broadcasting, reproduction on microfilms or in any other physical way, and transmission or information storage and retrieval, electronic adaptation, computer software, or by similar or dissimilar methodology now known or hereafter developed.
The use of general descriptive names, registered names, trademarks, service marks, etc. in this publication does not imply, even in the absence of a specific statement, that such names are exempt from the relevant protective laws and regulations and therefore free for general use.
The publisher, the authors and the editors are safe to assume that the advice and information in this book are believed to be true and accurate at the date of publication. Neither the publisher nor the authors or the editors give a warranty, express or implied, with respect to the material contained herein or for any errors or omissions that may have been made.

Printed on acid-free paper

This Palgrave Macmillan imprint is published by Springer Nature
The registered company is Macmillan Publishers Ltd. London

To all debased, enslaved, abandoned, despicable beings.

Introduction

This book aims to bridge the gap between normative theories and empirical research.

In social science and humanities, we can distinguish roughly three positions towards normativity. Especially in social and political philosophy, we are quite accustomed to scholars who adopt a clear, normative stance, offering compelling arguments for or against certain social and political institutions and ethical behaviour. The main problem is that we can find several, even contradictory, *reasonable* positions. Although the debate between these positions can lead to common views, it does not necessarily do so, and often, there remain reasonable but opposing viewpoints. This may lead to the suspicion that, ultimately, the scholars engaged in these debates are not following universal norms but a particular worldview.

In social science, however, we are quite accustomed to the claim of more or less objective, value-free, or impartial research. Scholars who follow this view often attempt either to describe reality or to encounter causal relations and underlying structures. We can find this approach in both quantitative and qualitative social research. The aim of this approach is to provide the most accurate information about social reality. Normative stances are outside the scope of the descriptions offered by these researchers. The information is provided to political institutions so that they can make informed decisions based on research outcomes and to the civil society that should be empowered through scientific knowledge. Although this approach claims to be value-free, it encompasses at least one normative stance, namely, that it is politics or civil society, not a particular researcher, that *should* decide the future of society. Moreover, having scientific knowledge at hand is *better* than not having that type of knowledge.

A third position combines both approaches. Scholars following this approach conduct empirical research on a social phenomenon and then use a normative position to denounce the encountered situation as unjust. For example, one could describe the structure, causes, and effects of discourses on migration and then denounce a specific discourse as racist. Sometimes the normative stance is defended very openly, but often the arrangement of the results merely presents suggestive images, thus leading the reader to the desired conclusion. This denial of the suggestive force of the presentation of scientific work can mislead some of the scholars working with this approach into seeing themselves as neutral observers.

Independent of whether normative claims and empirical research are presented together or separately, logically they are disconnected from each other in all of the cases described. On the one hand, a particular normative position might be that of a social and political philosopher, political and social groups, or the researcher; on the other hand, we have the sound elaboration of empirical research. In this book, I aim to overcome this division between the normative stance and "objective" social science. This overcoming goes back to the long tradition of immanent critique. The idea can be roughly understood as conducting an empirically sound analysis of the normative content pursued in everyday life by the social actors themselves, thus taking not an own, particular normative stance but the stance (implicitly) followed by the people.

The approach presented in this book aims to combine two intellectual traditions. On the one hand, we see the tradition of the Frankfurt School, with its Critical Theory and its theoretical elaborations of immanent critique. On the other hand, we see the empirical "toolbox" of Foucauldian discourse analysis. Over the last decade, this toolbox has received important input from sociology, broadening its analytical tools and, thus, enabling a combined and structured analysis not only of language use but also of other elements, such as practices or materialities.

These two traditions are clearly visible in the structure of the text. The first chapter, which addresses theoretical approaches to critique, brings us to the logics of immanent critique as present in the tradition of post-Marxism. However, whenever possible, I have attempted to bring this tradition into fruitful contact with Foucault and other post-structuralist authors. The aim of this part is to show the strand of the development of immanent critique and its connection points and controversies with post-structuralist approaches. As we will see, there is an important "empirical deficit" in this philosophically promising tradition.

In the second chapter, I develop the analytical tools that we can use to overcome the "empirical deficit". Although this chapter primarily draws on qualitative sociological discourse analysis in a post-structuralist tradition, its tools are discussed in relation to the previously presented theoretical approach so that they can be made to fit into a coherent approach. This approach, which I call Discourse Analysis as Social Critique, aims at social critique in the tradition of the Frankfurt School but does so with the help of analytical insights from discourse studies.

Although I attempt to develop neither the theory nor the analytical tools as detached from social phenomenon, the first two chapters might seem somewhat abstract, especially to the less-experienced reader. Therefore, the last chapter is dedicated to the presentation of concrete empirical examples. Each example will shed light on a specific aspect of the approach presented. The last chapter is roughly divided into two parts. Whereas the first part presents examples directly related to the first two chapters, the second part gives an outlook on alternative methods of application. It does so by theoretical reflection and practical examples on how aesthetic analysis could be used to perceive the injustices done to muted and therefore socially excluded subjects.

In bridging Critical Theory and post-structuralism, the text invites researchers from both traditions to critically examine the arguments presented in this book. Social critique must be both discussed and applied in empirical work. The discussion of this approach in the context of other theoretical traditions and empirical research in a wide variety of fields is a task that remains to be accomplished. The further development of society's ability to overcome situations of social injustice depends on the intellectual and practical work of its members. In that sense, I hope that this book makes a humble contribution.

Chapter 1

The chapter addresses theoretical approaches to social critique and leads to the logics of immanent critique as present in the tradition of post-Marxism, especially in the Frankfurt School. However, whenever possible, it attempts to bring this tradition into fruitful contact with Foucault and other post-structuralist authors. The aim of this part is to show the strand of the development of immanent critique and its connection points and controversies with post-structuralist approaches. The chapter shows that there is an important "empirical deficit" in the nonetheless promising philosophical tradition of post-Marxism.

Chapter 2

The second chapter develops the analytical tools to overcome the "empirical deficit" of current social critique. Although this chapter primarily draws on qualitative sociological discourse analysis in a post-structuralist tradition, its tools are discussed in relation to the previously presented theoretical approach so that they can be made to fit into a coherent approach. This approach, which is called Discourse Analysis as Social Critique, aims at social critique in the tradition of the Frankfurt School but does so with the help of analytical insights from discourse studies.

Chapter 3

The third chapter is dedicated to the presentation of concrete empirical examples. Each example will shed light on a specific aspect of the approach presented.

This last chapter is roughly divided into two parts. Whereas the first part presents examples directly related to the first two chapters, the second part gives an outlook on alternative methods of application. It does so by theoretical reflection and practical examples on how aesthetic analysis could be used to perceive the injustices done to muted and therefore socially excluded subjects.

Acknowledgements

Research processes often have no real start and only a provisional end. The thoughts presented here are the results of more than ten years of dedication to two strands of research: Critical Theory and Discourse Studies. These two poles also mark the writing process. This book was first conceived during a stay at the Institute for Social Research in Frankfurt in 2014 and was finished at the Centre for Applied Linguistics at the University of Warwick in 2016. I would like to warmly thank the Institute for Social Research, especially Sidonia Blättler and Axel Honneth, for giving me the ability to pursue my research in an intellectually challenging atmosphere. I also would like to thank the Centre for Applied Linguistics at the University of Warwick, especially Johannes Angermuller, Johannes Beetz, Ronny Scholz, Veit Schwab, and the rest of the astonishingly friendly DISCONEX team, for the uncomplicated manner in which they provided me with excellent work conditions. Furthermore, I want to express my gratitude to the University of Valencia, which financially supported both research stays.

I am also deeply in debt to Francesc Hernàndez, who has intellectually accompanied me in my research enquiries for more than ten years. He was and still is an inspiring teacher, an altruistic colleague, and a critical friend.

A special thanks to all of the students in my sociology of language courses and in my critical theory reading group. They showed an enormous interest in the topics treated here and forced me to order, explain, and reshape the arguments presented in this book.

I also want to thank Susana and Clara for their emotional support.

The work leading to this publication is part of the research project entitled "Validity, productivity and challenges of immanent critique in contemporary social philosophy", which is led by José Manuel Romero and financed by the Spanish Ministry of Economy and Competitiveness (FFI2013-47230-P).

Contents

1 Theoretical Approaches to Critique   1

2 Analytical Tools   67

3 Practical Examples   133

4 Conclusions   195

Index   199

List of Figures and Tables

Fig. 2.1	Second-order discourse and first-order elements	73
Fig. 2.2	The logics of structured sociological discourse analysis	122
Table 1.1	Types of critique	29
Table 1.2	Honneth's theory of recognition	47

1

Theoretical Approaches to Critique

1.1 Critique as Social Practice

When beginning to study subjects in social sciences or humanities, we often hear that we have to be "critical". We should "read critically" or write a "critical commentary" about particular issues treated in class. Entering deeper into our fields of study, we become familiar with theories, approaches, or methods that call themselves critical, such as critical sociology, Critical Discourse Analysis (CDA), critical theory (in lower-case letters), or Critical Theory (in upper-case letters). In this flood of imperatives, to be critical, it might appear that social science and humanities are critical per se. What else should they be? If the alternative to being critical is being uncritical, then of course everybody wants to be critical.

However, what exactly does being critical mean? What is critique? Certainly there are many important and interesting definitions. However, the point that I want to make attempts to lead to the very core of all of these definitions of critique. Everybody who claims to be critical refers ultimately to a bundle of critical *norms* or critical *methods*. One good first entry point into the analysis of critique can be the explicit definition of Michel Foucault, the French post-structuralist thinker. He describes

© The Editor(s) (if applicable) and The Author(s) 2016
B. Herzog, *Discourse Analysis as Social Critique*,
DOI 10.1057/978-1-137-56908-0_1

critique as the "art of not being governed or better, the art of not being governed like that" (Foucault 2007: 44). Later, he describes this position as "insubordination" or "desubjugation" (ibid.: 47).

It seems that at the beginning of critique, Foucault envisions an act of will. Where, however, does this act of will come from? Why does Foucault not want to be governed in that manner? These questions ultimately refer to the normative basis of Foucault's notion of critique. All critique refers to some type of prescriptive statement. Something should or should not be like this. My daughter should tidy up her room, my neighbour should turn his music lower, or the government should reduce taxes. When making these kinds of critical statements, we always refer to some norms—such as order, in the case of my daughter's room, or consideration in the case of my neighbour's music. In the case of tax reduction, the underlying normative basis perhaps is less obvious. Depending on why and which taxes we want to be lowered and for whom, the normative basis of this argument probably is related to equality, distributive justice, or liberty.

So let us have a look at the normative basis of Foucault's argument. Throughout his work, Foucault was quite critical of norms in general and hegemonic norms in particular. He was quite aware that norms are used as techniques of subjugation. Even unsuspicious norms, such as autonomy, liberty, or solidarity can turn into impositions. So, for example, the imperative of autonomy can be used to justify cuts in the welfare state to foster individuals' autonomy and responsibility. The same could even be said of solidarity. Reductions in social care for the needy can be justified by appealing to individual solidarity and solidarity through charity.[1] David Harvey resumes the contradiction that for Foucault (and for other thinkers) is inherent in the notion of freedom and liberty:

> For what classical liberal political economy proposes was not only some sort of utopian model for a universalized capitalism but a certain vision of individual liberty and freedom that ultimately came to underpin, as the French philosopher Michel Foucault acutely notes, a self-regulatory structure of governance that placed limits on the arbitrariness of stat power at

---

[1] Indeed, this was the argument of the German philosopher Peter Sloterdijk against the "tax State". Regarding his argument and the contestation, see also Herzog and Hernàndez (2009).

the same time as it led and enabled individuals to regulate their own conduct according to the rules of a market society. (Harvey 2014: 204)

However, even though Foucault was critical of all of the norms that he analysed, there is still a normative basis in both his writings and his political activities. In Foucault's work, we can find many reasons for his attitudes that could serve as a normative basis. Foucault discussed the consequences of a very wide range of techniques of power or governmentality as the *dispositif* of sexuality (Foucault 1979), techniques of surveillance and punishment in the judicial system, educational system and factory (Foucault 1975), and in treating mental "illnesses" (Foucault 2006). Although Foucault does not list the positive bundle of norms to which he refers, we can deduce these norms from his work. In all of Foucault's writings, he shows how social order, power relations, and subjugation are produced by humans' social actions and transformed into a relatively stable social structure. Individuals are usually unaware of the whole range of actions described by Foucault. When engaging in practices of discourse production, surveillance, or punishment, people think of those practices as "normal" or "natural" and do not acknowledge the violence present in the fact that specific discourses or practices are predominant in our society. Foucault himself described a series of these mechanisms in his inaugural lecture (Foucault 1981), showing the diverse mechanisms of exclusion necessary to create the existing order of discourse. From his series of writings, we can understand that Foucault implicitly defends norms related to autonomy or liberty, especially those related to the possibility of making free and conscious decisions. Ultimately, these are the norms of illustration. No wonder Foucault's definition of critique was first published in response to Emanuel Kant's question, "What is Enlightenment?"

We can say that there are plenty of reasons to criticize society, for "not being governed like that". All of these reasons ultimately refer to some norms. However, we must ask whether these reasons or norms are exclusive to Foucault and some of his followers. Perhaps other people have other reasons and other norms for why they refuse a specific type of government. And probably, there are many people who are quite happy with the existing social order. Now, if there are different stances towards the existing social order and even a different critical stance, which criteria do we have to want for a particular critique to be effective? What is the reason that the normative basis and argument of person A must be taken more seriously than those of person B?

This reasoning leads us to yet another characteristic of social critique: social critique must be universal—or at least widely shared by society—if it does not want to result in an imposition of norms by a particular social group. To be effective, social critique must be able to give a second-order reason that we want a critique. We can imagine a second-order reason or the corresponding second-order norm in analogy to Harry Frankfurt's second-order volitions (Frankfurt 1971). Following Frankfurt, the free will that differentiates persons from animals is essentially based on the capacity of having second-order volitions. I can have the first-order volition to eat the juicy and enchanting steak in front of me. However, at the same time, I can have the second-order volition of not wanting to eat meat. I do not want my first-order volition to become effective. I want to be a vegetarian and I do not want to be the type of person who eats animals. For Harry Frankfurt, non-human animals lack the capacity of having a volition over their first-order volitions. A cat cannot decide whether it wants to be the type of animal that eats mice. Although the cat can have other first-order volitions, which make not chasing a mouse at a particular moment like wanting to play or wanting to chase a bird, and so on, the cat cannot decide that it does not want his first-order volition to become effective.

In the same way, we can refer to second-order norms when realizing social critique. We do not want to be governed like that, but we understand that if most people prefer to be governed like that, we do not want to impose a change upon them. Too often in humanity's history, a particular social group has mistaken its particular situation, interests, and norms with those of the rest of society. The bourgeois class speaks in the name of the whole nation, or the communist party speaks in the name of society as a whole or—as is more subtle but more accepted today—a group of mainly male, mainly white, and mainly upper-class politicians speaks in the name of a national population. In other words, the norms to which social critique refers must be either universal norms or (at least) widely accepted social norms.

When criticizing, however, we do not follow only explicit or implicit normative assumptions. Apart from the often-unconscious or inexplicit normative basis of critique, there is another presupposition: When we criticize something or someone, we suppose that the *status quo* is suitable to change. In other words, we make an ontological statement about the object of critique, saying that it can be influenced by human behaviour. We can complain about the weather or lament the demise of a close relative, but both events are not subject to critique. What we can criticize is human behaviour and human-made circumstances. Critique is not about good wishes but about believing in the possibility of change. So when I criticize myself for not having brought an umbrella despite the cloudy sky announcing rain, I am believing that I could have acted differently and that next time in a similar situation, I should take an umbrella with me.

We will return to the point of the object of critique in the next chapter. Now, we want to take a deeper look at the questions around the problems of social change. Insofar as social critique expresses universal or socially accepted norms, it not only wants to evaluate or judge reality but also wants to *contribute* to change. Critique wants to change the criticized, that is, the persons, groups, or complex social structures being critiqued. A short glance at social reality shows that cognitive conviction is important in the process of change. Individual, groups, or societies must accept certain arguments and behave differently. However, we know from ourselves that this is not merely a matter of who has the better argument. We accept all of the reasons that we should not smoke, eat healthier food, or exercise more often. We want these reasons to be effective. However, we continue to behave in the criticized way. Are we not persons as described by Harry Frankfurt? Yes, we are; we want our unhealthy lifestyle to be ineffective. However, we often seem unable to make the change. Often there are practical or material impediments: the physical feeling of stress after a few hours without smoking, the mouth-watering pasta prepared by our mother-in-law, or the simple lack of time or money to enrol at a gym.

Therefore, critique is always more than a philosophical enterprise. Of course, although it must be fed by good reasons, it must also consider the real, practical, or material situation. It was exactly that point that caused Karl Marx to break with philosophy. The writing that best expresses Marx's move from philosophy to critique is perhaps his "Thesis on Feuerbach", in which Marx notes in his first thesis the need for a "'practical-critical' activity" (Marx 1970). Here, critique is a practice, an activity that changes both reality and the people involved in critique. For Marx, the role of practice and the material world is threefold:

First, material reality and practice are the starting points of critique. Critique is always practical. Second, critique must prove its truth both in relation to material reality and in practical activity. Thus, critique is not (only) about logical, cognitive consistency. Marx writes in his second thesis as follows:

> The question whether objective truth can be attributed to human thinking is not a question of theory but is a practical question. Man must prove the truth— i.e., the reality and power, the this-sidedness of his thinking in practice. The dispute over the reality or non-reality of thinking that is isolated from practice is a purely *scholastic* question. (Marx 1970: 121)

With the expression "this-sidedness" (*Diesseitigkeit*), Marx seeks to distance himself from what he criticizes in both religion and philosophy: theoretical thinking without it is not grounded in the existing social reality and has no impact on reality. Finally, in Marx's last, well-known eleventh thesis, he names the third and perhaps most important role of practice and reality for critique. "The philosophers have only interpreted the world, in various ways; the point is to change it" (ibid.: 123) Here, practice and reality are the objectives of critique. This quotation differs slightly from the better-known quote published in 1888 by Marx's friend, Friedrich Engels. In the more popular version published by Engels, the second part of the thesis states, "the point, however (*aber* in the original German version), is to change it." This "however" seems to open a space for contradiction between interpreting and changing the world, as if interpretation and change were two different activities. Nevertheless, for Marx, as we have seen in the first theses, interpretation and change come together in a practical-critical activity.

We have seen that the practical-material world is the starting point of critique, the criteria to prove the truth of critique and the end of the critical activity. However, the reverse of these theses does not mean that all change is the result of critique. There are several diverse reasons for change, such as natural development or development of a social system according to its own laws. Here, we could name the multiple processes of social differentiation in social systems, for example, the growing amount of laws, amendments, and law-like rules created to react in the logic of the juridical system to the challenges of reality. Nevertheless, critique is one very important *method of change*. It is important insofar as it is not only practical but also conscious. Critique is a conscious, self-reflexive method of change.

These considerations lead directly to questions related to critique as a method. What exactly is this critical method? What differentiates the specific practice of critique from other practices? We probably would avoid saying that a mechanic who changes the tires of my car is engaging in a critical practice, although undoubtedly, he is performing a conscious practical and material act aimed at changing the object of his acts. Or, if we prefer to remain with social objects of practice, traffic policemen whose practices aim at changing the flows of people at rush hour are engaged in a practice based on social reality and aim consciously at its change. Perhaps a short glance at the text of Max Horkheimer, the German post-Marxist, director of the Institute of Social Research in Frankfurt, and author of the famous 1937 essay "Traditional and Critical Theory", could help us further understand the difference between critical and non-critical activities. In the above-mentioned essay, Horkheimer states "that there is a human activity which has society itself for its object" (Horkheimer 1975: 206). In a footnote, he clarifies that he is referring to critique: "In the following pages this activity is called 'critical' activity. The term is used here less in the sense it has in the idealist critique of pure reason than in the sense it has in the dialectical critique of political economy. It points to an essential aspect of the dialectical theory of society" (ibid.; footnote 14). With the expression "dialectical critique of political economy", Horkheimer is referring directly to Karl Marx, although not mentioning him too openly. Horkheimer published the text from exile in the USA; thus, he only refers to Marx directly in a footnote, to avoid getting into too much trouble. However, how exactly is this activity to which he is referring a critical activity? Horkheimer goes on, "The aim of this activity is not simply to eliminate one or other abuse, for it regards such abuses as necessarily connected with the way in which the social structure is organized. Although it itself emerges from the social structure, its purpose is not, either in its conscious intention or in its objective significance, the better functioning of any element in the structure. On the contrary, it is suspicious of the very categories of better, useful, appropriate, productive, and valuable, as these are understood in the present order, and refuses to take them as non-scientific presuppositions about which one can do nothing" (ibid: 206f).

Horkheimer makes three main points here. First, he views critique as aimed at society. As he uses the term, critique refers exclusively to social critique, or at least it is only this type of critique in which he is interested. Second, when Horkheimer refers to society, he does not refer to one specific expression of a social phenomenon but instead to the very core of society. Therefore, we might think that Horkheimer is not referring to research aiming at improving migrants' access to the health system or making a more efficient information flow between citizens and government. For Horkheimer, all of these problems are "necessarily connected with the way in which the social structure is organized." Therefore, critique is always a critique of the whole social order, structure, system, or (to use a term that Horkheimer uses in the same essay) "social totality". The topic of structure leads us to the third point: the attitude of suspicion that, for Horkheimer, is related to critique. In all critique, there is an inherent suspicion that there is something behind the appearances, that reality is more than what we perceive at first glance. Marx expresses this suspicion in his famous sentence, "all science would be superfluous if the outward appearance and the essence of things directly coincided" (Marx 1962: 797).

Critique in this sense, as used by Horkheimer and Marx, therefore refers to the first and basic contradiction that both authors ultimately take from G.W. Hegel: the contradiction between appearance and essence. To our ears, the term essence sounds perhaps like essentialist, like there is a fixed, unchangeable, objective core of society. I think that we can easily translate this term for the needs of twenty-first-century science with "social structure", "social system", or simply "reality", acknowledging that all of these terms have different theoretical backgrounds and different intellectual histories. The contradiction between appearance and essence simply means that there is something behind the obvious. This is the attitude of suspicion to which Horkheimer refers.

The question now is as follows: how is it possible to uncover essence, social structure, or underlying reality? This is the big methodological question that the social sciences and humanities must address. Here, Hegel again gives us a first hint, stating that the essence must appear, otherwise it would not be the essence. Perhaps a practical example can help us disentangle this question, leading us directly from philosophy to the social sciences. When we ask, for example, what it is that characterizes a human being (avoiding the unwieldy term essence), we have no other choice than to begin our search with appearance, with real persons, with Peter and Mary, with my neighbour, my parents, and my colleagues. All of these real persons are appearances of what it means to be a person.

As noted above, these considerations lead us directly to the need for empirical research. When we want to know about the underlying reality or essence or structure of society, we have no other choice but to conduct research beginning with what we can grasp at first glance with our senses. Remember that the contradiction between essence and appearance also means that we cannot stop by just describing the surface. We must attempt to continue further. The very idea of contradictions as that term is used by Hegel (and in the tradition of Hegel until now) is that contradictions are not logical incompatibilities. Contradictions are the expression of certain tensions that usually do not have a solution but that are pushing and advancing an issue. In our case, it is the search for scientific knowledge that is pushed further by the contradiction between appearance and reality. Critique is pushed forward by the dialectical relation between reality and surface phenomenon and—remembering the second thesis on Feuerbach—must prove its truth in reality.

However, examining the relationship between surface and reality, which requires research to begin with the former in order to reach the latter, is not sufficient for anything more than a rough estimation, a compass for the direction of critique without a detailed approach. Horkheimer was quite aware of that problem: "To transform the critical theory of society into a sociology is, on the whole, an undertaking beset with serious difficulties" (Horkheimer 1975: 239). Critique always must work on the two levels at the same time: at the level of perceived social problems and at the level of society or social totality.

Foucault knows these difficulties well: "We identify a perpetual question which would be: 'how not to be governed like that, by that, in the name of those principles, with such and such an objective in mind and by means of such procedures, not like that, not for that, not by them'" (Foucault 2007: 44). It could be interesting to stop here for a moment and think about what Foucault means by "perpetual question". I think he does not mean that we should not attempt to find a solution because the question will always be there. The solution to this conundrum lies, I think, in the use of the verb "to govern". For Foucault, this verb does not, or at least does not exclusively, refer to the activity of a formal government. For Foucault, the notion of government and the notion of power is more impersonal. It means that there is a social order that is enigmatic to the individual. We are often not fully aware of the rules and obligations of that order. When Foucault refers to critique as "the art of not being governed like that", he is referring to a critique of a certain social order, with its duties and commitments. However, what is perpetual is not a specific social order but the fact that there is a social order at all. David Harvey explains what appears as a tension between critique and social order as a continuous contradiction between freedom and domination (Harvey 2014: 199ff). All freedom always requires a social order, meaning that it always requires some structure of duties and obligations or, as Harvey describes it, freedom requires domination. Of course, David Harvey is far from justifying the growing number of laws that restrict civil rights in the name of freedom. However, he makes an important point: even the best possible social order is full of structural impositions upon the individual. Through the process of socialization, we learn to accept these impositions.[2]

It is probably in that sense that Foucault describes the search for a way of not being governed like that as the "perpetual question". We are always governed because we are always part of a specific social order that precedes our existence. Moreover, we are always governed in a specific way. We are always governed "like that". Therefore, although the task of critique is a constant task, an unsolvable perpetual practice, it is not a useless or unnecessary task.

---

[2] Sigmund Freud has described this "uneasiness in culture" experienced by modern individuals as a permanent tension between immediate drive satisfaction and cultural stable patterns of long-term, sustainable drive satisfaction (Freud 2002).

Summing up the argument about the general characteristics of critique, we can say that critique always includes an approach to norms, methods, or proceedings and an approach to the object of critique. Critique refers to norms in a double sense. On the one hand, we always criticize from a normative point of view. Something *should* be or *should* be organized in a manner that is more functional, more autonomous, allows more freedom or equality, and so on. On the other hand, critique is performed in a field of what I call second-order norms. When criticizing something, I always need a reference to socially accepted or universal norms to justify why I want my critique to become effective (and perhaps why I want the critique of my neighbour not to become effective).

Critique is also a method for change. Insofar as social reality is the reason or starting point of critique, it is the objective of critique, and critique must prove its "truth" in the realm of reality. In that sense, critique is never a mere theoretical, cognitive, or philosophical enterprise. It requires the expertise of social scientists as experts in dealing with practical and material realities. Critique not only must address material and practical realities but also is a material practice in itself: In the modern language of social science, we would say that critique is performative. Again, critique must operate at two levels at the same time: it must focus on the practical need for change while analysing what Horkheimer called the "social totality", that is, the structural problems for change.

Finally, a minimum of information can be given about general aspects of the object of critique. The basic presupposition is that the object of critique can be changed by human action. This could be a directly human behaviour (e.g., racist speech) or it could be a natural phenomenon that makes humans suffer in a manner that can be relieved by human action, for instance, an earthquake. Because here we are talking only about a presupposition, critique must follow a double approach. It has to analyse reasons that a certain phenomenon may be the object of critique, for example, asking which type of suffering it is producing; simultaneously, critique has to justify why the phenomenon or the effects of critique may be changeable by human action.

Having established the general characteristics of critique with respect to its normative basis, method of change, and ontological claims, we must now confront a serious claim against general theories of critique. Are we not doing exactly what Marx was criticizing in his theses on Feuerbach, making philosophical observations on something without considering the real, material world? Judith Butler, in her lecture about Foucault's essay on critique, makes a similar argument:

> Can we even ask such a question about the generalized character of critique without gesturing toward an essence of critique? And if we achieved the generalized picture, offering something which approaches a philosophy of critique, would we then lose the very distinction between philosophy and critique that operates as part of the definition of critique itself? Critique is always a critique *of* some instituted practice, discourse, episteme, institution, and it loses its character the moment in which it is abstracted from its operation and made to stand alone as a purely generalizable practice. (Butler 2001)

As witness, Butler cites Adorno, who adopts a more Hegelian and Marxist approach: "Adorno makes a similar claim when he writes of the 'danger… of judging intellectual phenomena in a subsumptive, uninformed and administrative manner and assimilating them into the prevailing constellations of power which the intellect ought to expose'" (ibid.).

There seems no other way than turning our focus on the object of critique. This is necessary not only to learn more about that object but also to understand what critique means in the concrete case of *social* critique.

1.2　From Critique to Social Critique

We said that everything that is either human-made or can be influenced by humans in its effects can be the object of critique. As we saw, however, critique is always concrete and is always a practical activity engaged in a specific material-practical phenomenon. Therefore, we will limit our examination to one specific form of critique: social critique. In the course of this enquiry, we will learn not only about the object of critique but also about the specific form of critique. In other words, we will further our enquiry into critique and what critique is in the concrete case of social critique.

"Social" refers to society and its organization. Society is an everyday concept that seems self-evident and that seems not to require any further explication. However, when asking what exactly is society, what characterizes a society, what distinguishes one society from another, or what do we criticize when doing social critique, we probably notice that there is no clear definition of the concept. Definitions of societies usually refer to some shared form of living together, values, traditions, laws, organization, in short, to some form of community. Again, these secondary concepts are equally blurred. We speak colloquially about the French society, the European society, or the British society of criminology. We intuit that the societies' members have something in common, but we cannot list a bundle of values, traditions, and so on, that are exactly the same for all of those societies' members. The extreme position resulting from the incapacity to unambiguously define society is expressed in the classical, highly polemic statement by the former British Prime Minister Margaret Thatcher: "There is no such thing as society."

The incapacity to give a clear definition can be seen not only as a problem but also as a possibility when thinking about social critique. It can be problematic that different people may have different aspects in mind when talking about society. However, this fuzziness allows us to focus on diverse aspects when performing social critique. The fact that there is "no such thing as" an objective, independent definition of "society" requires us to justify our specific approach to the social order that we use for critique. When performing social critique, we are not criticizing the existence of society but a specific form of social order. We therefore must decide what we mean by the fundamental social order when we perform social critique. Is it a value system, an economic structure, a discursive order…?

Perhaps Margaret Thatcher was right in that sense that there is no widely accepted grand narrative of society. We can find structuralist and post-structuralist theories about societies, system theory, and theories that see capitalism as the centre of social order. All of these theories undoubtedly have enriched the debate about contemporary society, but none can claim uncontested truth. These considerations pose a challenge for social critique: social critique must always refer to some theory of the social, that is, one fundamental approach of how society is ordered. When performing social critique, we ultimately must criticize the social order.

Taking into account what was previously said about the ontological status of the objects of critique, we can understand that social critique is quite new in human history. We said that the object of critique has to be made by humans. This means conversely that, as far as we understand the social order as a natural or divine order, there is no social critique. Complaints about the divine or natural order are probably as old as human history. However, social critique as it is described here stems from Enlightenment. Someone who perhaps best expressed the possibility of social critique was Hegel when he spoke about the French Revolution in his *Lectures on the Philosophy of World History*:

> Never since the sun had stood in the firmament and the planets revolved around him had it been perceived that man's existence centres in his head, i.e. in thought, inspired by which he builds up the world of reality [...] not until now had man advanced to the recognition of the principle that thought ought to govern spiritual reality. This was accordingly a glorious mental dawn. All thinking being shared in the jubilation of this epoch. Emotions of a lofty character stirred men's minds at that time; a spiritual enthusiasm thrilled through the world, as if the reconciliation between the divine and the secular was now first accomplished. (Hegel 2004: 447)

From our perspective, we would probably brand Hegel as too idealistic. It is quite ingenious to think that reality can be built directly from our ideas. However, Hegel exemplarily expresses the possibility that human existence, that is, society, is ultimately built upon human will. With Enlightenment, the French Revolution, and the Industrial Revolution, people begin to understand history not only as a series of similar events (e.g., births, weddings, deaths, wars, coronations), but also as change, not only because of natural development but also because of human action. From the time that humans are aware that they are "doing society", they produce the very same order in which they are living, and critique as *social* critique becomes possible.

When Karl Marx asserts that "*criticism* of *religion* is the prerequisite of *all criticism*" (Marx 1843), he and his fellow colleagues in the "Young Hegelians" (a group of critical intellectuals that included both Marx and Feuerbach) understand the essence of religion as the essence of men. This group of intellectuals attempts to show that the origin of the divine lies in human beings. From there, discussions—especially those derived from the contributions of Ludwig Feuerbach, Bruno Bauer, Max Stirner, and

Karl Marx and Friedrich Engels—provide several insights that remain relevant. All of these contributions take Hegel a step further, showing not only that religion is a social product but also that for us, most of these processes of production are unconscious. It is important here to remember the relevance of their argument about religion for social critique: if religion is human-made, than the divine social order becomes a human-made social order; when this human social order is the result of a non-conscious process, then critique is (also) about bringing this process to awareness.

Feuerbach essentially provides the thesis of *projection*. Humans project what is important for them onto an external being. That is why some cultures have rain deities, others have war gods, and (following Feuerbach) the Christian god is characterized by love, wisdom, and power as important characteristics for Christian societies. Therefore, Feuerbach comes to the conclusion that "the secret of theology is [...] anthropology" (Feuerbach 1957: 207). The divine is human-made for Feuerbach in an unconscious process of projection. Human beings project the essence of mankind onto transcendental subjects.

Bruno Bauer (2002), another member of the Young Hegelians, adds motifs to the discussion. While Feuerbach's motif was projection, his contribution is that of *production*, reification, and alienation. The argument is essentially that the Bible is a human product. We even know the authors of the New Testament—Matthew, Mark, Luke, and so on. Now it seems that we have forgotten about the human nature of that product and treat a human-made text as a holy book. The book gathers power over human activities; people behave under the order of that specific text. It is a logic not only of production but also of forgetting that the text is a human production. This is the nucleus of the idea of reification. "For all reification is a forgetting: objects become purely thing-like the moment they are retained for us without the continued presence of their other aspects: when something of them has been forgotten", writes Adorno in a letter to Walter Benjamin (Adorno and Benjamin 1999: 32), meaning that we forget the original sense or the original process of production, and now, our product seems like an object that is alien to us instead of the result of a specific social relation or situation. Reification refers not only to products or human beings: it also refers to everything that we falsely treat as thing. We can see here the very elements of what will later comprise the Marxist analysis of capitalism as a human product that seems exterior to the individual and that has enormous power over him or her.

The Young Hegelians were a tremendously productive group of intellectuals (on the sociology of this particular group, see Eßbach 1988). They wrote, conducted passionate debates, and developed their collective thought. The state of the art of last week's debate might be overcome next week by a member's new text. Every critique was repeatedly criticized. Marx's expression of the "critique of the critical criticism" (Marx 1956) perhaps best expresses this ongoing process. Acknowledging this collective intellectual work, it is no wonder that the positions presented here were targets of important objections by components of the group itself. One of the most important critics was Max Stirner, an author often described as an individual anarchist, disdained by Marxists and social democrats and highly influential (but not openly acknowledged) to authors such as Friedrich Nietzsche and Michel Foucault. Saul Newman even describes Stirner as a "precursor to contemporary poststructuralist thought" (Newman 2003: §1).

Stirner criticizes what he understands to be a residuum of religion in Feuerbach's anthropology of the divine. Remember that Feuerbach replaced the essence of the divine with the essence of mankind. For Stirner, however, mankind is the last big lie (Stirner 1995). For Stirner, speaking about the essence of humanity or humanism in general is just another way to subordinate individuals in a specific way. In humanism, people are no longer subjugated by God but by what is supposed to be the essence of mankind. Although "in the name of humanity" replaces "in the name of the Lord", the consequences in terms of power and subjugation remain the same. Stirner makes a strong argument here, anticipating all types of uses of power in the name of the nation, the race, the community, humanity, freedom, and so on. All of these concepts independently—whether or not they seem appealing—ultimately are only concepts. Stirner rejects all domination in name of these concepts. For him, the only valid starting point is for the individual or the "ego" (as Stirner calls it) to avoid confusion with the *concept* of the individual.

Stirner's basic thoughts are highly relevant for our purpose of social critique and quite similar to Foucault's will "not to be governed *like that*, by that, in the name of those principles" (Foucault), "that" being principles of supposed divine origin or human-made concepts. Stirner describes two aspects important for social critique. First, our "human" principles do not express some type of natural essence of mankind; instead, they are made by humans. Whereas natural essences escape criticism, as human products, these principles can become the object of social critique. Second, Stirner shows that people are unaware of the social and powerful character of concepts, that is, that the religious way of thinking lives on in the belief in principles.

Marx and Engels' position on Stirner's critique is ambiguous. On the one hand, they have to admit Stirner's critique of the abstract concept of mankind in Feuerbach's work. Regarding that critique, in 1844, Engels clearly writes in a letter to Marx as follows: "Stirner is right" (Engels 1963: 11). However, Engels—and later Marx, in an extensive and (during his lifetime) unpublished response (Marx 1958: 101–472)—disagrees with Stirner about the consequence of that observation. Whereas for Stirner, the starting point for critique is the concrete individual, for Marx and Engels, these individuals are the products of *social relations*. In the same letter, Engels writes the following about Stirner's proposal: "This egoism is only the essence of the actual society and the actual mankind made conscious; it is the last thing what the actual society can say against us" (Engels 1963: 11). Instead of starting with the individual as given factuality, Marx and Engels start with the factuality of social relations. Following Wolfgang Eβbach (1982), we could say that whereas Stirner presents the materiality and thus the factual violence of the self, Marx and Engels present the materiality and factual violence of social relations.

Here, the circle of social critique of the young Hegelians comes to a provisional end. A critique of religion becomes a critique of social relations that produce wrong ideas, whether they are ideas about deities, abstract concepts of humanity, or the concrete individual. We now have another piece to add to our puzzle of social critique. The critique of ideas and (although using the term popularized some years later) the critique of ideology are fundamentally social critiques. In the Marxist tradition, ideology is more than a set of ideas. Today, we are accustomed to reading about left or right "ideology" or the "ideology" of a particular political party, politician, or institution. This popular use of "ideology" to mean a simple worldview is far from the Marxist notion of the term (for a good overview of the history and usage of ideology, see Lenk 1984). In the Marxist tradition, the set of ideas called ideologies have two additional characteristics. First, ideologies are wrong. Ideologies are a set of false comprehensions of the world. Second, ideologies are *necessarily* false. This means that ideology is not a simple mistake or carelessness in the thinking that produces ideologies. Instead, ideologies are produced by the given manner in which society is organized. It is exactly that which Engels meant when affirming that Stirner's incorrect argument, perceiving the individual as the starting point of critique, is ultimately the "essence of actual society and actual mankind". The bourgeois society, with its abstract relations among individuals, necessarily produces these ideas of isolated egoists, which are present not only in the text of Stirner but also in what Marx calls the "robinsonades" of political economy.

In that sense, ideologies are false and true at the same time. They are false because they distort social reality. However, they are true because they are the "normal" response to the deformed social order. Ideas are the "reflex in consciousness" of the social order. György Lukács brings this argument to a point with an example of the discussion of the isolated individual:

> Of course, this isolation and fragmentation is only apparent. The movement of commodities on the market, the birth of their value, in a word, the real framework of every rational calculation is not merely subject to strict laws but also presupposes the strict ordering of all that happens. The atomisation of the individual is, then, only the reflex in consciousness of the fact that the 'natural laws' of capitalist production have been extended to cover every manifestation of life in society; that – for the first time in history – the whole of society is subjected, or tends to be subjected, to a unified economic process, and that the fate of every member of society is determined by unified laws. [...]
>
> However, if this atomisation is only an illusion, it is a necessary one. That is to say, the immediate, practical as well as intellectual confrontation of the individual with society, the immediate production and reproduction of life—in which for the individual the commodity structure of all 'things'

and their obedience to 'natural laws' is found to exist already in a finished form, as something immutably given—could only take place in the form of rational and isolated acts of exchange between isolated commodity owners. As emphasised above, the worker, too, must present himself as the 'owner' of his labour-power, as if it were a commodity. His specific situation is defined by the fact that his labour-power is his only possession. His fate is typical of society as a whole in that this self-objectification, this transformation of a human function into a commodity reveals in all its starkness the dehumanised and dehumanising function of the commodity relation. (Lukács 1971: 91f)

Summarizing the argument until now, we can say that social critique requires an idea of what society is. Social critique needs to adopt an approach to the basic, underlying aspects of social order. Furthermore, it must prove—as the excurse on criticism of religion has shown—that these aspects of social order are not natural, divine, or fixed. Critique must show that these aspects are human-made and therefore can be changed by human action. However, we have also seen how deeply rooted some ideas about the apparently immovable nature of some aspects of human societies are. However, these two considerations—the need for both an idea about basic social order and arguments about the possibility of changing this order—do not justify social critique. As we have seen, critique always requires a normative stance towards its object. We therefore need two more steps to complete the puzzle of social critique. First, we need arguments about why we think something went wrong in society. We must take a look at the surface of society to find social phenomena with which we disagree, such as injustices, inequalities, and disrespect.[3] Second we require a logical connection between the surface problem that we want to change and the social (changeable) order. Otherwise, we are not doing *social* critique.

Therefore, when doing social critique, in a first step, we are not concerned with the social order at all. First, we are concerned about a specific social problem. When saying that something is a social problem, we are saying three things. First, we are saying that the problem affects more than one person: it affects whole social groups or societies as a

---
[3] In Sect. 1.3 we will see the complexity of the task of justifying our normative stance.

whole. Otherwise, it would be an individual or psychological problem and not the object of social research. However, a social problem can *appear* first in one or a very few persons as a symptom of social wrong. Second, saying that something is a social problem refers to the fact that the problem and/or the solution are highly influenced by collective action. Third, when speaking of social problems, we are saying that the problem is related to the underlying social order. Otherwise, we only experience collective problems. Examples include the problem of how to handle the flows of football supporters to and from the stadium every game day. This problem affects a huge collective of hundreds of thousands of supporters every weekend. However, it seems more a problem of correct traffic management than connected to a fundamental, criticizable social order.

Therefore, we must operate on both levels: the level of general social order and the level of the appearance of normative problems. If we only worked on the general level, we would fall into general theoretical considerations about society with no real impact on material reality. If we worked only on the level of visible problems, we would fall in what Marx called "that kind of criticism which knows how to judge and condemn the present, but not how to comprehend it" (Marx 1990: 528, footnote 324).

From a post-structuralist viewpoint, Judith Butler goes a step further, mistrusting the specific social situation from which critique could originate:

> Further, the primary task of critique will not be to evaluate whether its objects—social conditions, practices, forms of knowledge, power, and discourse—are good or bad, valued highly or demeaned, but to bring into relief the very framework of evaluation itself. What is the relation of knowledge to power such that our epistemological certainties turn out to support a way of structuring the world that forecloses alternative possibilities of ordering? Of course, we may think that we need epistemological certainty in order to state for sure that the world is and ought to be ordered a given way. To what extent, however, is that certainty orchestrated by forms of knowledge precisely in order to foreclose the possibility of thinking otherwise? (Butler 2001)

Here, Butler opens an important debate about the immediacy of problems and the possibility that social problems themselves could be ideological.

They could be the correct expression of the wrong social situation. The learned and used categories can have distorting effects on people's perception of reality and even of immediate suffering. For example, we can easily imagine how vast swaths of the white population suffered from status loss and fear after segregation was officially abolished in the USA. There was an enormous group of people who perceived abolition as a social problem. However, from our point of view, we would probably argue that the problem was not abolition, but racism or xenophobia. In other words, when starting with salient social problems, we experience the normative difficulty of what counts as a social problem and the methodological problem of how to separate ideological problems from "real" ones. The first question will be discussed in Sect. 1.3, and the second question will be discussed in Sect. 1.6.

Butler's proposal not to stay with the immediate evaluation of the object of critique but to ask for the framework of that evaluation seems both correct and insufficient at the same time. It is insufficient insofar as it simulates that this approach does not imply a normative position. However, even if we attempt to escape first-order normative evaluation, we confront a second-order normative position in Butler's proposal: opening the view for alternative readings or an alternative social order without even saying whether these other social orders are preferable implies the normative position that being conscientious about the social order and having the choice about how society is organized are preferable to the status quo.

Social critique, we can say by now, requires three main steps, all of which involve risks and pitfalls. First, we criticize a specific situation. Here, we need a first criterion for normative critique. What is wrong with that situation? Why do we want the situation to be changed? The danger here is what we could call an ideological or wrong sense of justice. How can we distinguish the correct from the incorrect form of justice or injustice and therefore decide what constitutes a social problem and object of social critique? In the end, this is a *meta-normative question*, a question about how to decide about the norms that we want to use for social critique.

Second, we have to be able to draw a logical relation from that somehow-unjust situation to a general social order. Here, we face a double methodological problem of showing the existence of an underlying social order, which is an economic or value system, a social or discursive structure, or any other method of understanding social order. However, we have to show how to relate a particular injustice to that general social order. How does a social order generate injustices? Here, we must always be open to the alternative hypothesis that specific situations are not produced by the social order but by other, even casual factors.

Third, we must then criticize that social order. From a normative perspective, this critique should not be to complicate any solid, normative critique developed in the first step. Here, we must explain what we think is wrong with the social order. What we have to show at that third and final stage is the possibility of changing the social order that is ultimately responsible for the injustice in question. This includes not only demonstrating that the social order is human-made and can be influenced by (collective) human action but also analysing the difficulties of change. These possibilities could refer both to material problems and to ideological problems preventing individuals from understanding both social order and their role in it.

We have seen that these problems could be summarized both as *normative* problems of how to perform a fundamental social critique and as *methodological* problems of how to proceed. Normative problems include the question of what is wrong with the social order and the related question of what is wrong with certain social phenomenon. Methodological questions concern the detection of social problems, the relation of these problems to the social order, the development of a general theory of social order, and the ability to demonstrate possibilities and problems when attempting to change the social order. We essentially wish to dedicate the next two chapters to normative problems so that afterwards, we can see how to proceed in terms of a practical social critique, that is, how to transform social critique into social research or how to use social research in social critique.

1.3 Normative Justification of Critique

When formulating normative judgements, we are confronted by a certain contradiction, as Stahl (2013a: 12) notes. When participating in a process of critical thinking about norms, about how society should be, it is supposed that we are referring not only to the uncovering of natural laws but also to some statements of how we want society to be. Therefore, we need good reasons for our statements. However, normative judgements are not only about "what *we* think or feel personally about a certain state of art but also about what we *should* feel or think" (ibid.). In other words: we simultaneously engage in normative and meta-normative considerations.

In what follows, I do not want to discuss all of the possible good reasons that one could have for criticizing a particular social situation. This would be far beyond the scope of this short overview on social critique. Instead, I will ask what *kind* of good reasons are usually used when engaging in critical practices. Essentially, we can differentiate between external, procedural, and internal or immanent forms of critique.

When performing *external critique,* we apply reasons that do not stem from the object of critique itself. One of these forms of critique would involve criticizing contemporary society based on the Bible. In this case, we could consult the Bible to determine how community should be and how people should behave. We then would compare the ideal of the Bible with our society and criticize the difference between claims and reality. The same logic would be to take the Quran instead of the Bible, performing a social critique based on Islamic rules. Although these foundations of external critique do exist in our societies, they are quite marginalized. Particularly in the academic field, they would not be considered admissible. However, academics often invoke another textual ground as the basis of an external critique: the Universal Declaration of Human Rights. However, in that case, too, we are following the same logic as in the case of the Bible or the Quran when comparing real societies with the description of how societies should be according to the Universal Declaration of Human Rights.

I call this type of critique an external critique, arguing that it is external to the object of critique—in this case, external to society. However, as we have seen in the classical critique of religion by Bruno Bauer (2002), none of these texts is really external. They are produced by humans in a particular social environment. Nevertheless, I call it external because the criteria stem from a specific person or group of persons, not from the social situation that we want to criticize itself. Even human rights are not necessarily an expression of what contemporary societies want; instead, they are the result of world leaders' political negotiations after World War II. In the same way, we could ask, why should what was written by Luke and Matthew approximately 2000 years ago be valid for my everyday behaviour or how we should organize society now? Why should a text written by powerful men more than 60 years ago have any impact on how we want to organize how we live together in far more complex contemporary societies?

Another form of external critique is also quite popular: the use of utopias as justification for social critique. Utopia literally means no-place, a society that does not exist.[4] Philosophers, science fiction authors and average people have often imagined—in more or less detail—ideal, peaceful and harmonious societies. Social critiques based on utopias, then, compare existing society with the ideal, showing the deficiencies of the former. The translation of utopia as the place that does not exist clarifies that here again, we experience a form of external critique, which is normatively based not in society as it exists today but in a future, ideal society.

Other forms of external critique include that of the classical social and political philosopher thinking about the best way to organize society and arguing for or against certain basic rules. Independently, regardless of whether we agree with the position and regardless of whether the proposals are well-argued, the position remains a particular position. Even if we could argue that the philosopher is not completely external to society (because like every other human being, he is a product of society), I still call this type of critique an external one. It is one particular person with a particular way of arguing. Even if the argument is shared by a group of persons, they are still a particular group. Neither the philosopher nor the group of philosophers is representative of society.

From this external foundation of norms that we use for social critique, we can distinguish the *procedural* approach. Procedural means that which makes norms suitable for the foundation of critique is the procedure that we use to establish the norms. These procedures can be either hypothetical or real and pragmatic.

---

[4] In English, there is the homophonous word "eutopia", which means good place, and which may be partly responsible for the consideration of utopias as better or even ideal societies.

Perhaps the most influential hypothetical procedure for justifying how an ideal society works and which norms we can use to criticize society was introduced in the 1970s by John Rawls (1971, 1999). Rawls' basic hypothetical procedure works as follows: imagine you live in a society in which you do not know which gender, religion, ethnicity, abilities, and so on, you have. Rawls calls this procedure the veil of ignorance. Then, decide how your society should be organized. Which type of inequalities would you allow as just and which inequalities would you abolish as unjust? For Rawls, the "natural distribution [of capacities, gender, etc., B.H.] is neither just nor unjust […] these are simply natural facts. What is just and unjust is the way that institutions deal with these facts" (Rawls 1999: 87). Rawls elaborates over several decades the social order to which we would agree under this conditions. One of the best known principles is his difference principle: "Social and economic inequalities are to be arranged so that they are both (a) to the greatest expected benefit of the least advantaged and (b) attached to offices and positions open to all under conditions of fair quality of opportunity." In other words, Rawls states that we would agree to inequalities when initially everybody would have a fair possibility to obtain the positions that provide better living standard, and these inequalities would also help the worst off in that society.

Although the procedure intuitively may be convincingly just and producing just results, several criticisms of Rawls' proposal have been formulated, especially in the course of the debate between liberals and communitarians (see also Honneth 1995a). For our purpose, two arguments are important. Remember that our purpose was to find types of justifications for normative judgements in particular social situations or a general social order. The proposal made by Rawls seemed to be norm-free at first glance because he is not primarily arguing for a particular norm but instead for a procedure to elaborate the normative basis (of critique). However, Rawls' proposed procedure is not norm-free. It is the expression of norms of a liberal society committed to certain values, such as non-discrimination or equality of opportunity. The procedure presupposes what it is about to show: the justice of non-discrimination and equal opportunities. The very idea of the veil of ignorance is thought in the way that all what in liberal democracies is thought to be the ground for unjust discrimination is part of what participants do not know about society. A second argument stemming directly from communitarian authors (MacIntyre 1984; Taylor 1989; Walzer 1990) is that we need communities—that is, communities with more or less elaborated normative orders—to make reasoned decisions. It is impossible for us to disregard our profound identities, including our normative convictions.

Jürgen Habermas can be seen as one of the main authors defending a pragmatic procedure for justifying the normative ground of social critique. In his *Theory of Communicative Action*, Habermas (1984, 1987) claims that the original mode of every speech act includes three validity claims: the claim for empirical truth, the claim for moral rightness and the claim for personal sincerity. When engaging in free discourses with others, all of the participants have the ability to negate, challenge and therefore redefine the three claims. We can discuss whether what was said before is empirically correct, whether we agree to how it is expressed to us—that is, the interpersonal relationship between the participants—or whether we think it is a sincere expression of the speaker. And in his discourse of ethics, Habermas claims that only those norms should be valid "that could meet with the consent of all affected in their role as participants in a practical discourse [...]. For a norm to be valid, the consequences and side effects of its general observance for the satisfaction of each person's particular interests must be acceptable to all" (Habermas 1990: 197). In other words, the normative grounds for social critique are those norms that could be found in a discourse free of coercion in a free interchange in which "forceless force of the better argument" is the only thing that governs (Habermas 1971: 137).

Here again, it seems at a first glance that we see a reasonable procedure to find norms that can guide us for our purpose of social critique. Therefore, it is no wonder that Habermas' theory was acclaimed by new social movements in the 1980s. Feminists, anti-racists, and ecological groups—that is, those who do not have the economic lever of the working class—found their capacity to argue as exactly that characteristic able to ground social critique and therefore to change the world. However, severe doubts arise when seriously addressing Foucault's considerations about the order of discourse (Foucault 1981). In Foucault's inaugural lecture, we can find two main arguments against the procedure proposed by Habermas. The first is that even the ideal, power-free space of free discourse is already pre-structured. There is a specific order of discourse. In that space, we can find (for example) arguments that count as valid, accepted ways of performing, and so on. In *The order of discourse*, Foucault describes a series of these powerful mechanisms that definitively exclude ways of speaking. "We know perfectly well that we are not free to say just anything, that we cannot simply speak of anything, when we like or where we like; not just anyone, finally, may speak of just anything. We have three types of prohibition, covering objects, ritual with its surrounding circumstances, the privileged or exclusive right to speak of a particular subject" (ibid.: 49). Foucault even mentions mechanisms as inconspicuous as "reason and folly", thus saying that the fool and the foolish are excluded through the order of discourses. When thinking a bit more about that mechanism, we find a whole set of discursive dispositions that define what has to count as foolish and what is a reasonable argument. These are only some examples why there are good reasons to think that the Habermasian discourse is a pre-structured, powerful, particular and exclusive way of interacting with its own normative basis.

The second argument against Habermas' proposal comes from a democratic perspective. Not all people are able to engage in public arguments in the same way. Discourses are a conflict-resolution technique that clearly favours those with more educative or cultural "capital", that is, those accustomed to engaging in critical debates. Those (often marginalized) people who are unable to engage in social or political debates about justice are structurally excluded. This argument is even stronger given that those who are excluded from debates are often the same people in whose name others claim for justice.

From these two forms of normative foundation—the external foundation and the procedural foundation—I would like to differentiate a third form, the *internal or immanent foundation*. Internal and immanent critiques are directly related to the analysis of the object of critique. However, when taking a closer look, internal and immanent critique do not have exactly the same meaning. They have different normative implications. Additionally, there are quite diverse theoretical ideas about how to understand immanent critique.

When speaking of *internal* critique, we are really speaking of coherence (see also Herzog 2016a). Internal critique would then be the analysis of internal incoherencies or contradictions. Thus, such an internal critique would reveal, for example, in the discourse of a right-wing European political party the complaint that migrants come to Europe to enjoy the benefits of the welfare state, whereas the same discourse claims that migrants are employed in jobs that otherwise would be held by natives. Thus, this approach simply highlights incoherencies in discourses. It seemingly does not use specific norms other than positing that discourses should be coherent. Of course, according to this approach, a racist but coherent discourse would not be subject to criticism. So even if internal critiques directly and empirically analyse the object of those critiques, they do not take their normative position from that object. The normative position, for example, that a discourse should be coherent, is taken from outside and then applied to the material. Confusion may arise because of the fact that in discourse analysis, the term immanent critique is sometimes used to describe what we call internal critique. So for example, Reisigl and Wodak (2001) state that "'*text* or *discourse immanent critique*' aims at discovering inconsistencies, (self-) contradictions, paradoxes and dilemmas in the text-internal or discourse-internal, for example, lógico-semantic, cohesive, syntactic, performative, presuppositional, implicational, argumentation, fallacious and interactional (e.g., turn-taking) structures" (p. 32). This is exactly what I described with the term internal critique.

From this internal form of critique, I will differentiate another form that will finally lead us to the unfolding of our social critique. I am speaking here of *immanent* critique, which proceeds quite differently than an internal critique. Immanent critique means a normative position that is developed from existing society that not only reveals prospects for social change but also contributes to that change. This notion perhaps can help us find a solution to the problem of how to justify normative critique (see also Browne 2008; Romero 2013; Stahl 2013b, c). In this type of critique, the norms that we use are not taken from outside or from a specific procedure but directly from the object of critique. The basic form of this critique is the "if… then" form noted by Rosa (2009). If what society wants or accepts is X, then society should be organized in a specific, different form according to its own norms. For example, if

Table 1.1 Types of critique

	Starting point	Basis of critique
External critique	External	Contradiction between external criteria and existing practice
Procedural critique	External	Contradiction between criteria stemming from fair procedures and reality
Internal critique	Internal	Contradiction in the sense of inconsistencies between internal ideals and reality
Immanent critique	Internal	"Dialectical" contradiction inside society, crisis

Source: Adaption of Jaeggi (2014a: 309)

society wants radical equality, then all discrimination (whether based on race, class, gender, etc.) must be abolished. The existence of racism, classism, or sexism is incompatible with the self-proclaimed norm of radical equality. However, the first problem of this approach is to identify society's basic norms. Table 1.1 summarizes the basic differences among external, internal, and immanent critiques.

Immanent critique now needs both a theoretical approach to what society is and a practical approach to identify or extract the norms from that society that we want to use to criticize the social order. Regarding the social form of capitalism, Rahel Jaeggi (2014b: 323f) notes three main argumentation patterns that we can understand as normative grounds for critique and that could be applied for other types of social formation. The *functional* strategy criticizes something for being intrinsically dysfunctional. Something does not work as it is supposed to work. The *moral* argumentation claims that a specific social order is unjust. The *ethical* critique argues that a given social order does not allow individuals to live a good or complete life.

In all three cases, we encounter important problems when identifying "capitalism" as a basic social order, as if this description would be self-evident. First, what functions is capitalism supposed to fulfil? Is capitalism supposed to bring freedom and liberty, wealth, growth, and quick access to basic goods and services for all? Capitalism is not a subject that is able to state clearly what it is supposed to stand for. We could criticize a teapot made of chocolate arguing that it does not carry out the function a teapot should have. The chocolate would melt when entering in contact with hot liquid. However, who said that the original or main function of the chocolate teapot was to contain hot liquid? Perhaps the function was to serve a sweet, and instead of having the form of Santa Claus or an Easter bunny, it was given the form of a teapot. Functions are not inherent characteristics of objects but ascriptions we make to objects. The function of an apple is not to serve as food for humans. However, if we ascribe that function to apples, then we can complain about all apples that do not perform that function. We can criticize the serving of specific apples for being too small, not tasty, not healthy, rotten, and so on. The argument is only slightly different when criticizing objects produced by humans. The process of production usually implies the ascription of a function. If I build a guitar, I want it to sound good. If it does not, you can criticize the guitar (or the builder) on the basis that the guitar does not perform its declared function.

Coming back to the critique of a specific social order, regardless of whether the order is capitalism, we have to ask if it was either consciously made by human beings with the idea of performing a specific function or a mere secondary effect of what people were doing? It is likely that most social orders meet both criteria. Next, we must ask which functions people ascribe to a specific social order. Finally, we have to analyse whether the specific social order performs the ascribed function. However, Jaeggi introduces yet another argument that is very common in the critique of capitalism: It is possible that although a social order meets its function *now*, it cannot do so in the future. Therefore, the social order must be changed. We can find this critique, for example, when warning about the near-term ecological consequences of our way of production and consumption (Harvey 2014: 246ff). Again, this argument's basic structure would be, "If X is seen as basic function of a social order Y, then the social order is not meeting this criteria now or will not be able to meet this criteria in the future and, therefore, has to be changed."

Second, we could see that similar problems do arise when using the moral argument that a given social order is either unjust or producing unjust social relations. Here, we have to ask what is justice or better yet (remembering that we are attempting to uncover the immanent critique): what is justice *for a specific society*? Is it equality, liberty, access to health care, the right to private property, and so on.? Here again, we would have to find the moral reasons that dominate in a particular society and then analyse whether society can provide the specific moral goods and whether or not it could do better. Again, this argument could have a historic component. It could be possible for a society that provides basic moral goods—for example, an acceptable form of equality—to lose the ability to fulfil this moral claim in the future for reasons of its own dynamics.

Third, the problems with the functional and moral approach are also a true *mutatis mutandis* for the ethical argument. Here again, the basic structure of the argument would be as follows: If a specific way of life is good, then we could criticize a social order on the ground that it does not or cannot provide the possibility of living a good life, either now or in the future. In summary, we can say that whether we use functional, moral, or ethical norms, we always experience the problem of identifying what this society and its social order are intended to fulfil. If we do not want to make either exterior or procedural justifications (which, as we have seen, are ultimately based on exterior norms that justify the procedure) for the normative ground of critique, then the normative question of justification turns into a methodological problem. In the "if… then" scheme of immanent critique, we first have to find the norms that we use in the conditional clause. Only in the second step can we turn our analysis to the question of whether society lives up to its norms. However, to find the normative basis, we also must turn our attention to society because the basic idea of immanent critique is that norms should stem from society. The methodological problem is that society overall is not a conscious actor. We cannot ask society about its underlying norms. We can ask members of that society, perhaps especially distinguished members. However, if what was said before about ideologies is true, then members of a society are often or even mostly unaware of the underlying reasons, processes, and norms of society. People follow norms in everyday life but seldom do so consciously.

Even if we could clearly identify immanent norms to compare with society, the question of how to evaluate social order would remain. Only as an example—and staying strictly with moral norms—could we cite the last century's debates about the moral influence of markets (Herzog and Honneth 2014). Here, we find arguments about the goodness of markets as having the ability to create and distribute wealth, providing the possibility of limiting destructive individualism, fostering social integration, tempering violent passions, and creating more rational social organization (see, e.g., the classical moral argument of Smith 1977, 2002). Conversely, there are good arguments that criticize social disintegration caused by markets, social and structural violence, and the creation of inequality and extreme poverty (here, the classical opponent of Smith would be Marx 1990). Moreover, it is theoretically possible that both positions are right. A social order can produce justice and injustice simultaneously. In such a case, we would have to analyse the need for these justices and injustices and the possibility of abolishing the unjust part of the order without losing any moral goodness. Regarding social order, there are two, apparently opposite, positions that could be true at the same time. For the first position, we could paraphrase Charles Taylor, arguing that it is likely that all social orders "that have animated whole societies over some considerable stretch of time" have important positive characteristics with regard to function, morality, or ethics. However, we could reverse this argument with Foucault (see, e.g., Foucault 1994, 1975, 2010). We can suppose that in every more or less stable social order, there are power relations and oppression that run contrary to liberty but that guarantee stability over time.

Regarding the first problem, the identification of the norms that we want to use in our conditional sentence to criticize society, we can find a change in arguments over time. Perhaps the most important line of developing the immanent critique is that of the tradition of left Hegelianism as presented by the Frankfurt School. We therefore turn to Marxist and post-Marxist Critical Theory to detect social norms that are immanent in society. Before we do so, however, let us take an even closer look at the concept of immanent critique.

1.4 Untying Immanent Critique

The notion of immanent critique—a normative position that is developed from existing society that not only reveals prospects for social change but also contributes to that change—represents a solution to the problem of how to justify normative critique (see also Browne 2008; Romero 2013; Stahl 2013b, c). This type of critique is also described as immanent transcendence (Honneth 2000), context-bound universalism (Sauerwald 2009), or inner-worldly transcendence (Fink-Eitel 1993). Immanence, context-bound, or inner-worldliness refers to the attempt "to give the criterion of critique an objective support in pre-scientific practices" (Honneth 2000: 92). This is what Marx called the "this-sidedness of his thinking" (Marx 1970: 121). The notions of universalism and transcendence refer to the possibility of an emancipator change of given social relations in the sense of social self-liberation.

The notion of immanence and the notion of critique or transcendence can be divided into two aspects: norms and methods. Norms stem from the normative potential of the existing society (i.e., immanence) but point simultaneously towards a future society (i.e., transcendence and critique). As a method, the results not only should be developed completely out of the empirical material (i.e., immanence) but also should either indicate a practical path or be a powerful tool to change society (i.e., transcendence and critique).

We can distinguish three types of questions regarding norms. First, there are questions involving the notion of immanence and immanent norms: What are immanent norms? What degree of real or potential consciousness do subjects have regarding these norms? Are immanent norms accepted *de facto*, explicitly, entirely, or only partly? The second type of question refers to the notion of transcendence, that is, the normative stance that goes beyond existing social relations. These questions thus refer to the scope of the critique. Can we perceive and criticize only minor social mistakes and obvious misunderstandings, or is it possible to criticize society on a fundamental level? Does transcendence necessarily point in the direction of emancipation; in other words, is immanent critique necessarily progressive in the tradition of the Enlightenment? Finally, there are questions about the *relation* of immanence and transcendence. Can immanent norms have a transcendent character? Are all or only some (and if so, then which?) of the implicitly *de facto* or explicitly accepted norms of a transcendent nature?

For social philosophers, these normative aspects are particularly important (see also Romero 2013; Stahl 2013b). In addition, for social scientists, the methodological aspects of immanent critique are highly relevant. Here, several questions arise: How can immanent norms be detected and made visible (i.e., immanence as method)? What is the influence of criticism on its subjects, and what influence do subjects have on the criticized social relations (mode of action of critique)? How can social critics develop transcendent aspects from immanent norms (i.e., the subject of the research)? If we want to engage in critique as social scientific practice, we have to find answers to these methodological questions. However, let us turn first to the more theoretical questions of immanent critique.

Titus Stahl (2013c) differentiates two types of immanent critique: "hermeneutic" and "practice-based". The *hermeneutic immanent critique* takes its critical norms from a re-interpretation of explicitly accepted standards such as liberty, equality, or fraternity. This type of critique attempts both to use the "normative surplus" (Honneth 2011a, 2013)—which we can find, for example, in the mentioned norms—and to attempt to allow the full potential of these norms to flourish. Perhaps it is easier to understand the idea of "normative surplus" using an example: We can say that the norm of democracy has been widely accepted in most Western societies for more than a century. However, when people took this concept seriously, they began to notice that it is not enough to merely have the right to vote. To exercise one's democratic rights, one has to be able to participate in democratic debates to form political objectives and to participate in decision-making processes. Therefore, a basic right to an education was needed. To make use of the right to education and to participate in political debates, one must be free of both basic material needs and fear. Both needs and fears undermine a person's ability to do his or her best for the community. This insight was part of the beginning of social rights and the welfare state. Following actual debates accompanying social movements, it is easy to see that there is a broad perception of a democratic system being not democratic enough. Voting rights for migrant populations, relief from obstacles to plebiscite elements, or critiques of the economic influences in politics and media are only three of the claims for democratic extension accomplishing the normative surplus of the concept of democracy (on this argument, see also Herzog and Hernàndez 2009).

Remember that immanent critique meant not only to find socially accepted norms but also that these norms should point to another, future, more emancipated society. The norms should also have a transcendent character. Therefore, we could distinguish merely corrective immanent critique on the one hand from transcending immanent critique on the other hand. A corrective immanent critique of an affirmative critique (Romero 2013: 65) would then be a critique that refers to the norms crystallized in institutions without questioning the institutions themselves. As an example, we could cite norms such as those embodied in the discussion of same-sex marriage. Arguments that support same-sex marriage typically refer to the ideal of equality, which is accepted not only implicitly but also explicitly in many national and international legal systems. By referencing a type of equality that remains unrealized in our society, civil rights activists claim that same-sex couples should enjoy the same rights as heterogeneous couples, particularly with respect to marriage. The relatively smooth introduction of the right to same-sex marriage into the national laws of a dozen states and several sub-states during the last decade indicates that discrimination against homosexuals is not (or no longer) systemically important. In this argument, it is irrelevant how close a society comes to overcoming this type of discrimination. Imagine if someone had claimed legal equality for same-sex couples a century ago. Because homosexuality was criminalized and pathologized at that time, there was no systemic need for legal discrimination against homosexuals. Thus, both now and then, the claim for equal rights for same-sex couples is a corrective critique.

From this corrective critique, we can differentiate the transcending critique, which is characterized by the fact that the social change that is the target of such a critique encounters systemic resistance, such as the social norm of the recognition of individual merit in the labour market. The principle of merit is widely accepted. For example, because we accept that income should depend on the individual employee's achievements, we demand the same salary for the same performance and accept that individuals with higher merit should receive higher incomes. This merit principle becomes problematic when we consider what should count as individual merit. Many so-called "individual achievements" are the result of social constellations that do not depend on the individual but instead are the result of inherited material and cultural capital (see also the debate involving Honneth vs. Sloterdijk, Herzog and Hernàndez 2009). Thus, for example, a medical student's apparently objective marks do not precisely indicate the student's real and individual learning performance and life achievements. The son of a medical professor and a lawyer who always had sufficient cultural and material capital[5] to enable him to study under ideal conditions is compared via the grading system with a female, working-class student who is the child of immigrants and who first had to learn the language and then had to work to finance her coursework. Paraphrasing Marx, we might say that to relate their evidence of achievements to one another as meritorious, men must first equate their various life achievements and learning performances. They do not know it, but they do it.

Thus, if we want to realize the "normative surplus" of the merit principle, there are two challenges. On the one hand, biographical inequalities must be considered when measuring individual merit. In certain fields, we can already observe positive discrimination, which is known as affirmative action. To the extent that this type of discrimination is practiced in our societies, it is corrective, that is, it is a corrective immanent critique. On the other hand, birth privileges must be abolished or compensated for. This proposal refers to inheritance laws or the promotion of underprivileged children. This approach is also implemented in practice, particularly in the social-democratic version of capitalism. Here again, we only have a corrective immanent critique. However, this critique becomes transcending when we think these proposals through towards their logical end. Ultimately, these proposals refer to the impossibility of accumulating capital (either material or cultural) or more correctly: to use the accumulation as capital. Although certain forms of discrimination, such as discrimination against ethnic minorities, might be abolished without transcending the frame of a given society (because the discrimination is not relevant to the existence of the system), not all discrimination can be abandoned, particularly not discrimination based on class. The thesis that I would like to defend here is that the consequent compensation for accumulated cultural and material capital would disturb the basis of our social and economic system, which rests on the possibility of the creation of capital (it is exactly this feature the term *capital*ism stands for). Although

---

[5] I do not want to ignore that there are strong arguments against the use of Bourdieu's concepts of social, cultural, educative, and so on, capital (see e.g. Harvey 2014: 185f).

this type of critique also originates in a contradiction between claims and reality, it surpasses the corrective critique by revealing the systemic difficulties of fulfilling the demands; therefore, it is transcending immanent critique. I will return to both examples, that of the homosexual marriage and that of the merit principle, in the third chapter, in which I explain the empirical procedure of critique. At this stage of the argument, only the formal aspects of these examples are of interest.

The example provided here is very similar to Romero's (2013) proposal for the solution of the problem of the relation between immanence and transcendence. Although he suggests the use of immanent normative concepts, such as liberty or equality, he proposes not to do so in its institutionalized version. Following Romero, the institutionalized form would create the risk of producing only an affirmative critique. He instead proposes a re-interpretative or emancipator version of these concepts to reach the aim of a transcending position. However, here again, we experience the problem of the immanence of those re-interpretative or emancipator versions, which perhaps are defended only by a small emancipator or intellectual elite. If those normative versions that are about to bring the transcending stance are not representative of a large part or even a majority of society, but only a minority, then we face the question of the real immanence of these norms.

Nonetheless, the proposal I made here with the example of the consequences of the merit principles is slightly different from Romero's suggestion. I propose not to use an alternative or emancipator form of merit nor a re-interpretation of the existing norm, but instead to bring the already accepted version to its logical conclusion. The principle of non-discrimination is already accepted, although in practice, it is not yet completely abolished, which, as we have seen, is caused by systematic resistance.

Remember that we have been speaking here only about the specific case of a hermeneutic immanent critique, that is, that case of critique in which the detection of society's normative basis is not too complicated. However, Stahl (2013b) differentiated from that type of critique the *practice-based* form of immanent critique. This "practice-based" type of immanent critique is identified by Stahl as belonging to the Marxist tradition, particularly as articulated in the tradition of the Frankfurt School. Thus, the critic "must not only draw on the cultural meaning or the rules accepted in a given community, but also on his or her knowledge about the community's *objective practices and institutions*" (ibid. 535). In other words, this type of immanent critique always presupposes the existence of normative elements in social *practices* that are beyond the conscious understanding of the participants and upon which immanent critique can draw. For social analysis, such presupposing would mean a change in attention. Although practices are always discursively created, shaped, and interpreted by social actors, the primary focus of the analysis required for this type of critique must be practices and not more or less conscious language use, as seems to be the case for hermeneutic critique.

When looking not only for affirmative critique but also for real, transcending immanent critique, we have to seriously consider not only some of the insights made in this chapter but also those insights derived from practice-based immanent critique. The norms to which a critique refers are not always as obvious as those taken from the example that is embodied in the merit principle. Often, these norms are only implicitly present in practices and must be uncovered by social researchers. The proposal that I will make in Chap. 2 is that for the task of uncovering, we can draw on the toolbox from sociological discourse analysis, that is, those types of discourse analysis that have a focus beyond that of language and conversation. Here, we face serious methodological problems, which will be discussed in Sect. 1.6. However, we must first turn to those authors who are already working with what Stahl called the practice-based immanent critique. What are their responses to the pre-scientific practices that embody norms that can be made conscious and then used to criticize society in a transcending way? What are these practices, and which norms do they embody? As Stahl says, this approach is primarily followed by the Marxist and post-Marxist traditions of the Frankfurt School.

1.5 Post-Marxist Traditions: The Frankfurt School

We can roughly identify three generations of the Frankfurt School with three answers regarding the practical, pre-scientific, moral experiences that can be used to extract norms that help us criticize society. The first generation, which has provided intellectual leadership to the Institute for Social Research in Frankfurt since the 1920s, during the exile and again in Frankfurt until the end of the 1960s, is inseparable from the names of Theodor W. Adorno and Max Horkheimer, although other researchers such as Walter Benjamin, Erich Fromm, Siegfried Kracauer, or Herbert Marcuse were also highly relevant for the Institute's intellectual development. Their work remains influential in both the humanities and the social sciences. The main author of the second generation, who attempts to overcome what he calls the "sociological deficit" of the Frankfurt School, that is, the impossibility of empirically grounding a normative critique of society, was Jürgen Habermas. The most influential work of the Frankfurt School is that of Axel Honneth and his Theory of Recognition. What all of these generations have in common is that they attempt to perform immanent critique. However, the Frankfurt School's development is characterized by obvious ruptures with its former proposals.

1.5.1 First Generation: Adorno and Horkheimer

For the first generation, at least until the catastrophe of Auschwitz, the central practice that could help to overcome society was work. Following a classical Marxist argument, work was the key experience that puts those who work— that is, the working class—into a privileged position to understand and change society. The centrality of work in the Marxist tradition stems from the classical fragment about the master and the slave in Hegel's *Phenomenology of Spirit* (Hegel 1977). In this section, Hegel conceptually examines how true self-consciousness is built, that is, how knowledge about ourselves is created. To know about myself, I have to contact my limits, that is, my environment and other persons. In the section about the master and the slave, it is not love or friendship that influences how self-consciousness is created; instead, it is struggle. To learn about themselves, two self-consciousnesses fight. The struggle to the limits, over life and death, is seen as a possibility to confirm their self-consciousness. In the language of the twenty-first century, we could perhaps talk of a "stress test". One can never be sure of the limits (e.g., how much weight a rope can hold) unless these limits are tested. Hegel also contemplates the possibility of one of the fighters being killed, but this would not generate self-knowledge because there is no dialogue partner left to create self-consciousness. Therefore, the struggle ends with the fear of death of one self-consciousness, which then becomes the slave while the other becomes the master.

In the same way that we have to confront material reality to experience ourselves as physical beings with concrete limits, we also have to encounter other persons to understand our limits as persons. In this process of creating awareness, we need the other as a mirror for our self to create a "correct" self-image. What does this mean for self-knowledge? Hegel surprises us with the statement that "the truth of autonomous Consciousness is the consciousness of the slave" (ibid.: §192). Nevertheless, it becomes immediately clear what Hegel means when thinking about acknowledgement under the threat of punishment. In unequal power relations, those with more power cannot be sure that they will receive a "correct" self-image. Think about subordinates laughing at the boss's bad jokes. They are not in a position to mirror back a sincere opinion about the boss's humour. As a consequence, the boss does not receive an undisturbed self-image. For Hegel, the master never can be sure about himself because: (a) he is now recognized because of the fear of the slave (and therefore never can be sure if this is true recognition); (b) he is recognized by a "loser"; and (c) he has not experienced his own limits. Conversely, the slave who has experienced the fear of death knows about himself and has experienced his limits.

What is important in this section is the relation between subordination, self-consciousness, and consciousness on the one hand and the exterior, natural, and social context on the other hand. It is through his work that the slave or bondsman knows about reality. Hegel calls the work concrete negation, in contrast to the mere abstract negation or consumption of the master. Using a Marxist notion, it is the worker who relates to external nature, the production process, and social relations because of his work and his subordinated situation. And it is through his work that the worker can overcome this situation of serfdom. Following Hegel, "Through his service he [the slave/bondsman] rids himself of his attachment to natural existence in every single detail; and gets rid of it by working on it" (ibid.: §194).

For Marx and the first generation of the Frankfurt School, it is through the work process that the proletariat obtains a fuller consciousness about itself, nature, and society. This knowledge, and of course the fact that the vast majority of people belong to the category of the "working class", is one of the main justifications for the belief in the historic mission of the working class. With the help of the intellectual, workers can become more conscious of their situation because they have a specific interest in social change. Or, in the words of immanent critique: the working process is the practical, pre-scientific, moral experience that is used by Marx, Horkheimer, and Adorno (e.g., Marx 1990; Horkheimer 1975; Adorno and Horkheimer 2002) to criticize society as it exists. Society does not fulfil the claims for a more emancipated life inherent in the fact that people work and relate both to each other and to nature through work. Therefore, we can say that the working class has both an ontological and an epistemological centrality in Marxist and post-Marxist theory. The working class has a specific capacity and a privileged access to knowledge because of the practice of work. Moreover, for Marx, the working class was the "universal class", that is, a class whose interest coincides with the needs of the entire society. In this sense, the immanent critique in Marxism always makes universal claims.

This conviction of the historic mission of the working class passed relatively intact through the multiple historic setbacks in the 50 years after the death of Karl Marx. The most important setback perhaps was the First World War, in which workers of all lands did not follow the slogan of Marx to unite but killed themselves in the European battlefields. Workers and vast swaths of their parties, including the German social democrats, fought wars between nations instead of class struggle. Even the use of poison gas—that is, the first use of weapons of mass destruction—did not destroy the belief in both the general process of historic progress (understood also as moral progress) and the power of the working class. Of course, although theoretical debates had to recognize these debacles for the workers' movement, they mainly did so by including some elements of ideology and contexts of delusions. Authors such as György Lukács (1971) and Adorno and Horkheimer (2002) included social psychological comprehensions in their theoretical models to explain the working class's difficulty in understanding their "objective" class position or mission.

This generally positive view of the capacity of the working class changes rapidly and profoundly with the catastrophe of Auschwitz. For Horkheimer and Adorno, Auschwitz as the synonym for the industrial extermination of the Jewish population[6] was not just a hiatus in history after which social and political philosophy could continue with the same premises as before the Holocaust. Auschwitz profoundly changed the Frankfurt School's members' perception of philosophy, history, and the working class. As early as in their exile in California, Horkheimer and Adorno finish their "Dialectics of Enlightenment" (2002). In that text, they follow the supposition of barbarity not as the opposite of Enlightenment but as a fundamental part of the rational domination of nature and humans enabled by Enlightenment. According to Horkheimer and Adorno, the totalitarian character of Enlightenment and the growth of human power create alienation from the objects of that power: "The absurdity of a state of affairs in which the power of the system over human beings increases with every step they take away from the power of nature denounces the reason of the reasonable society as obsolete" (ibid.: 31f). Power of humans over nature turns into power over humans by humans and by some abstract social "system".

Regarding the working class and the possibility of using the work experience as a practice with normative content that can be used for immanent social critique, the authors of the first generation of the Frankfurt School are quite sceptical after Auschwitz. The German working class cheerfully supported the totalitarian regime and entered into the Second World War similar to the European working class less than 40 years before. For Horkheimer and Adorno, however, it was the Holocaust that made the distinction or showed a more profound error in the conception of the working class. Work, the capacity of organization and collaboration, the knowledge about nature and others, was not used for building up a better future but for its opposite: the industrial organization of death. Moreover, it was exactly work's capacity that enabled the "rational" organization of that barbarity.

We can understand Hannah Arendt's (2006) observation of the trial against Adolf Eichmann as a good example of the lack of emancipator norms in the working process. Eichmann used all of his effort, skills,

---

[6] It should not be forgotten that in the concentration camps, political enemies, including trade unionists, socialists, communists, and anarchists were murdered together with homosexuals and the mentally disabled. Furthermore, ethnic and religious minorities, such as Gypsies and Jehovah's Witnesses, were also exterminated.

and knowledge in a rational manner to organize trains. In other circumstances, he would have been an excellent worker. However, there was one decisive difference between him and contemporary railway workers: Eichmann was responsible for organizing the deportation of the mainly Eastern European population to the concentration camps.

With the loss of faith in work as practice with immanent emancipator content and in the working class as a privileged subject for social change, Critical Theory withdrew from the attempt to identify emancipator normative content in empirical, observable reality. In the totally administered world, "there is no standpoint outside of the whole affair which can be referred to, from which the ghost could be called by its name" (Adorno 1979: 369). Sometimes, it seems that for Adorno, art and especially music can be the transcending instance because it "is magic delivered from the lie of being truth" (Adorno 1964: 222). However, the overall picture is that of a negative theory unable to provide a critical normative instance for moral emancipator progress. The image that Adorno especially liked to use was that of a message in a bottle: the Hegelian foundation that cannot be deciphered, that is, which cannot be employed in contemporary society, is kept in a bottle and thrown into the ocean of history, hoping that someday humanity will be able to decipher the foundations and use it for emancipation. However, in the time of Adorno, neither he nor his colleagues were able to take that revolutionary step.

1.5.2 Second Generation: Habermas

It is this impossibility of grounding normative critique in empirical social research that Jürgen Habermas, the most prominent author of the second generation of the Frankfurt School, described as "sociological deficit". His opinion about the message-in-a-bottle-situation of the Critical Theory in the 1960s was quite negative: "For me there was no Critical Theory, no consistent theory. Adorno wrote essays on culture criticism and gave seminars on Hegel. He presented a certain Marxist background – and that was it" (Habermas 1981: 128). Habermas' own approach, most famously presented in the *Theory of Communicative Action* (Habermas 1984, 1987), attempts to overcome the intellectual blockage of Critical

Theory. His theoretical offer presents a change of paradigm from work to communication (quite common in social theory of the 1970s and 1980s and present in other theoretical traditions such as System Theory (Luhmann 1997) or post-structuralism (Foucault 1981, 2002)). In the practice of communication, Habermas observed an underlying normative content that could be used for social critique. Immanent critique can be based on the practical, intuitive, pre-scientific experiences of communication. For him "reaching understanding is the inherent telos of human speech" (Habermas 1984: 287). Following Habermas, the original mode of communication includes three validity claims[7]: the claim of rightness, that is about the normative correct interpersonal relation between the participants in the communication process; truthfulness, a claim about the true intentions of the participants; and a claim on truth, that is, a claim about the truth of the content of communication. At the beginning, we discussed the Habermasian discourse as a pragmatic procedure of grounding normative critique (see Sec. 1.3). However, we can also understand his proposal as practice-based immanent critique. What is important now for our argument is that in an ideal speech situation, we can engage in a type of meta-communication. We can question each of the validity claims and therefore discuss empirical truth, moral rightness, and personal sincerity. Understanding Habermas' proposal as immanent critique, we now can see that the practices of competent speakers present exactly the pre-scientific anchor that we sought. The practice of speaking has a normative content because "understanding", for Habermas, is seen as a practice of emancipation. This emancipation as an objective is already accepted by people when engaging in communication. Thus, we have here an example of practice-based immanent critique. Insofar as communication is a universal practice, the Theory of Communicative Action makes a universal claim similar to that of Marxism.

However, as we have seen before, the Theory of Communicative Action has attracted sharp criticism from diverse sources. Whereas the Luhmannian system theory generally doubts the possibility of normative social critique (e.g., Luhmann 1997: 229), for our argument post-structuralist and later, Frankfurt School, critics are more interesting. Both coincide in the basic comprehension that there is no space in society for

---

[7] Later, Habermas includes comprehensibility as a fourth validity claim.

free discourse. Speech acts are pre-structured by powerful norms that limit the space of the expressible. As Foucault states in his famous inaugural lecture (Foucault 1981), several mechanisms exclude people, topics, and ways of speaking from the discourse. Furthermore, there are mechanisms that constantly produce and reproduce discourses in a specific order. For the omnipresence of these mechanisms that precede all our speech acts, a free discourse or a free meta-discourse as imagined by Foucault is impossible. Discourses always fall in a normatively nourished context.

If this is true of every speech act, it is true *a fortiori* of the highly structured space of public debates. Axel Honneth, Habermas' disciple, who wrote his Ph.D. thesis about the early works of Foucault and the first generation of the Frankfurt School, writes in 1981 before publishing his thesis, "My supposition is that the social theory of Habermas is constituted in the way that it has to ignore systematically all the forms of social critique that are not recognized by the public political-hegemonic space" (Honneth 2000: 112). Here, we can see two critics of Habermas: first, the criticism of the notion of avant-garde. In the normative debate, the possibilities of being heard are unequally distributed. The higher an individual's linguistic, intellectual, and social, resources for using language in the public sphere, the more likely the individual is to be considered in the debate that, according to Habermas, should lead to understanding and universal emancipation. Other forms of expressing critique (or more generally, discomfort) that are not articulated in the dominant form in public space are not considered in the Theory of Communicative Action. Second, as we have said, the public space is pre-structured in a way that strongly influences the possibility of a free understanding. Public space is not a neutral field. It is a field of established social relations, power structures, and normative backgrounds.

1.5.3 Third Generation: Honneth

In his own proposal, Honneth does not break completely with his master Habermas. Moreover, his own Theory of Recognition can be understood as a development of the Habermasian theory attempting to compensate for two criticisms. In an interview with Luc Boltanski and Robin Celikates, he claims,

As far as I was concerned, there was no going back to the time before Habermas's 'communicative turn'. With the benefit of hindsight, it would be fair to suggest that, in my case, the development of a distinct approach has been an intensification of, rather than a break with, the Habermasian model. [...] I became aware of my discontent with Habermas only when I sought to identify the limitations of early critical theory myself. In a way, Habermas regards a sociological limitation of early critical theory as the main problem: Adorno and Horkheimer create an utterly distorted picture of society, since they fail to understand that people act communicatively and participate in practices of justification. It took me some time to realize that precisely this criticism can be levelled against Habermas himself. His focus on the linguistic structure of communication and on its underlying rationality means that he pays insufficient attention to the social experiences with which they are entangled. People's everyday experiences have no place in Habermas's theory. (Honneth in: Boltanski and Honneth 2009: 86f)

In his own theoretical approach, Honneth does not identify the practices of communication as pre-scientific moral experiences for immanent critique but instead as emotional reactions to disrespect. In his Theory of Recognition (1992), Honneth identifies three spheres and three modes of recognition. Following Hegel, in the family, individuals are recognized as having concrete needs in the mode of love. In civil society, the formal autonomy of persons is recognized by their rights. In the state, affective intuition about the family and the cognitive concept of rights are somehow sublated (*aufgehoben*)[8] in intellectual intuition (or the "affect made rational"). Here, the mode of recognition is solidarity between subjects with specific individuality (see also Hernàndez and Herzog 2011a; Pippin 2007). Unlike Hegel, whose early work inspires Honneth's use of the concept of recognition, Honneth does not see these three spheres as partaking in a process in which one sphere leads to the creation of another and that finally comes to an end with the (Prussian) state. For Honneth, modern societies have three parallel, interwoven spheres with three equally important modes of recognition.

---

[8] For information regarding the complex meaning and translation of *aufheben* and *Aufhebung*, see Froeb (2012).

Table 1.2 Honneth's theory of recognition

Sphere of recognition	Family	State	Society
Mode of recognition	Emotional support	Cognitive respect	Social esteem
Dimension of personality	Needs and emotions	Moral responsibility	Traits and abilities
Forms of recognition	Primary relationships (love, friendship)	Legal relation (rights)	Community of value (solidarity)
Developmental potential	Freedom from economic restrictions, for example	Generalization, de-formalization	Individualization, equalization
Practical relation-to-self	Basic self-confidence	Self-respect	Self-esteem
Forms of disrespect	Abuse and rape	Denial of rights, exclusion	Denigration, insult
Threatened component of personality	Physical integrity	Social integrity	"Honour", dignity

What is important for Honneth is that every sphere corresponds to a specific dimension of personality and practical self-relation. For successful self-relation, one must experience recognition in all three spheres. Otherwise, one component of one's personality is threatened. Honneth summarizes his approach as shown in Table 1.2. (Honneth 1992: 129—slightly expanded):

Here, we can observe the three spheres of recognition and how each of these spheres corresponds to different modes of recognition: emotional support, cognitive respect, and social esteem. In our society, each of these modes is linked to a specific form of recognition. This is why most authors, such as Thompson (2006), do not differentiate between modes and forms, and instead, speak directly of the following three modes: love, respect, and esteem. As we can see, for Honneth, there is a developmental potential in the different modes of recognition, which is one reason that the process or "struggle" for recognition has not yet come to an end: love in families can be liberated from economic pressures (Honneth in: Fraser and Honneth 2003: 139), and rights can be generalized or esteem can be distributed in a more individualized way. What is important is that all of these modes refer to specific dimensions of personality and that if one part of a person's personality is disrespected, that disrespect can lead not only to social disintegration but also to serious damage to one's self-relation.

Coming back to our original question of how to empirically ground the norms that we use to criticize society, we can now say that the moral, pre-scientific experience upon which we rely is the *capacity of suffering of disrespect*. This capacity overcomes some theoretical problems of the Habermasian approach to discourses. It is democratic in the sense that everybody has the ability to feel social suffering. Suffering is not limited to those able to discursively articulate that suffering or to articulate even a coherent approach to a social order where that suffering has been abolished. However, for the critic, this suffering points to a pathological social order, that is, an order that does not allow the individual to become fully autonomous. Moreover, unlike suffering that is neither made by humans nor can be abolished by humans, social suffering is only possible because individuals, often unconsciously, have claims of recognition. For example, it is only because I claim that my neighbour should greet me when he sees me on the street that I can feel disregarded when he fails to do so. Here, we can see how people's pre-scientific reactions towards disrespect are relegated to the normative claims inherent in social practices. With the Honnethian relation of claims of recognition and successful self-realization, these affective reactions and normative claims point towards emancipation—in this case, towards a society that allows its members full or at least broader autonomy. This approach, therefore, is not only immanent but also transcendent because it exceeds the given social order. We could therefore reformulate the famous Habermasian sentence in recognitional terms: *Autonomy or emancipation is immanent as the objective of social suffering.*

This form of critique could be either an affirmative or a corrective immanent critique if it relied only on the actual interpretation of norms and did not point towards a structural social change. However, there are two reasons to think that the sociology of disrespect, that is, the sociological analysis of social suffering, can lead to real, transcending immanent critique. We can find the first reason in the *necessary* character of some social pathologies. Remember that by necessary, we mean that specific pathologies and therefore specific forms of disrespect are related to the fundamental social structure. One example could be that capitalism, at least as we know it, cannot provide equal recognition in all of its forms to all members of (world) society. Therefore, certain forms of abolishing disrespect would require a fundamental change in social order. Social suffering whose abolition points towards the sublation of necessary contradictions would then transcend critique. Those sufferings that could easily be abolished within the given social order, in contrast, are mere corrective critique.

The second reason justifying the speaking of transcending critique is noted by Stahl (2013b), who argues that suffering does not refer to *actual* interpretation of norms but instead to the *correct* interpretation of those norms. This orientation towards the future is the orientation towards another society. In his "rediscovering of hope" (Stahl 2013b: 457), the critic uncovers the hope that is immanent in social action and social relation but that until now has not been recognized by social actors.

What is important from a methodological perspective is that although we are discussing often silent, unarticulated, or at least not discursively articulated suffering, other people can still understand that suffering. Honneth argues that we can empathically read others' feelings of disrespect. We therefore can understand—as Honneth does—this approach as a type of theory of silent communicative action. The capacity of empathy points towards a shared normative horizon; otherwise, we would be unable to understand others' suffering.

At first glance, the Theory of Recognition seems unable to overcome the sociological deficit of the Habermasian approach. The current task is to elaborate a "Sociology of Disrespect" (Herzog 2013a) to identify the multiple feelings of disrespect and transform them—like a photo negative—towards their inherent claims for recognition. This sociology of disrespect would reconstruct the norms inherent in social suffering and its corresponding claims of recognition. Here, we are considering genuine social critique because in the second part of this sociology of disrespect, existing society is to be criticized for not fulfilling claims of recognition.

Perhaps the Theory of Recognition, or better yet its reverse, the theory of disrespect, can close the gap with the post-structuralist notion of critique. Remember that for Foucault, critique was the "will not to be governed like that". However, Foucault was surprisingly silent about the reasons for that will. Foucault's problem with naming his normative standpoint would have been that *every* normative position might be made the object of critique. Nonetheless, although not openly following a normative approach, Foucault too argues from a certain position with normative implications. Probably his will not to be governed like that is grounded in the experience of social suffering. This suffering need not necessarily be his own. However, he had an empathic understanding of others' suffering. In particular, Foucault's political work and his research on people in prison, people with marginalized sexualities, and people in psychiatric wards made him sensitive to the negative consequences of the existing social order. Foucault's will to criticize existing society or forms of government (remember that he uses the term "government" in a very broad sense) is therefore based on moral, pre-scientific experiences of human suffering, which Foucault is able to read empathically.

It is now the task of social research to uncover the normative basis of society, a basis that we can find not only in manifest and even discursive practices but also in silent social suffering and institutionalized practices (Honneth 2011a). If we want to uncover the norms that we can use for social critique, we therefore must perform a "normative reconstruction" of institutions, institutionalized practices, and silent and manifest suffering. In that sense, it could seem that practical immanent critique is the same as sociology of critique. Although it is true that immanent critique must uncover the hidden sources and structures of critique, it goes a step further in a double sense. Immanent critique is interested not only in practices of critique (or justification) but also in everyday practices, assuming these too have a normative background. Additionally, immanent critique clearly wants to be transformative, overcoming a moment of crisis in society (on that point, see also the debate between Boltanski and Honneth 2009). However, in that enterprise of immanent critique in the sense of recognition theory, the social scientist will experience at least two major methodological problems that can be described as the sociological deficit of recognition theory (Herzog and Hernàndez 2012).

The first problem involves the epistemological status of the silent affective reactions mentioned above. Not all suffering or all sublation of suffering points towards emancipation. Here, Honneth also speaks of an "ideology of recognition". As an example, he mentions the "recognition" that a young neo-Nazi receives from his or her peer group (Honneth

2004). However, this recognition is possible only under the premise of disrespect for other social groups. Here, we face a problem: if not every suffering or every recognition points towards a development in terms of recognition, then the question arises of how to differentiate legitimate claims of recognition from unjustified or ideological forms of recognition.

The second problem is methodological in nature. It is not enough to say that the claim or the possibility of recognition is immanent in affective reactions of disrespect; the theory has to be made operative for empirical research to capture and understand the diverse forms of (silent) suffering. In the same way that the Theory of Communicative Action had problems taking into account claims that are not formulated in public arguments, the Theory of Recognition is also confronted by questions. First, how can we perceive the feelings of disrespect of others, especially when those feelings are not publically, verbally, or even manifestly expressed? Second, how can we "give voice" to those silently suffering without falling into the trap of Habermasian, pre-structured discourses? Would critics not hold exactly the same non-democratic, privileged position that those with more cultural capital hold in the Habermasian theory?

1.6 Overcoming the Sociological Deficit of the Frankfurt School with the Help of Discourse Analysis

The thesis that I want to defend in this book is that the recent proposals of sociological discourse analysis can serve, if used consciously, to overcome the sociological deficit of recognition theory. Discourse analysis can be the missing link between social, political, and philosophical considerations and empirical social research that we need to formulate normative social critique. Discourse analysis, as proposed originally by Foucault, was developed in the 1980s and 1990s mainly from linguists who saw in the Foucauldian notion of discourse a helpful tool for more social analysis. However, their work continued to concentrate primarily on language. If they referred to non-linguistic reality, they often did so by simple parallelisms or by referring to existing social research. There was seldom a direct link between the research on linguistic aspects of discourses and what we perhaps can call "extra-discursive realities".

With the beginning of the new millennium, a new wave of discourse analysts from a more sociological background attempted to overcome that shortcoming of the existing approaches. These approaches took seriously the Foucaultian demand to analyse the conditions of discourse production—the practices and material and symbolic realities that enable a certain discourse. Here, we can find Reiner Keller, with his *Sociology of Knowledge Approach to Discourses* (Keller 2005a, b), who differentiates between the material and symbolic order of discourses and who, like Foucault, is especially sensitive to the relationship between power, knowledge, and discourses. The *dispositif-analysis* (Bührmann and Schneider 2007, 2008) approaches the *net* between the elements of the discourse universe, that is, between discourse formations, knowledge, power, and social reality (relations, experiences…). Gutiérrez-Rodriguez (2007) proposes an approach to *reading affects* that is especially interesting for the purpose of understanding silent and silenced suffering. Other approaches exist between social science and linguistic attempts to include extra-discursive reality by analysing pre-constructions necessary for the understanding of speech acts. This is the case of Angermuller's approach in *Discourse Analysis After Structuralism* (Angermuller 2007, 2014).

These sociological approaches to discourses can help us to simultaneously analyse both implicit and explicit claims of recognition at the same time and to understand the materialities, practices, and institutions that produce and reproduce both material and symbolic disrespect. These approaches are not limited to helping us understand each of the parts mentioned. Instead, the original, broad, Foucauldian approach to discourses facilitates our understanding of the *relations* between the parts. Moreover, sociological approaches to discourses could be used not only to "read" recognition and disrespect but also to relate the production of both discourses to the social structure. Sociological discourse analysis, with its attention to symbolic and material reality, could simultaneously analyse the obstacles that arise when one attempts to fulfil the claims of recognition inherent in social suffering.

One of the challenges of such an analysis is that the empirical research must show whether or not the reasons for not meeting the claims of recognition are systematic. In the former case, we talk about transcending social critique; in the latter we talk about a corrective one. We can understand claims for recognition either as discourses or as discursive games or conflicts about claims of recognition. Furthermore, we must understand that these games or conflicts have to be analysed not only on the language level; they also must consider the "discursive infrastructure", that is, the symbolic and material contexts of discourses. This approach can help differentiate systemic or structural problems in keeping the promises of recognition from problems that are mere historic particularities. In particular, the reference to the discursive infrastructure, understood as the crystallization of recognition orders and orders of disrespect in institutions and institutionalized practices, seems appropriate to show the deep incrustation of recognition claims and structural disrespect.

1.7 On Critical Discourse Analysis

When writing about critique and discourse analysis, it seems that the natural ally of such enterprises would be the well-known approach that already includes all of the relevant terms in its name: Critical Discourse Analysis (CDA). However, as I argue in this chapter, CDA struggles with two problems: the methodological problem of analysing non-linguistic realities and the normative problem of the source of the standpoint of its critique.

Researchers who perform CDA (most prominently Fairclough 1995; van Dijk 1993; Wodak 1996) openly aver that they follow a critical approach. By offering methods to reconstruct social senses that are implicit and unnoticed by the social actors involved, these scholars offer tools for understanding social reality in general and the power effects of specific discourses in particular. However, it should be acknowledged that there are both theoretical and methodological differences between these "classical" authors. Whereas the socio-cognitive model of van Dijk is centred on the analysis of social cognition and mental models perceived as fundamental for mediation between discourses and the social, Wodak focuses on the historical context as important for understanding actual discourses. Discourse practice is at the centre of Fairclough's approach because it fulfils functions similar to van Dijk's mental model, that is, it "straddles the division between society and culture on the one hand, and discourse, language and text on the other" (Fairclough 1995: 60).[9]

As we have seen, since the beginning of the new millennium, sociology has contributed critical input regarding discourse analysis, leading to further developments in the relationship between text and material and between practical and/or institutional infrastructural elements and consequences (Bührmann and Schneider 2007, 2008; Keller 2005a; see also Bührmann et al. 2007; Keller et al. 2005). Although other theoretical inputs are important for all of these approaches, whether they are from linguistic or sociological backgrounds (e.g., Habermas for Wodak and Fairclough, Gramsci for Fairclough, Berger and Luckmann for Keller), the one author central to all of these works is surely Michel Foucault. The problem here is that the existing approaches on discourse follow, often implicitly, Foucault's notion of critique. Although even critical discourse analysts seldom work directly on the notion of critique, by following Foucault's post-structuralist approach they tacitly accept the notion of critique inherent to post-structuralism.

As we have seen, Foucault understands critique both as the "art of not being governed or better, the art of not being governed like that" (Foucault 2007: 44) and as "insubordination" or "desubjugation" (ibid: 47). In these formulations, there is something negative (e.g., being governed in a certain way or subjugation) from which Foucault would like to distance himself because he was suspicious of all existing—and particularly hegemonic—norms and values. Furthermore, Foucault was aware that even concepts such as liberty, autonomy, democracy, and emancipation can become instruments of repression, power, and/or governance. Both Foucault and contemporary discourse analysts did great work uncovering the hidden power relations in the most diverse and initially unsuspicious discourses. They often can show how identities, subject positions, knowledge, power relations, and even material realities present logical

---

[9] Unfortunately, the insights of discourse theory and analysis have not yet been systematically analysed by the most important authors of the Frankfurt School (for a systematic analysis of the relation of discourse, critique, and the Frankfurt School, see also Forchtner (2011) and Forchtner and Tominc (2012)).

outcomes of the discourse order. For most of these works, we understand that the discourse analysts want not only to describe discourse orders and their outcomes but also to condemn or criticize that order. In other words, they do not want to be governed like this. They do not want the existing discourse order to persist.

However, insofar as discourse analysis wants to be critical, it faces a serious problem of justification of the will of not being governed like this. In the post-structuralist view, power is immanent in all social relations. However, if there is simultaneously an inherent distrust of authoritative power, social relations, and even the values and norms of illustration, then there is a problem for one's *own* normative viewpoint. Should we strive for no normative viewpoint? Is it possible to argue without adopting a normative stance? Or does pretending to have no normative stance only mean failing to recognize one's own (implicit) normative viewpoint? Where does the will not to be governed come from if not from some norms about what is right and wrong, what is a good and bad way of organizing our living together?

At this juncture, we face the problem of an infinite regress. Even if discourse analysts frequently assume a critical stance towards hegemonic norms, their research is typically based on implicit ideals of freedom or autonomy, including when these researchers expose the contingencies of hegemonic discourses or propose alternative interpretations and/or emphasize oppressed discourses. Such scholarly work implicitly refers to a normative viewpoint, that is, to a position that can be employed as a positive and normative point of reference. They do so, for example, by presenting informed alternatives saying implicitly that it is either good or better to have alternatives to choose from, and that the freedom of fully aware decision making is a positive value. However, even if we can show that there is an implicit normative posture espousing freedom and autonomy in the studies of many discourse analysts, the problem of the critique of liberty and autonomy remains. For example, in neoliberal discourses, liberty and autonomy are frequently employed as tools to transfer responsibility for certain problems to various individuals (Fairclough 2004). Freedom of choice can turn into the imposition of choosing. It can be used to blame people for their situations if those situations are understood as the result of a considered choice.

Furthermore, liberty and autonomy are used to abolish social solidarity and collective responsibility. We could easily form the suspicion that even liberty and autonomy are specific historic ideals that have certain power effects. Therefore, we might be able to transform the values and norms of the discourse analyst into the object of a second-order discourse analysis, thus revealing the power structures and power effects of discourse researchers. In addition, if "critique is the movement by which the subject gives himself the right to question truth on its effects of power and question power on its discourses of truth" (Foucault 2007: 47), then we can repeatedly question our own position with respect to its power effects. We would end up with an infinite regress and never arrive at an irrefutable normative ground.

Another approach often used by critical discourse analysts is to openly defend a particular normative standpoint. Although critical of hegemonic norms, such researchers defend particular norms that also can have (undesired) power effects. When adopting a normative viewpoint before performing discourse analysis, these researchers must assume a normative position outside of the criticized material. In any event, it is *their* normative point of view, not necessarily that of society. One example of such a position would be the "sociodiagnostic critique" defended by the Discourse-Historical Approach (DHA), which "aims at detecting problematic – 'problematic' from the analyst's normative-ethical perspective [...] – social and political goals and functions of discursive practices" (Reisigl and Wodak 2001: 32). Similarly, to reveal the ambiguity of this procedure, we can cite the proposal of van Dijk regarding the normative position of critical discourse studies (CDS):

> One of the tasks of CDS is to formulate the norms that define such 'discursive injustice'. [...] Such a research policy presupposes an ethical assessment, implying that discourses as social interaction may be *illegitimate* according to some fundamental *norms*, for instance, those of international human and social rights. At the same time, critical analysis should be aware of the fact that such norms and rights change historically, and that some definitions of 'international' may well mean 'Western'. As a criterion, we thus call any discourse unjust if it violates the internationally recognized human rights of people and contributes to social inequality. (van Dijk 2009: 62)

Thus, van Dijk presents the dilemma faced by most critical discourse analysts. Although they are aware of the problems related to Eurocentrism and particular norms and values, there seems to be no alternative to insisting on a specific foundation of particular rules, such as human rights (as in van Dijk). Most of us would certainly agree that the development of human rights represents important progress in human history. Ultimately, however, human rights are a bundle of norms developed by a specific social group at a specific historic moment that cannot be considered a timeless, context-independent point of reference for social criticism.

Thus, criticism based on human rights argumentation is simply a specific type of *external critique* that adopts an external normative position and analyses social reality based on the degree to which it differs from that external benchmark. We have seen that other ways of referring to external ideals include basing the critique on one's own (reasoned) arguments. Independent of how well these arguments are grounded, they nonetheless reflect a particular external position. Similarly, critiques based on the Bible, the Quran, or any utopian ideal are ultimately forms of external critique.

To summarize the problem of critique in discourse studies, we can say that we are confronting the classical Münchhausen trilemma: justifications based on first principles either lead to an infinite regress or logical circle or must break off from the process of justification by taking an arbitrary point (Albert 1968: 13). If we do not want to refer to particular external norms and values, we have to ground our "will not to be governed like that" in socially accepted norms and values. In other words, we have to make society's normative breeding ground coincide with our standpoint of critique. The ultimate ground of critique cannot be our personal "will" imagined as detached from society; it must be society itself. We called this procedure immanent critique. Therefore, we could perhaps reformulate the famous statement of Foucault's definition of critique as "the social will not to be governed like that" or "the will not to be governed contrary to the norms and values of society".

Judith Butler (2001) attempts to obtain a deeper understanding of what is critique for Foucault by analysing not only what he says but also what he does. The specific procedure of Foucault's analysis is for Butler his way of *doing* critique. When Foucault asks about the procedures of exclusion (e.g., Foucault 1981), the procedures through which a field of knowledge is structured and the procedure through which categories either come into play or are suppressed, then what is important for Butler is the practice of asking. "For the very question, 'what is critique?' is an instance of the critical enterprise in question, and so the question not only poses the problem—what is this critique that we supposedly do or, indeed, aspire to do?—but enacts a certain mode of questioning which will prove central to the activity of critique itself" (Butler 2001). For Butler, the questions recognize both that there is no "correct" normative standpoint and that it is only possible to perform several approximations of the object of critique, thus showing alternative social orders without saying that they are somehow "better". However, following Butler, Foucault is not surrendering to either the problem or the normative origin of critique but instead recognizing that the person who criticizes is him- or herself the result of subjection and subjectivation. There is "no self-forming outside of a mode of subjectivation, which is to say, there is no self-forming outside of the norms that orchestrate the possible formation of the subject" (ibid.). Having recognized this and still insisting on critique is, for Butler, a "virtue". Acknowledging that there is no appropriate discourse and no appropriate social order, virtue consists of showing the fractures in the existing discourses and the existing social order.

1.8 Summarizing the Possibility of Empirically Grounded, Normative Social Critique

We have seen that discourse analysis, even when calling itself critical, encounters difficulties in normatively justifying its own procedure. It seems impossible to engage in critique, that is, to engage in practices that value what should and what should not be without taking a normative stance, regardless of how weak this stance may be. In discourse analysis, we find two main forms of normative stances. On the one hand, we have unacknowledged normative positions. In this case, researchers attempt to avoid committing themselves to normative positions. As we have seen, however, in every normative statement, that is, in every critique, there is a normative position.¹⁰ Therefore, not naming the normative position is nothing but an unconscious or unacknowledged normative position that—ironically—is inconsistent with the very same normative position of making aware the unacknowledged. Conversely, we can find the open defence, often with very good reasons, of a normative point of view in discourse analysis, whether it be general norms such as liberty, equality, or solidarity or written norms such as laws, constitutions, or the human rights charter. Nonetheless, every norm may or may not coincide with the implicit normative basis of society, that is, with those norms consciously or unconsciously accepted by the vast majority of a given group of people. Moreover, every norm that coincides at a given historic moment with the normative basis of society in another historic situation could be outdated. Normative claims, like claims of recognition, change with time and with social and normative possibilities and achievements. Therefore, we can only criticize society on the ground of our *actual expectations of future*. Once the first step is taken, once the first social change is achieved, we have to be open to modify our normative coordinate system. Norms themselves change through critique. There is a need to transform the norms themselves. Moreover, both practices and the critic herself change in this process of critique. In other words: critique is a self-changing practice (see e.g., Jaeggi 2015). Here, we can close the gap to what Foucault called the "perpetual" question of how not to be governed like that. Because the critic, the norms, and the practices change, the process of critique will always continue and cannot be anticipated but must always arise out of the specific historic and social situation. Moreover, because critique points to structural problems and systematic insufficiencies, it shows the immanent crisis of society and therefore is an accelerant of social crisis. It makes systematic failures conscious and pushes towards an overcoming of deep structural problems.

If we want to overcome the normative shortcoming of discourse analysis then we must turn to immanent critique, a critique that takes its normative standpoint from the norms implicit in social practices and confronts society with these norms to change the social order. However, what seems

---

¹⁰ We could even argue with Habermas that in every statement, in every act that can be understood by others, there is a normative position regarding the normative rightness of the communicative act.

complicated in theory—because we do not know in which social, pre-scientific practices we can find implicit norms—is even more complicated in practice. We are confronted by the methodological problem of how to uncover the normative content of moral experiences. We have seen that the post-Hegelian, post-Marxist approach of the Frankfurt School has turned its attention from work experiences (Marx, Horkheimer, Adorno…) to discourses as speech acts (Habermas) and finally to affective reactions to disrespect (Honneth). In this last theoretical proposal, we can see the ultimate social norm, namely, that social suffering should not exist. Therefore, social critics must analyse the normative content of suffering while researching the social structure with respect to both its systematic production of suffering and its potentialities and resistances related to overcoming the production of disrespect.

For the integrated analysis of social structure and social suffering, I again pointed to discourse analysis. Especially in its more sociological version, with its attention to practices, material realities and even affects, discourse analysis can offer exactly the integrative approach that is needed to uncover the normative breeding ground of social relations and simultaneously use the norms found in this procedure to hold them against the existing social order. However, to use discourse analysis for social critique, we need some analytical tools that help us in that task. The analytical tools—mainly concepts that guide us in the organization of empirical work—can be found in the vast literature on (sociological) discourse analysis. For our purpose, they have to build either a conscious unity or (at least) conscious relations between the elements of analysis. Furthermore, we should not forget the aim of the analysis proposed here. We do not want to show only discourses or discursive infrastructure; we also want to criticize social structure using the very norms of society. The missing link between the social theory on critique as presented in this chapter and the analytical tools as presented in the next chapter represent a coherent theory on social reality that we can find in discourse theory, namely, the theory of the discursive construction of realities (Keller et al. 2005). Therefore, the next chapter will start by explaining how discourse theory offers an approach of what "the social" or social reality can mean.

References

Adorno, T. W. (1979) *Soziologische Schriften I, Gesammelte Werke, Vol 7*, (Frankfurt/Main: Suhrkamp).
Adorno, T. W. & Benjamin, W. (1999) *The Complete Correspondence 1928–1940*, (Cambridge, Mass.: Harvard University Press).
Adorno, T. W., & Horkheimer, M. (2002) *Dialectic of Enlightenment*, (Stanford: University Press).
Arendt, H. (2006) *Eichmann in Jerusalem: A Report on the Banality of Evil*, (New York: Penguin).
Albert, H. (1968) *Traktat über kritische Vernunft*, (Tübingen: J.C.B. Mohr).
Angermuller, J. (2007) *Nach dem Strukturalismus. Theoriediskurs und intellektuelles Feld in Frankreich*, (Bielefeld: Transcript).
Angermuller, J. (2014) *Poststructuralist Discourse Analysis: Subjectivity in Enunciative Pragmatics*, (Houndmills: Palgrave Macmillan).
Bauer, B. (2002) *English Edition of Bruno Bauer's 1843 Christianity Exposed: A Recollection of the 18th Century and a Contribution to the Crisis of the Nineteenth Century*, (New York: EMP, Lewiston).
Boltanski, L. & Honneth, A. (2009) 'Soziologie der Kritik oder Kritische Theorie? Ein Gespräch mit Robin Celikates', in: Rahel Jaeggi, Tilo Wesche (eds.), *Was ist Kritik?*, (Frankfurt/Main: Suhrkamp), pp. 81–114.
Browne, C (2008) 'The End of Immanent Critique?', *European Journal of Social Theory* 11(1): 5–24.
Bührmann, A. & Schneider, W. (2007) 'More Than Just a Discursive Practice? Conceptual Principles and Methodological Aspects of Dispositif Analysis', *Forum: Qualitative Social Research*, 8(2).
Bührmann, A. & Schneider, W.(2008) *Vom Diskurs zum Dispositiv - Eine Einführung in die Dispositivanalyse*, (Bielefeld: transcript).
Bührmann, A., Diaz-Bone, R., Gutiérrez-Rodríguez, E., Schneider, W., Kendall, G. & Tirado, F. (2007) 'Editorial FQS 8(2): From Michel Foucault's Theory of Discourse to Empirical Discourse Research', *Forum Qualitative Sozialforschung / Forum: Qualitative Social Research*, 8(2), http://nbn-resolving.de/urn:nbn:de:0114-fqs0702E10.
Butler, J. (2001) 'What is Critique? An Essay on Foucault's Virtue', in: *eipcp – european institute on progressive cultural policies*, online resource available at http://eipcp.net/transversal/0806/butler/en.
Engels, F. (1963) 'Brief an Marx – 19. November 1944', in: *Marx-Engels Werke*, 27 (Berlin: Dietz), pp. 9–13.

Eßbach, W. (1982) *Gegenzüge. Der Materialismus des Selbst und seine Ausgrenzung aus dem Marxismus,* (Frankfurt a.M.: Materialis).
Eßbach, W. (1988) *Die Junghegelianer. Soziologie einer Intellektuellengruppe.* (Munich: Wilhelm Fink).
Fairclough, N. (1995) *Critical Discourse Analysis,* (London: Longman).
Fairclough, N. (2004) 'Critical discourse analysis in researching language in the new capitalism: Overdetermination, transdisciplinarity and textual analysis', in: Harison, C. & Young, L. (eds.) *Systemic functional linguistics and critical discourse analysis,* (London: Continuum), pp. 103–122.
Feuerbach, L. (1957) *The Essence of Christianity,* (New York: Harper & Row, Publishers).
Fink-Eitel, H. (1993) 'Innerweltliche Transzendenz', *Mercur* 47(3), 237–45.
Forchtner, B (2011) 'Critique, the discourse-historical approach and the Frankfurt School', *Critical Discourse Studies,* 8(1): 1–14.
Forchtner, B & Tominc A (2012) 'Critique and argumentation. On the relation between discourse-historical approach and pragma-dialectics', *Journal of Language and Politics,* 11(1): 31–50.
Foucault, M. (1975) *Discipline and Punish: the Birth of the Prison,* (New York: Random House).
Foucault, M. (1979) *The History of Sexuality Volume 1: An Introduction,* (London: Allen Lane).
Foucault, M. (1981) 'The order of discourse', in: R. Young *(ed.) Untying the text: A post-structural anthology,* (Boston, MA: Routledge & Kegan Paul), pp. 48–78.
Foucault, M. (1994) *The Order of the Things. An Archeology of Human Sciences,* (New York: Random House.)
Foucault, M. (2002) *The Archaeology of Knowledge,* (London and New York: Routledge).
Foucault M. (2006) *History of Madness,* (New York: Routledge).
Foucault, M. (2007) *The politics of truth,* (Los Angeles: Semiotext(e)).
Foucault, M. (2010) *The Government of Self and Others. Lectures at the Collège de France 1982–1983,* (New York: Palgrave Macmillan).
Frankfurt, H.G. (1971) 'Freedom of the will and concept of the person', *The Journal of Philosophy,* vol. 1xviii, no.1 January 1971.
Freud, S. (2002) *Civilization and Its Discontents,* (London: Penguin).
Froeb, K. (2012) 'Sublation', in: *hegel.net,* online resource. Available at: http://www.hegel.net/en/sublation.htm. Date of access: 02/06/2015.
Fraser, N. & Honneth, A. (2003) *Redistribution or Recognition? A Political-Philosophical Exchange,* (London: Verso).

Gutiérrez-Rodríguez, E. (2007) 'Reading Affect—On the Heterotopian Spaces of Care and Domestic Work in Private Households', *Forum: Qualitative Social Research,* 8(2). http://nbn-resolving.de/urn:nbn:de: 0114-fqs0702118.

Habermas, J. (1971) 'Vorbereitende Bemerkungen zu einer Theorie der kommunikativen Kompetenz', in: Habermas, J. & Luhmann, N.: *Theorie der Gesellschaft oder Sozialtechnologie. Was leistet die Systemtheorie?,* (Frankfurt/ Main: Suhrkamp), pp. 101–141.

Habermas, J. (1981) 'Dialektik der Rationalisierung', Interview with Axel Honneth, Eberhard Knödler-Bunte and Arno Widman, *Ästhetik und Kommunikation,* 45/46: 126–155.

Habermas, J. (1984) *Theory of Communicative Action Volume One: Reason and the Rationalization of Society,* (Boston, Mass.: Beacon Press).

Habermas, J. (1987) *Theory of Communicative Action Volume Two: Liveworld and System: A Critique of Functionalist Reason,* (Boston, Mass.: Beacon Press).

Habermas, J. (1990) 'Ethics, Politics and History', from an interview conducted by Jean-Marc Ferry, in: D. Rasmussen *(ed.), Philosophy and Social Criticism,* (Cambridge, Massachusetts: MIT Press).

Harvey, D. (2014) *Seventeen Contradictions and the End of Capitalism,* (London: Profile Books).

Hegel, G. W. F. (1977) [1807] *Phenomenology of the Spirit,* (Oxford: Clarendon Press).

Hegel, G. W. F. (2004) *The philosophy of history,* (New York: Dover).

Hernàndez, F. & Herzog, B. (2011a) 'Axel Honneth: Estaciones hacia una teoría crítica del reconocimiento', in; Honneth, A., *La sociedad del desprecio,* (Madrid: Trotta), pp. 9–38.

Herzog, B. (2013a) 'Negation of Social Recognition. From Theory of recognition towards sociology of disrespect', *Contribution at the conference "Crisis, critique and change",* Torino, September 2013.

Herzog, B. (2016a) 'Discourse analysis as immanent critique: Possibilities and limits of normative critique in empirical discourse studies, *Discourse & Society,* 27(3): 278-292.

Herzog, B. & Hernàndez, F. (2009) 'Honneth vs. Sloterdijk – Duelo sobre el futuro del mundo', *Posdata, supplement of the newspaper Levante-EMV,* 6 November.

Herzog, B. & Hernàndez, F. (2012) 'La noción de «lucha» en la teoría de reconocimiento de Axel Honneth. Sobre la posibilidad de subsanar el «déficit sociológico» de la Teoría Crítica con la ayuda del Análisis del Discurso', *Política & Sociedad,* 49(3): 609–623.

Herzog, L. & Honneth, A. (eds.) (2014) *Der Wert des Marktes. Ein ökonomisch-philosophischer Diskurs vom 18. Jahrhundert bis zur Gegenwart*, (Frankfurt/Main: Suhrkamp).
Honneth, A. (1992) *Der Kampf um Anerkennung. Zur moralischen Grammatik sozialer Konflikte*, (Frankfurt: Suhrkamp). [English: Honneth, A (1995) *The Struggle for Recognition: The Moral Grammar of Social Conflicts*, (Cambridge: Polity Press).]
Honneth, A. (ed.) (1995a) *Kommunitarismus – Eine Debatte über die moralischen Grundlagen moderner Gesellschaften*, (Frankfurt: Campus).
Honneth, A. (2000) *Das Andere der Gerechtigkeit*, (Frankfurt/Main: Suhrkamp).
Honneth, A. (2004) 'Anerkennung als Ideologie', *WestEnd Neue Zeitschrift für Sozialforschung*, 1: 51–70.
Honneth, A. (2011a) *Das Recht der Freiheit*, (Berlin: Suhrkamp).
Honneth, A. (2013) 'Theorie der Anerkennung als kritische Theorie der Gesellschaft? – Ein Interview mit Axel Honneth', *Soziologiemagazin* http://soziologieblog.hypotheses.org/4000.
Horkheimer, M. (1975) 'Traditional and critical theory', in: ibid. *From Critical Theory: Selected Essays*, (New York: Continuum Publishing), pp. 188–243.
Jaeggi, R. (2014a) *Kritik von Lebensformen*, (Berlin: Suhrkamp).
Jaeggi, R. (2014b) 'Was (wenn überhaupt etwas) ist falsch am Kapitalismus? Drei Wege der Kapitalismuskritik', in: Jaeggi, R. & Loick, D. (eds.) *Nach Marx – Philosophie, Kritik, Praxis*, (Berlin: Suhrkamp), pp. 321–349.
Jaeggi, R. (2015) 'Objektive Kritik und Krise. Überlegungen zu einer materialistischen Grundlegung von Sozialkritik', in: Martin, D., Martin, S. & Wissel, J. (eds.) *Perspektiven und Konstellationen kritischer Theorie*, (Münster: Westfälisches Dampfboot), pp. 14–28.
Keller, R. (2005a) 'Analysing Discourse. An Approach From the Sociology of Knowledge', *Forum: Qualitative Social Research*, 6(3).
Keller, R. (2005b) *Wissenssoziologische Diskursanalyse – Grundlegung eines Forschungsprogrammes*, (Wiesbaden: Verlag für Sozialwissenschaften).
Keller, R., Hirseland, A., Schneider, W. & Viehöver, W. (Eds.) (2005) *Die diskursive Konstruktion von Wirklichkeit: Zum Verhältnis von Wissenssoziologie und Diskursforschung*, (Konstanz: UVK).
Lenk, K. (1984) *Ideologie. Ideologiekritik und Wissenssoziologie*, (Frankfurt a.M.: Luchterhand).
Luhmann, Niklas (1997) *Die Gesellschaft der Gesellschaft*, (Frankfurt/Main: Suhrkamp).
Lukács, G. (1971) *History and Class Consciousness*, (London: Merlin).

MacIntyre, A. (1984) *Is Patriotism a Virtue?*, (Kansas City: University of Kansas, Dept. of Philosophy).
Marx, K. (1843) *Critique of Hegel's Philosophy of Right*, Marxist Internet Archive, on-line resource https://www.marxists.org/archive/marx/works/1843/critique-hpr/intro.htm.
Marx, K. (1956) *The Holy Family or Critique of Critical Criticism. -Against Bruno Bauer and Company*, (Moscow: Foreign Languages Publishing House).
Marx, K. (1970) 'Thesis on Feuerbach', in: Marx K., Engels F. *The German Ideology*, (New York: International), pp. 121–123.
Marx, K. (1958) 'Die deutsche Ideologie', *Marx-Engels Werke*, Vol. 3, (Berlin: Dietz).
Marx, K. (1962) *The Capital*, Vol. III, (London: Lawrence and Wishart).
Marx, K. (1990) *Capital, Volume I.*, (London: Penguin Books).
Newman, S. (2003) 'Stirner and Foucault: Toward a Post-Kantian Freedom', *Postmodern Culture* 13(2) http://muse.jhu.edu/journals/postmodern_culture/v013/13.2newman.html.
Pippin, R. (2007) 'Recognition and Reconciliation: Actualized Agency in Hegel's Jena Phenomenology', in: van den Brink, B. & Owen, D. (eds.) *Recognition and Power. Axel Honneth and the Tradition of Critical Social Theory*, (Cambridge: University Press), pp. 57–78.
Rawls, John (1971) *A theory of justice*, (Cambridge / London: Harvard University Press).
Rawls, John (1999) *A theory of justice – Revised edition*, (Cambridge / London: Harvard University Press).
Reisigl, M. & Wodak, R. (2001) *Discourse and Discrimination. Rhetorics of Racism and Antisemitism*, (London: Routledge).
Romero, J. M. (2013) 'Sobre la pretensión de trascendencia de la crítica inmanente', *Diálogo Filosófico*, 85: 55–75.
Rosa, H. (2009), 'Kapitalismus als Dynamisierungsspirale - Soziologie als Gesellschaftskritik', in: Dörre, K; Lessenich, S. & Rosa, H., *Soziologie, Kaptialismus, Kritik: Eine Debatte*, (Frankfurt/Main: Suhrkamp), pp. 87–124.
Smith, A. (1977) *An Inquiry into the Nature and Causes of the Wealth of Nations*, (Chicago: University of Chicago Press).
Smith, A. (2002) *The Theory of Moral Sentiments*, (Cambridge: University Press).
Stahl, T. (2013a) *Einführung in die Metaethik*, (Stuttgart: Reclam).
Stahl, T (2013b) *Immanente Kritik. Elemente einer Theorie sozialer Praktiken*, (Frankfurt M./New York: Campus).
Stahl, T (2013c) 'Habermas and the project of immanent critique', *Constellations*, Vol. 20(4): 533–552.

Stirner, M. (1995) *The Ego and Its Own*, (Cambridge / New York: University Press).
Taylor, C. (1989) 'Cross-Purposes: The Liberal-Communitarian Debate', in: Rosenblum, N. L. (ed.) *Liberalism and the Moral Life*, (Cambridge: Harvard University Press), pp. 159–182.
Thompson, S. (2006) *The Political Theory of Recognition. A Critical Introduction*, (Cambridge: Polity).
van Dijk, T. (1993) 'Principles of critical discourse analysis', *Discourse & Society*, 4: 249–283.
van Dijk, T. (2009) 'Critical Discourse Studies: A Sociocognitive Approach', in: Wodak, R. & Meyer, M. (eds.) *Methods for Critical discourse Analysis*, (London: Sage), pp. 62–85.
Walzer, M. (1990) 'The Communitarian Critique of Liberalism', *Political Theory*, 1: 6–23.
Wodak, R. (1996) *Disorders of discourse*, (London: Longman).

2

Analytical Tools

2.1 The Discursive Construction of Realities

We were able to see a relationship—or as Foucault calls it, a "relation of brotherhood"—between critical discourse studies and Critical Theory, with its core of immanent critique. However, there was a sociological or empirical deficit of contemporary approaches on immanent critique, along with theoretical deficits on critique in discourse studies. If we want to bridge the gap between the theory of social critique and empirical discourse analysis, we need an approach that captures society, social structure, or more generally, reality in discourse theoretical terms on the one hand and that offers analytical tools to carry out social research on the other hand. We can find such an approach in the thesis of the discursive construction of realities (Keller et al. 2005).

Behind that thesis, we can identify a long discussion dating back to 1932 with Alfred Schütz and his work on the "meaningful construction of the social world" (Schütz 1967). For Schütz, "real" means considering that a phenomenon has a specific, significant relation with us. Although every individual has different experiences or "streams of consciousness", we can essentially share significations with others through communication. This shared, common, or social meaning between two or more individuals is never completely identical because of the participants' various background experiences. Therefore, we can find something like an ontological uncertainty of meaning. However, the common meaning is strong enough to allow social interaction in everyday life.

Schütz strongly influenced Peter Berger and Thomas Luckmann, who published their book *The Social Construction of Reality*" in 1966 (Berger and Luckmann 1967). Those authors, who influenced a generation of sociologists, analyse the *social* construction of knowledge and its *institutionalization*. In their work, they underline the important role of language for the creation, conservation, and transmission of knowledge. Human language objectifies, that is, makes present, so that people can relate to themselves events in other regions of the world that occurred in the past or will take place in the future. However, language cannot transcend only time and space; it can also transcend reality. We can easily speak and therefore either make present or objectify hypothetical reality for example, by speaking of a green dog. Furthermore, language is a stock of knowledge. Words precede us, and although we are able to create new words and new meanings, they force us to use these words with their more or less fixed meanings if we want to communicate.

Regarding this strand of the sociology of knowledge, the "discursive construction of realities" presents three important enhancements. First, it includes the post-structuralist approach to discourses as developed by and in the tradition of Michel Foucault (e.g., 1981, 2002). The notion of "discourse" as it is used here refers to a structured and institutionalized way of speaking in which the rules of creation can be brought to light and can be the object of social analysis (Foucault 2002; Link 1986). These rules limit and structure how subjects use language. In this sociological discourse model, it is assumed that discourses and non-discursive reality (e.g., social action, institutions) influence each other. Discourse theory gives us an approach to *how* social realities are constructed. This points towards *discourse analysis* for researching the processes of social construction of realities and analysing the results of these types of processes.

Second, we no longer think of reality in the singular, as if there were one "objective" reality to be uncovered by social researchers. Rather, we must identify diverse discourses about the same object, which thus constitute different realities for different social groups. In any event, this does not mean that there are as many realities as there are subjects. Usually social perceptions are shared between members of a group. Moreover, there are often hierarchies and hegemonies giving one discourse or interpretation of social reality priority over others. Therefore, when performing discourse analysis we are always doing social analysis. We are usually uninterested in what a particular person says. Even when discourse analysts research a particular person's talks or writings, they do so taking into account the *social* sources and the *social* effects of the production of texts and talks. Foucault would say that discourse expresses *itself* through persons. Finally, there is also a limitation related to the thesis of the "discursive construction of realities". Social researchers working with that approach only focus on the part of reality that is constructed through discourses (Keller et al. 2005: 8).

2.2 On the Relation Between Discursive and Non-discursive Realities

This final limitation mentioned leads us to the question of which part of social reality is *not* constructed through and by discourses. Here, different scholars have given different answers for the last few decades. For example, in his book *The Construction of Social Reality* (1995), John Searle distinguishes between facts that depend on language and facts that do not. For him, it is institutionalized reality that depends on language, whereas non-institutionalized facts are independent of language. Therefore, a mountain can have snow in winter or two birds can form a couple independent of language. However, for institutionalized facts, that is, facts that express norms, we need the existence of language. Thus, when human beings marry, they relate to each other in a normatively significant way. There are many specific norms regarding the roles of husbands and wives, that is, what they should do and what they should not do.

Perhaps it would be helpful to point to the extreme positions in the debate on the distinction between discursive and non-discursive reality. On the one hand, we have the approach by Ernesto Laclau and Chantal Mouffe (2014), who state that everything is discourse or, more accurately, that objects cannot constitute themselves outside of discursive conditions. In other words, although there may be many phenomena independent of discourses, we currently constitute them as objects of knowledge; they are already included in the discursive games. On the other hand, we can find authors who argue for a clear differentiation between the discursive and the non-discursive (e.g., Fairclough 1992; Wodak 1996). These authors, who hail primarily from a linguistic background, usually concentrate on language and its use when performing discourse analysis (van Dijk 1993). Therefore, especially in the Anglo-Saxon world, "discourse analysis" and "conversation analysis" are often used as synonyms whereas in a sociological, Foucaultian tradition, there are clear differences.

However, let us have a deeper look at the very challenging and coherent approach of Laclau and Mouffe on discourses. In their theoretical work on hegemony, they write as follows:

> Our analysis rejects the distinction between discursive and non-discursive practices. It affirms: a) that every object is constituted as an object of discourse, insofar as no object is given outside every discursive condition of emergence; and b) that any distinction between what are usually called the linguistic and behavioural aspects of a social practice, is either an incorrect distinction or ought to find its place as a differentiation within the social production of *meaning*, which is structured under the form of discursive totalities. (Laclau and Mouffe 2014: 93—emphasis B.H.)

To understand their approach to hegemony, it is important to recall the authors' distinction between moments and elements. We can say that moments are articulated elements. This distinction means that we can find elements to be a pre-discursive phenomenon. However, at the very instant elements become articulated, they constitute moments. In other words, we cannot speak or even think of elements without converting them into moments and thus including them in discourses.

To come back to the question of a social structure, system, or totality, we note that articulatory practices create a "structured totality" or simply, a discourse. This totality is not a casual accumulation of moments but has a necessary character. "Whoever says system says arrangement of conformity of parts in a structure that transcends and explains its elements. Everything is so *necessary* in it that modifications of the whole and of the details reciprocally condition one another" (ibid.: 92). However, discourses are never fixed entities. There is always a space left for new articulatory practices, that is, for converting elements into moments and creating discourses.

With these basic vocabularies in mind, we can now understand Laclau and Mouffe's approach to materiality. We have seen that there are elements that are not discursively structured. Laclau and Mouffe cite the example of an earthquake that is independent of human action, discourses, or either individual or collective will. However, as an object, it is already part of discourses—that is, discourses of risk and uncertainty, of international interrelations, of the natural environment, or divine actions. What Laclau and Mouffe deny "is not that such objects exist externally to thought, but that rather different assertion that they could constitute themselves as objects outside any discursive condition of emergence" (ibid.: 94). This finally means that every discourse has a material character and that discourses are not just mental or linguistic constructs but that they are at the very core of what reality is. No material aspect of reality can be understood without discourses. In other words, materiality is nothing (for us) without discourses; every discourse has a material character. With this complex but coherent approach, we finally abolish the distinction between the discursive and the material or between the discursive and non-discursive. Every object insofar as it is an object for us, whether it is speech acts or other acts, material reality, ideologies, knowledge, or power, is part of discourses and can be the subject of discourse analysis.

As I said, the approach is coherent. However, it is neither new nor helpful for empirical research. It is not new: similar approaches have a long-standing tradition in philosophy. The motto "Everything is discourse" bears a very close resemblance to the apparent radicalness of "everything is phenomenon", "everything is spirit", or "everything is consciousness". Of course, there is no phenomenon that is not phenomenon and there is nothing that we can perceive consciously that is not consciousness. It is the same circular—but coherent—argument that we cannot engage in discourses on objects without that object being part of discourses. Understood in this manner, the theses defended by Laclau and Mouffe are true—but tautological. They do not help make a distinction for empirical analysis. Understanding everything as discourse does not introduce analytical differentiation between elements that can be helpful for discourse analysis. Moreover, Laclau and Mouffe's discourse theory threatens to blur the differences between parts of discourses.

However, this must not be the case. Saying that everything in the basket is fruit does not necessarily mean that everything is the same, that everything must be eaten in the same way, or everything tastes identical. Although we accept the objects in the basket as fruits, we can introduce several distinctions on a new level, which logically arises even prior to the concept of fruit. In the same way, we can accept that everything is discourse as a second-order truth. The differentiation between logical orders means that it still makes sense to speak of language, practices, materialities, social actors, ideology, and knowledge, power, or social structure. Although strictly speaking, in a general sense, all of these concepts and their underlying social phenomena may be objects of discourses: these objects, *analytically*, can be differentiated and classified. Even in the words of Laclau and Mouffe, we can justify these separate concepts "as a differentiation within the social production of *meaning*, which is structured under the form of discursive totalities" (p. 92, emphasis mine). In other words, there may be an overall concept of discourse or discursive structure that includes all articulated objects. However, for analytical purposes, we can distinguish these objects based on either our research interests or our research questions (Fig. 2.1).

Because the purpose of this chapter is to make available the tools of discourse analysis for social critique, that is, to prepare the ground for empirical social research, I will follow the approach of Laclau and Mouffe only in one very generic way: Because everything is discourse, everything can be analysed from a discourse-analytical approach. In a similar

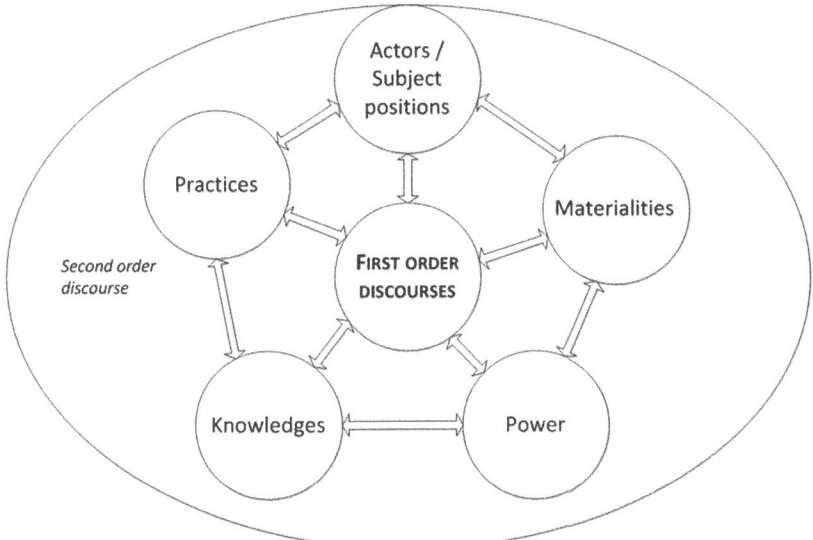

Fig. 2.1 Second-order discourse and first-order elements

(but slightly different) manner, Ruiz Ruiz (2009) understands discourse as "every practice used by subject to give meaning to social reality" (§3). Nonetheless, in what follows, I want to insist on the distinction between discourse and non-discursive reality for analytical purposes. *Therefore, I will understand discourse as an "institutionalized way of speaking"* (Link 1986). However, keeping in mind that even what is classically called non-discursive reality can be understood as discourse, I will show how we can use the very logics of discourse analysis to understand what I call non-discursive realities, that is, practices, materialities, knowledge, and so on.

However, it is the notion of institutionalization that relates speech acts, language, and language use directly to what I will call the discursive infrastructure, the non-discursive aspects of discourses. In other words, discourses (in a narrow sense) cannot be analysed without reference to their conditions of emergence and their place in the social order, or in the words of Ruiz Ruiz (2009), without "contextual analysis". That is why discourse analysis is always more than a linguistic enterprise. It is a fundamentally *social* research. This is why in practice, it seems impossible do draw a clear line between these concepts. When doing research on discourses, we must always consider the non-discursive infrastructure and conversely, when doing research on non-discursive aspects of the social, we must always consider the discursive production of meaning that gives sense to non-discursive aspects.

I understand practices, materialities, social actors and their identities, ideology, and knowledge, power, and social structure as non-discursive reality. As noted, however, these aspects of non-discursive realities must be seen in relation to the field of language and discourses. Analysing discourses means analysing both language and non-discursive reality. Discourses have to be understood in a field of actors, practices, materialities, and so on. The possibility of the appearance and the effects of such discourses go far beyond the analysis of language. Discourses not only represent the world but also give it meaning and signify it (Fairclough 1992: 64). The very same object can be embedded in different discourses and therefore can have different conflicting meanings. Or, in the words of Laclau and Mouffe: "Yet, a discursive structure is not a merely 'cognitive' or 'contemplative' entity; it is an articulatory practice which constitutes and organizes social relations" (Laclau and Mouffe 2014: 82). These articulatory practices depend on the material and symbolic resources for articulation (or discourse production). In this articulation, we can find power relations, repressive social norms, and emancipator ones. The task of our analysis will be to uncover the content of discourses and non-discursive reality.

It is for this complete, holistic character that discourse analysis seems especially appropriate for doing research on social critique. As noted at the end of Chap. 1, this sociological version of discourse analysis can show the normative content of practices, material realities, and even affects. Here, the normative content is part of the *social meaning* of these objects of analysis. This social meaning can exceed the individual understanding of the objects and can be uncovered with interpretative discourse analysis. As we have been, the normative content must be simultaneously held against social reality, against social practices, the material organization of society, and so on. Again, this reality can only be understood in the context of its discursive production, that is, the social production of the meaning of these contexts. When performing these two steps simultaneously, we can immanently criticize social order. We criticize social structure with the norms immanent in both discursive and non-discursive reality. By unfolding the conditions of production of the norms on the one hand and the—perhaps opposed—social order on the other hand, we will be able to show the distance between both or (in a manner that is the same) we will show whether there is a possibility of reconciliation within the social order or whether the critique transcends society.

2.3 Analytical Concepts

Discourse analysis usually understands itself as existing in the tradition of post-*structuralism*. Although post-structuralism emphasizes the possibility of discontinuities, I will insist that the elements of analysis—that is, language, practices, materialities, and so on—are structured. Structuralism does understand structures as doing more than repeating patterns that are contrary to casual events. Being structured refers first to the fact that the elements in question appear in relation to other elements, being either of the same type or of a different type. This appearance typically takes place in a field. So, for example, practices are related to other practices, to subjects typically performing these practices, to knowledge about the field, and to the material and discursive conditions and effects of those practices.

When doing discourse analysis—that is, when interpreting the field of appearance as a discursive field—we therefore can never separate one of the analytical concepts presented here as if it were an independent unit of analysis. However, it is impossible to analyse all aspects, all elements of a given social phenomenon. Social phenomena, especially those in which we are interested for social critique, were once enormously complex. Moreover, social research is not about describing a highly complex situation but instead is about reducing its complexity to make the situation understandable both for oneself and for others. Below, we will present some of the possible elements of discourse analysis as social critique. However, it is the researcher who must choose and relate those elements that most suit her object of interest.

2.3.1 Practices

2.3.1.1 On Practices

As we have seen, practices are especially important for immanent social critique. Stahl (2013c) even presents the "practice-based immanent critique" as the primary and original theoretical tradition of Critical Theory. Practices, this tradition generally supposes, can have normative contents that can be used to criticize social order. Even if people are not aware of this content, the normativity inherent in practices can point towards a future, more emancipated society. However, there were many differences regarding which practices contain that special normative content. Labour, art production, speech acts, or practices of recognition and disrespect are the most common suspects for grounding normative social critique. To have the ability to analyse practices regarding their normative content, we must first understand what practices are.

In sociology, we are accustomed to differentiating terms that seem synonymous in everyday speech. This is the case, for example, for action and practices. The term "action" is at the very core of the classical definition of sociology by Max Weber (1978): "Sociology […] is a science concerning itself with the interpretive understanding of social action […] We shall speak of 'action' insofar as the acting individual attaches a subjective meaning to his behaviour - be it overt or covert, omission or acquiescence. Action is 'social' insofar as its subjective meaning takes account of the behaviour of others and is thereby oriented in its course" (ibid.: 4). For Weber, what distinguishes an action from a mere doing is that the former includes a subjective meaning. By his definition, even doing nothing—that is, an omission—can be an action when it is related to an individual meaning, when the omission is conscious. So, for example, when I hear cries for help but decide not to intervene, I would be making a conscious omission and therefore acting. However, when I am unable to perceive the cries and therefore do not help, I would not be acting because there is no subjective sense in my omission. This definition is the very core of the sociological conception of understanding [*verstehen*]. Again, in everyday life, we often use explanation and understanding as synonyms although for a sociologist, they are not synonymous.

The difference between explanation and understanding is that we can only understand what has meaning. So, for example, we can understand human actions. Although we might be able to explain the eruption of a volcano using geological terms, such as tectonic plates and magma chambers, we will not be able to understand a volcano. Unlike our ancestors, we do not believe that there is a subjective meaning involving some deistic entity in the rupture of the volcano. However, when we attempt to understand a friend's behaviour, we attempt to understand the particular sense or meaning of the action for him or her. Weber writes the following about meaning: "'Meaning' may be of two types. The term may refer first to the actual existing meaning in the given concrete case of a particular actor, or to the average or approximate meaning attributable to a given plurality of actors; or secondly to the theoretically conceived *pure types* of subjective meaning attributed to the hypothetical actor or actors in a given type of action. In no case does it refer to an objectively 'correct' meaning or one which is 'true' in some metaphysical sense" (ibid.).

There is one main methodological and one important theoretical problem related to the understanding of actions.

Methodologically, it is difficult to know the meaning of an action for another person. Sometimes we can ask the person. However, even in the case that we receive the best and most sincere answer that the person is able to give, we still experience the problem of understanding the person's words. Do the words really mean exactly the same for the other person as for us? This is the general problem of the impossibility of understanding what Schütz (1967) has noted. We can end up in an infinite regress, attempting to understand the explication of the given explication … or we can assume that at some point, we must *interpret* the information received. For the necessity of interpreting to understand, Max Weber is seen as one of the founding fathers of *interpretative sociology*. Interpretative sociology and the interpretative paradigm, which in most cases leads to qualitative research, assumes that there is an ultimate, ontological impossibility of being certain about the meaning interpreted/understood. This is one main reason that qualitative techniques are often seen as "soft", "less objective", or "less scientific" than those that operate with numbers. However, if we want to *understand* others' actions—whether in everyday life or as part of a research project—there is no alternative to the precarious process of interpretation. Therefore, independently of whether we analyse actions or the explication people give for their actions, we must interpret what we perceive.

Additionally, there is a theoretical problem: Namely, it is not at all clear whether we can situate meaning within the individual. This problem will ultimately lead us to our notion of practice as opposed to action. The notion of practice is a social term in a triple sense, adding three important aspects to the notion of individual action. The first is that often actions are repeated doings, whether by the same person or by others. Millions of people cycle, chat with each other, and wash their dishes. The notion of practices comprehends a structure or pattern in most human actions. Actions are seldom events in the sense that they are new, previously unseen creations of behaviour. When we talk about practices, we therefore talk about institutionalized, somehow social forms of behaviour. What we are interested in when doing research on practices is not why Paul or Mary behave in a specific manner but why members of a social group collectively behave as they do. In other words, the term "practice" focuses on social order, that is, on the fact that actions repeat in a structured way.

Furthermore, "practices" are also social in a secondary sense. Are we really conscious about our repetitive daily actions? And if we are conscious of those actions, are we really aware of all of their meaning to us? The discovery of the unconscious is not the only way to accept that we might not be fully aware of a practice's meaning for us. We accept that there are underlying impulses and therefore something like a "hidden meaning" in our behaviour. Furthermore, practices that once had a meaning for us now become mere traditions and conventions, and we repeat certain behaviour without being conscious of the original meaning. In other words, on the one hand, we can forget about a meaning and still perform a practice. On the other hand, although the circumstances that gave rise to a practice and its meaning may have changed, we still perform it because we are accustomed to the practice. When I said that this adds a second social aspect, I am referring to the fact that these often not-fully conscious practices are learned in contact with others, for example, in the process of socialization. This social learning process may include practices for which there is not a full awareness of their original sense. The meaning of such a practice therefore need not be sought in individuals but in processes of social appropriation. However, we have to be aware that practices are not only repeated but also creatively appropriated, modified, and adapted to the concrete social situation.

Finally, the third social aspect of practice is related to the social dimension of "meaning". The meaning of a practice, like the meaning of words, is not capable of individual definition. As Wittgenstein says, there is no such thing as a private language. What the words man or woman, drug, big, or small mean depends only on the individual. It depends on the specific socio-historical context. In the same way, the meaning of a handshake, walking, or cooking depends not only on the individual sense but also on a specific, context-bound meaning. So, for example, when I am driving on the right side in Britain, although I am intending to express my pro-European attitudes, others would probably understand my behaviour as dangerous, antisocial, and even criminal. However, if properly socialized, I probably know that people would not understand me driving on the right side in the manner that I intend to be understood. In other words, the individual is usually quite aware of how his or her behaviours are understood by others. Exceptions include all of the cases that produce misunderstandings. "Oh, I did not mean to…" is the typical sentence that indicates a difference either between individual meanings or between individual and social meanings.

For empirical analyses all three dimensions are important: the fact that practices point towards a structure, that is, they are related to some aspects of social order; individual unconsciousness about meaning, even about the individual meaning of some practices; and the social character of meaning. If practices were not ordered structures and every behaviour were an individual event, then no *social* analysis of practices would be possible and no relation of the analysis of practices and *social* critique could be drawn. If the individual meaning of practices in all of their dimensions were always clear, there would be no difference between appearance and reality, and we would just need to ask individuals about their behaviour. The same is true if meaning were always individual. In this case again, we would be unable to do *social* research and *social* critique because there would be no nexus between individuals and either society or the social structure.

Furthermore, practices are usually chains of action (Jaeggi 2014a, b: 95f). The practice of cooking, for example, could consist of the actions of putting water in a pot, adding noodles, slicing tomatoes, and so on. The meaning of every action can only be understood in the context of the other actions, that is, on the horizon of the entire practice. However, it is never quite clear when the practice is finished or whether it is ever finished. Perhaps the cooking was only one part of the practice of organizing a family reunion, the organization of a family reunion gains its sense only in the practice of raising a family, and so on. What is important here is that practices could be understood only in their meaning as part of social institutions, as standing in relation to other, normative elements of our lives.

2.3.1.2 Practices and Discourses

The social aspects of practices turn social actions into a type of language. Practices can be intersubjectively "read", that is, perceived, interpreted, and understood. For social researchers, this means that they must interpret practice to understand social dimensions and meanings. This is the reason that Laclau and Mouffe understand practices as discourses. However, we began this chapter with the idea of analytically dividing discourses from non-discursive realities, such as practices. Nonetheless, in the analysis of practices, we must use interpretative techniques similar to those used for an interpretative linguistic discourse analysis. Furthermore, we have seen that sociological discourse analysis means analysing discourses in their social contexts with respect to their causes, content, and effects. When analysing practices in the frame of discourse theory, we are explicitly acknowledging these three aspects of practices. Practices comprise a structured, meaningful ensemble. Just like discourses, practices are often not fully conscious and are a social—instead of an individual—product. Therefore, we can draw four types of relations between practices and discourses or what in this case is the same: we can differentiate four types of practices (for the first three practices, see also Keller 2005a).

First, we can identify *practices of discourse production*. These include all practices in which text and talk are produced directly, such as political declarations, news reports, academic papers, or discussions with neighbours and friends. Here, it is not only the strict linguistic outcome of these practices that is important but also a whole set of mechanisms that regulate practices of discourse production. Foucault (1981) shows us how the production of discourses is, on the one hand, limited through certain mechanisms, and on the other hand, enabled and guided through mechanisms of power. So, for example, not everybody is allowed to speak in every situation about every topic. Consider the production of legal discourses in courts, which have strict rules about who has the privilege to speak and how those speech acts must be performed. Conversely, there can be imperatives to produce discourses. So, for example, in an academic setting teachers and researchers are obliged to engage in discourse production and re-production. They *have to* refer to prior discourses, and they *have to* create new speech acts. In Luhmaniann terms, we could even say that discourses produce discourses.

Therefore, when analysing practices of discourse production, we can certainly analyse the linguistic outcome of those practices. However, we can analyse many more aspects. We can and must analyse the practical conditions of discourse production: the persons involved in the practices, their disposition in the space, the manner in which they must behave while producing text and talks, the reasons for discourse production, and so on. And we must do so, *interpreting* all of these aspects of practices: What does it mean that professors in law schools seem to have to wear ties to produce discourses? What is the meaning of the "corporal language" when politicians speak? What is the meaning of people engaging in small talk about the weather when they meet in elevators? These are only some examples of questions that we can ask when performing interpretative research on practices in the frame of discourse theory.

Second, we can identify *practices produced by the discourse.* Discourses say what people should do. Sometimes they do so quite openly, as in the case of the Ten Commandments in Christian discourse or the demand to vote for a certain political party during election campaigns. However, very often, the invitation to behave in a certain way is quite subtle. The Western discourse on the beauty ideal, for example, does not directly demand certain actions but is related to eating practices, sports practices, practices related to the so-called work-life balance, personal hygiene practices, and consumption practices involving beauty-care products or clothes. In these cases, where a discourse does not directly say what to do, the need for interpretation by social actors is quite important. Here, we must consider that different social actors can interpret the behavioural invitations of a certain discourse in different ways. And once again, an analysis of the context and conditions of a certain discourse that fosters a specific practice is indispensable. The concrete practice depends, inter alia, on the material infrastructure. So, for example, one factor that is very important to engaging in consumption practices is an individual's material resources. When analysing practices produced by discourses, we must therefore analyse the discourse in a narrow sense, the real existing practices, and the material conditions of these practices. We have to ask questions such as the following: Which practices are demanded by a certain discourse and which practices are suggested by discourses? However, we must also ask other types of questions: Which practices are finally performed by individuals and why? The difference between discursive claims and reality can be especially revealing for social researchers.

The third type of practices that we can identify involve *practices independent of specific discourses.* Although every practice is a part of a certain discourse, not every discourse includes all possible practices. The practice of shaving my beard is probably quite external to the discourse on nuclear energy or the practice of cycling seems not directly related to the discourses of drug consumption. For sociological discourse analyses, it is interesting to understand which practices are a part of a specific discourse and which are not. Furthermore, we have to ask questions about why certain practices are excluded in discourses, whereas others are not.

Here, we are confronted by very interesting mechanisms of inclusion and exclusion of practice with respect to certain discourses. The mechanisms of inclusion differ from those of exclusion in an important way: whereas the discursive inclusion of practices can be identified by the existence of discourses about a certain practice, discursive exclusion is usually not argued. Exclusion here means ignoring certain practices, not their discursive devaluation. Here, we can ask questions such as why a certain practice is completely ignored by a specific discourse. So, for example, housework seemed largely ignored by early discourses on the national economy. However, there may be cases in which this exclusion is not a simple ignoring but a discursive argument. The differentiation between argumentative exclusion and exclusion for structural omission can be highly revealing.

Finally, a fourth set of practices does not produce discourses and is not produced by a specific discourse but nonetheless is part of that particular discourse. I am referring here to *practices* that are not produced by a specific discourse—although they may be produced by other discourses—but *to which discourses give a specific social sense*. For example, there may be cases in which stealing a handbag is socially interpreted as drug-related crime. Stealing a handbag is not producing text or talk; although it is not the result of a drug discourse, it is interpreted by society as part of drug reality (i.e., as drug-related behaviour). This set of practices can be understood as the opposite of excluded practices. So, for example, we can see that in recent decades, the practice of smoking has been included in discourses on solidarity. Western countries now prohibit smoking in public, closed spaces. Moreover, the practice of smoking seems to be a problem for social solidarity because it is seen as increasing costs to the community because of its responsibility for higher healthcare costs. Similarly, we can see how several practices that were once relatively detached from economic debates now must be justified in monetary terms. This is what we know as mercantilization, for example, of public services.

It is important to underline that differentiation into four types of practices is only an analytical support. In reality, most practices are of various types at the same time. This is especially true of reflexive practices. For example, the discourse on academic excellence demands that researchers produce journal articles. In other words, a discourse produces a certain practice of discourse production. At the same time, this "discourse producing practice produced by discourses" might be external to other discourses, such as the discourse on recycling.

A basic assumption of discourse theory is that discourses are not the product of independent, individual wills. Instead, discourse theory understands the proliferation and order of discourses as related to the non-discursive infrastructure. Keeping in mind that discourses produce social meaning, we can see that how society understands a practice depends on the material and ideal infrastructures both of the particular practices and of the corresponding discourses. The questions here are the following: Which discourses are at hand to interpret a specific practice? How are the materialities to which practices refer constructed? What types of social actors are involved in the practices? The interpretation of a practice in itself depends not only on the practice and the discourses available but also on other aspects of what I called the discursive infrastructure: knowledge, social status of actors performing a certain practice, power, material infrastructure, and so on So, for example, the valuation of a practice can vary. depending on whether the social group performing it is of low or high social status (see also Reinarman and Levine 2004; Herzog 2009; Herzog et al. 2008).

2.3.1.3 Analysing Practices and Immanent Social Critique

For discourse analysis, these conceptual distinctions mean that we can differentiate four aspects of analysing practices. First, we can research the practices as infrastructure or *causes* for discourses; what practices have an effect on discourse production or can be used as strategic resource for that purpose? This would chiefly involve analysing practices of discourse production and practices surrounding discourse production. Second, we can analyse the practical *effects* of discourses; what are the results of a specific discourse? This includes not only practices produced by discourse but also practices valued positively and negatively by discourses. We then can analyse questions of *belonging*; which practices do not belong to a particular discourse? As we have seen, the question of belonging is a question of inclusion and exclusion along with a question of discursive and non-discursive exclusion, that is, structural exclusion by omission (see Herzog 2011). Third, we can analyse the content of a discourse about a specific practice; what does a practice mean in a specific discourse? In discourse analysis, however, questions of belonging and content fall together as the discursive interpretation of a content of a practice decides about its belonging (or not) to a discourse.

Let us return to our original question of performing immanent social critique. Armed with the conceptual tools of analysing practices as part of discourse studies, we have yet to see how these tools can help us formulate an immanent critique. Therefore, we made two basic and necessary assumptions: First, some practices have a normative content, that is, they refer to how things should be, how persons should behave, and how society should be organized. Second (and indispensable to critique), practices often have something like a "normative surplus" (Honneth 2011a, 2013). In other words, the normative claims included in some practices are not always completely accomplished by society.

For empirical social research, the notion of immanent critique means that social researchers must analyse and reconstruct the normative basis of society. In other words, the task of discourse analysis is first to describe discourses and practices in a specific way, that is, to arrange the analysis and therefore the description in such a way that the normative content of practices can arise. As far as this reconstruction refers to the official and explicit normative point of reference of specific practices, it seems not to be too complicated for discourse analysis. Here, we might consider analysing the discourses of powerful political, economic, and social institutions and revealing the normative basis of their arguments. However, especially with regard to the possibility of a normative surplus of daily practices, as some Marxist authors suggested for work-related practices, we could consider analysing not the dominant discourses but the popular ones. Here again, to the extent that people involved in these practices can think out loud about the normative content of their doing, discourse analysts do not experience major problems.

Such discourse analysis becomes slightly more complicated when we seek to emphasize the implicit normativity in these discourses. However, for discourse analysts, revealing the implicit structures of discourses is everyday work and should not be overly complicated. We could consider analysing the implicit normative surplus both in dominant and in popular discourses. A first problem arises when we have to decide the discourse in which practices are likely to lead to those elements we require for social critique. Critical thinkers point to work practices (classical Marxism), speech acts (Habermas), justification practices (Boltanski), or recognition and disrespect practices (Honneth) as candidates for a deeper social analysis. However, other practices are thinkable. Or, in Axel Honneth's terms, we could also think of the recognitional content of many everyday practices that at first glance seem quite unsuspicious but can have an important normative content. Then, we would have to analyse discourses on these practices.

Nonetheless, if we accept the important thesis that socially accepted normativity is immanent in *social practices* and do not necessarily have to be expressed in speech acts surrounding these practices, the analysis becomes more difficult. We must then conduct an interpretative analysis of the normative (or recognitional, if we want to follow Honneth) content and normative surplus of these practices.

Here, we are confronted by at least three major problems. First, how should such an analysis proceed? How can we analyse those "silenced discourses" that are the result of silent or silenced suffering? In more general terms, how can we analyse the normative content of practices that do not involve discourse production or, more precisely, that do not involve discourse production by those performing the practices? When discourses do not appear, when they are reduced to silence before they are even articulated, how can the social researcher access the normative content of this silence?

A second issue involves not only that the possibilities of expression of practices are pre-structured but also that practices themselves are not immediate experiences. Practices are always already mediated. We can perfectly imagine a practice of recognition of neo-Nazis in a group of peers. In the same way that Honneth speaks of the ideology of recognition (Honneth 2004), we can speak of ideological normative practices. Therefore, when we accept that the normative content of affective reactions, practices, and institutional orders, for example, can be ideological, then the second problem becomes clearer: How can we differentiate ideologically normative content from that content that the critic wants to use as a foundation for an immanent critique? The problem here is how to determine the normative status of a practice.

Finally, there is a third problem, which references the previously discussed relation between immanence and transcendence in a double sense and involves the question of how to effectively transcend society with actual immanent norms. The norms must point towards other (better) social relations, and the analysis of these norms must contribute to social change becoming effective.

All of these problems refer to what we have called the "sociological deficit" of immanent critique (see also Herzog and Hernàndez 2012). As we have seen, presenting the possibility of immanent norms in social phenomena requires an epistemic and methodological approach to those norms that might be found in sociological discourse analysis. To analyse practices, we could use interpretative, that is, qualitative, techniques of social research. However, as we have seen, it is also possible to understand every practice as a type of language that can be analysed in a manner similar to that of linguistic expression. Practices and language share similar characteristics: both are structured, both include social meaning and individual meaning that are similar but not identical, and to a certain degree, both are intersubjectively understandable through empathic interpretation. Again, we can think about the analysis of the normative content of two types of practices: everyday or "universal" practices on the one hand, such as work, speech acts, or practices of recognition, and disrespect or, especially, public practices that enjoy a high social status or recognition on the other hand.

It is important to underline the indirect interpretation of all practices. We cannot look into individuals' conscious or even subconscious. Often we cannot even see practices. This can be because some practices are performed in private. Additionally, there are practices that are performed in apparent inactivity. Just consider the practice of thinking. At first glance, an outsider will be unable to differentiate thinking about mathematical problems from staring at the wall or dreaming of a lottery win. Here, two basic approaches are thinkable: asking about the practice and observing its consequences.

On the one hand, the problem for empirical analysis is not to overestimate the capacity of the subjects involved and to imagine them as subjects with the almost absolute freedom to use and interpret practices. On the other hand, the problem is also not to understand practices and discourses as systems that leave no liberty at all to individuals and determine their behaviour. If discursive—and therefore normative—struggles were conscious, no deeper analysis would be required. However, when practices and discourses are interpreted as in independent systems, the possibility of social actors engaging in discursive (i.e., normative) struggles and finding consensus is undermined. This impossibility of engaging in normative struggles or "games" makes it impossible to determine a "moral" viewpoint from which society can be legitimately criticized. Even "truth" or "reality" is now nothing more than discursive constellations and cannot be used as empirical anchors to ground normative critique.

However, after additional sociological discourse analysis, we can understand the (implicit) interpretations that social actors elaborate from specific situations. Such a discourse analysis of language and practices can perform controlled interpretation, can use reflexive methods, and can analyse the socio-historic context of these interpretations. For Foucault, individuals are permanently involved in social struggles, that is, in discursive struggles, which are primarily struggles for truth or resources and often have normative effects. These struggles (or the participation in discursive practices) are often unconscious. Therefore, when individuals engage in practices, whether practices of discourse production (e.g., speaking) or practices produced by discourses (e.g., taking up cycling as the result of a discourse on health and well-being), they are frequently unaware of the normative implications of those practices.

At the same time, discourse analysis as social critique must also focus on the other side of social critique. The critical approach requires simultaneous research on the development potential, obstacles, and systemic or structural limitations that impede the unfolding of these normative claims. We can differentiate transcending immanent critique from corrective critique only through this second element. In other words, we must perform a social analysis of the structural conditions of social change. This could be performed with the help of the diverse research traditions in social science.

The problem here is that we have two different pieces of research: the discourse analysis of discourses and practices on the one hand and the analysis of social structures on the other hand. It is likely that we can create suggestive narratives that relate each part of the analysis to the other. Indeed, this is how most linguistic discourse analysis works: by creating a parallelism between discourses and social reality. One—admittedly simplified—example would be to say that there is racism in social structures because there is racism in discourses—or the other way around, that racist discourses are the result of racist social structures. The most interesting research questions arise, however, when racist discourses *do not* lead to racist behaviour or when racist social structures *do not* produce a coherent racist discourse. What we need in order to understand such a phenomenon and to relate the analysis of normative contents and potentials to the analysis of structural obstacles is a common, coherent, integrated approach. In my understanding, a broad sociological approach to discourses can provide such a common attempt.

We can understand structural obstacles again in terms of discourse analysis as structured, meaningful objects that are understood intersubjectively. What is needed to understand the possibility or impossibility of changing structures is an approach in the social sense, the meaning of these structures as changeable or static, and what it takes to change the perception of a social order as a "natural", eternal, static state towards the perception of the possibilities of fundamental change of social orders. Therefore, what we can perform is a discourse analysis on social structure and a discourse-like analysis of these structures. With the more sociological approaches, which simultaneously focus on texts and on non-textual aspects of social life, such as practices, we can make explicit the normative pretensions of individuals engaging in all types of interaction (Angermuller 2007, 2014; Bührmann and Schneider 2007, 2008; Keller 2005a, b). Concurrently, we can reveal the normative implications of their often-unconscious struggles.

The more sociological approach of discourse analysis not only helps us with the methodological problem but also can contribute to the differentiation of ideological and non-ideological normative claims. Alternatively, those who only present particular solutions are differentiated from those who lead to emancipation and justice. However, although the analysis of discursive and extra-discursive realities cannot offer unambiguous, second-order normative criteria for immanent critique, it can reveal the social effects of possible criteria. Therefore, discourse analysis offers the possibility of adopting a reflexive, informed position regarding different normative claims and their respective discursive and extra-discursive expressions.

The simultaneous analysis of the normative claims of practices and its structural obstacles can ultimately help us assess the transcending character of the normative claims that are either openly or latently inherent in practices. If it is possible to show that our everyday practices include a normative potential or normative surplus that requires fundamental social change to become effective, then we are confronted by real immanent transcendence. However, we should be open to the possibility that either there is no normative surplus in some practices or there is only a surplus that points towards slight corrections within the given social order.

We have seen that practices—in social science in general and in discourse analysis in particular—can be analytically differentiated. Next, we can simultaneously perform a basic analysis of discourses and an analysis of practices as the infrastructure of discourses, as the causes and effects of language use. As I noted in reference to Foucault (1981), a sociological discourse analysis requires not only analysing discourses but also analysing the conditions of discourse production. However, we are not experiencing two different types of analysis, one of language and one of practices. Practices are also institutionalized, that is, they are structured forms with social and individual meaning that are intersubjectively understandable. This common ground between language and practices allows us to simultaneously perform both an analysis of the normative content of practices (whether through discourses on practices or qualitative interpretation of observed behaviour) *and* an analysis of practical possibilities and obstacles to the normative surplus's becoming effective. This is how the discourse analysis of practices can become social critique.

2.3.2 Materialities

Once the analytical logics of discourse analysis of discourses and non-discursive realities are understood, we can apply the very same idea to other aspects of non-discursive phenomena. In what follows, we will turn to materialities as analytical objects that can be analysed in the frame of discourse theory. The analysis, similar to the case of practices, includes the analysis of discourses on materialities and the analysis of materialities as structured, meaningful objects.

Similar to the notion of discourse, the notion of materiality allows a very broad and general approach. Since the so-called material turn, social and cultural sciences turn not only to the analysis of physical objects but also to the analysis of knowledge, power, discourses, and so on, because these units of analysis also have material effects. In that sense, we could even echo Laclau and Mouffe's assertion that everything is material because everything (language, practices, knowledge…) has material consequences and conditions. The question is whether this general approach to materiality is helpful in regard to the analysis of social reality. Similar to the debate about discourses, we can probably accept that everything can be understood as having relation to materiality and therefore that we can speak of the materiality of every object or phenomena. However, for analytical purposes, I propose to accept this truth on a second order. This means accepting a first-order differentiation (for the sake of analysis) between physical materialities such as objects, landscape, and so on—that is, materialities—as they are used in everyday language on the one hand and other phenomena such as discourses (but also practices, knowledge, etc.) on the other hand. This analytical division can help us not only organize and structure our research but also to focus on those aspects that seem promising for our task of developing social critique. Therefore, we should conduct a closer analysis of what materialities can mean.

Similar to the example of practices, physical materialities can be divided into four analytical types. First, although physical materialities cannot produce discourse on their own, they can be used for discourse production and distribution. This is true not only of pen and paper, which were invented to produce and distribute discourses but also of radio, television, and (partially) the computer. Materialities that help create and distribute discourses are highly relevant to both social stability and social change. Material control of the press has always been important to totalitarian regimes. Similarly, much has been written about the importance of new technologies, such as mobile devices (with applications such as Twitter, Facebook, and Whatsapp), especially for the organization of youth protests, for example, during the Arab Spring. The control of the means of the diffusion of discourses must be an essential part of the analysis of discursive infrastructures.

Second, materialities are produced by the discourse. Foucault's (1975) classical example is that of the panoptical prison as part of a specific discourse on education, discipline, and punishment. However, almost every material production is (of course) preceded by a discourse about it. Nuclear weapons are unthinkable without a discourse on war, risk, and geopolitics. Recycling technologies are embedded in discourses on environment, progress, and resources. Discourses tell people what they should produce and how they should produce it. Should a society produce churches for the glory of God, social housing for the worst off, or emblematic buildings to show the greatness of the society? Typically, these questions are at least partially negotiated through discourses. Similar to the case of practices, we need to be well aware that material production is not always the direct result of a single discourse. There could be conflicting discourses either on the same level or within a power hierarchy (e.g., the dominant discourse versus the popular discourse). There could be errors or casualties in the development process. Many actual inventions are the result of casual observations that were not intended. One of the most prominent cases is that of the discovery of Viagra, which was originally developed to fight hypertension.

Third, we can also find materialities that are entirely unrelated a specific discourse, such as the above-mentioned prison buildings, which are not part of the discourse of academic excellence. Finally, materialities, whether or not they are "originally" part of the discourse, can be included in and shaped by the discourse, and the discourse gives meaning to materiality. People give meaning to physical materialities independent of whether they are produced by human beings. Even a mountain, a rock, or a volcano can have meaning as part of a tourist discourse, a spiritual discourse, a discourse on landscape, and so on. For our purposes, questions of the inclusion and exclusion of materialities in discourses are highly relevant. They show both the limits of discourses and the social perception of their extension.

When differentiating the four types of materialities for discourse studies, we must also differentiate between the discourses on these materialities and the materialities themselves. In other words, we must simultaneously analyse discourses about materialities on the one hand and research material aspects of social reality on the other hand. That said, analysis of materialities should be framed by discourse theory in a double sense: first, we must analyse the relation of materialities to discourses. This means that we must understand materialities not only as infrastructures and causes of discourses but also as effects and consequences of discourses. Second, for our purposes materialities could be understood as sharing important characteristics with language so that we can analyse materialities in a manner similar to how we analyse language. Materialities are structured, meaningful phenomena. There is not only one car—as an exception, historical accident or "event"—on our streets. Instead, cars on our streets are repeated phenomenon. Their distribution follows certain, potentially illegible structures. Additionally, cars have meanings for people—that is, their owners or bystanders. Although meaning has an individual component, there are a limited number of socially available meanings. Cars represent not only liberty and status but also danger and ecological problems, depending on the (socially embedded) eye of the beholder.

For discourse analysis, these analytical divisions mean that we can distinguish the same aspects of the analysis of physical materialities that we have already distinguished in the case of practices. First, we can research the material infrastructure used for discourses (buildings, technical tools, spatial distribution, etc.), that is, we can analyse resources as *causes* of the entry or exit of a certain discourse. Second, we can analyse the material *effects* of discourses; what changes in physical materiality are caused by a specific discourse? Third, we can ask questions of *belonging*; is a certain materiality part of a particular discourse? Fourth, we can analyse the *content* of a discourse about a specific materiality; what does a materiality (mountain, building, artefact…) mean in a specific discourse? Again, we must insist that these are only analytical divisions that should help organize the analysis itself. In practice, the diverse components of discourse analysis often overlap.

We should not lose track of the aim of such a "discourse analysis of materialities". Because we want to use the examination of materialities for social critique, we must simultaneously analyse the normative content of material realities and material realities as inert objects that make difficult, limit, or impede social change. The main methodological problem here is that material objects cannot be asked. Interaction with objects is quite limited. However, the fact that objects are inanimate does not mean that they do not have any normative content. Usually we have quite clear ideas about what an object *should* do, or what we *should be able* to do with an object. So, for example, a car should be fast, secure, robust, nice, and practical; moreover, it should not consume too much and it should be as ecological as possible. Here, we can raise questions similar to those of Jaeggi (2014b), who asks the following question about the analysis of capitalism: who decides how a car should be? Perhaps what is important about a car for one person is not important for others. As in the case of car shows, perhaps there is not only one ideal of a car, but several. However, the number of normative approaches towards cars is probably quite limited and shared by social groups. The silence and complexity of materialities require them to be analysed in their social context, in their use and, of course, in their discursive embeddedness. Although we can obtain some idea about objects by "just staring" at them and attempting to interpret their normative content, a more profound analysis requires us to consider both the discursive and the non-discursive contexts of materialities.

The car example shows that material products can also have a normative surplus. Every claim that we formulate towards a car points towards its further development. Indeed, it seems that cars are made faster, more secure, and so on. However, there can also be a transcendent moment in normative claims of materialities. The claim of fast cars points not only towards the cars themselves but also towards the infrastructure, that is, roads that permit rapid locomotion. The imperative of being resource conserving ultimately points towards a profound social change, not one that regards only transport policy.

2.3.3 Actors, Identities, and Subjectivities

We have seen how practices and materialities are surrounded by symbolic orders that often are difficult to decipher. Objects usually do not speak for themselves; instead, they must be understood in context. Practices—such as the practice of thinking—could be not just silent but even unnoticeable. At first glance, the case of social actors as an analytical unit is far easier to handle. Social actors are usually visible persons of flesh and blood, that is, they can easily be perceived. Additionally, they usually have the capacity to make themselves understandable. Nevertheless, for the practice of discourse analysis as social critique, actors can be even more difficult to analyse than practices or materialities.

In most cases that are relevant to our purpose of social critique, we are not interested in the physical aspects of actors, whether tall or small, dark-haired or blonde, or wearing trousers or skirts. Usually social researchers are more interested in social identities or—more generally speaking—in subject positions. The term "subject positions" refers to the result of a positioning practice in which an individual positions him- or herself and is positioned by society and therefore occupies a social place, that is, a place within a social structure. Or, as Davies and Harre (1990) describe it,

> A subject position incorporates both a conceptual repertoire and a location for persons within the structure of rights for those that use that repertoire.

Once having taken up a particular position as one's own, a person inevitably sees the world from the vantage point of that position and in terms of the particular images, metaphors, storylines and concepts which are made relevant within the particular discursive practice in which they are positioned. At least a possibility of notional choice is inevitably involved because there are many and contradictory discursive practices that each person could engage in. (p. 46)

Therefore, a subject position is both the result of social and discursive construction and the ground from which discourses are produced. Subjects are other than objects; they are not only autonomous instances that can act and react but also the result of a powerful process of subordination that makes them how they are. The notion of the subject is somehow situated between the notion of individual identity and social role. It focuses on the often-unconscious mediation between these two poles. The logic of subjectivation adds a circular or dialectical aspect to our problem of how to ground social critique normatively. Remember that this seemed like the origin of normative critique not only by post-Nietzschean[1] authors such as Foucault but also by Antonio Negri o Laclau and Mouffe, which lies in the subject as given entity. The notion of subject position now adds the insight that the positions of Foucault, Negri, Laclau, and Mouffe, like any other positions, are the result of a positioning practice and not some type of pre-cultural, pre-social, somehow "original" or "authentic" characteristics. In this practice, the individual is in dialogical contact with his or her social environment. Identity is built in dialog with the image of alterity.

A subject position includes a whole set of mental schemes about how reality is to be interpreted, about norms of behaviour, including norms about speech acts, and certain ideas about one's own place in the social structure. When I said in the beginning that we are usually uninterested in the physical aspect of persons, that is not the whole truth. Not only how someone dresses but also how people wear their hair, display

---

[1] It could easily be argued that the origin of radical individualism lies not in Nietzsche but in the young Hegelian Max Stirner (see Sect. 1.2, p. 16).

piercings and tattoos, or build their body can be the result of a specific subject position. It is a common fun among university students to mock how students and professors from other departments dress. It seems that with the subject position "sociology student" or "law professor", there are related dress codes and codes of conduct.

Every subject position faces three major challenges that are interesting for our purpose insofar as they are related to normative expectancies. First, everybody usually has several subject positions, similar to several social roles. One can be—at the same time—mother, vegetarian, anthropology student, Christian, and supporter of the Barcelona Football Club. This means that a person positions him- or herself in the world in various, sometimes conflicting, ways. Being a mother sometimes can mean not being able to do all of the work that one is supposed to do as a student, and being an active supporter of a football club can equally produce conflicts about time and loyalty with other roles. What is important for our purpose of normative, social critique is that using our language, we can say that every subject position has a normative surplus. This refers to more than a single, concrete situation. We expect certain coherencies of subjects, even when we are not in that concrete social situation.

Social expectancies towards one specific subject position can also be considered an important problem. Individuals must both negotiate expectancies and adapt them to their personal identity. Although my fellow Christians can expect me to go to church every Sunday, I can decide not to do so and continue to feel, speak, and behave (or just "be") as a Christian. Following the normative language, social norms form, often almost unrecognizable for individuals, that is, the specific subject position. Here we are facing the power of the more "social" aspect of positioning practices.

The more "individual" aspect of these practices can be understood as the problem of inner tensions in every subject position. There is no fixed meaning or repertoire of behaviour: just as individuals have always had to interpret their social roles, they have always had to fill the ontological openness of subject positions. Does being a good mother mean enrolling one's children in as many after-school activities as possible to offer them the greatest possible variety of life chances or does it mean, on the contrary, spending a great deal of time together? It is this principal openness of the subject position that transformed the notion of subject into an interesting object of analysis for purposes of social change.

To analyse subject positions, we can perform differentiations similar to those used for the analysis of practices and materialities. There are subject positions that produce certain discourses. Indeed, we can say that discourses are produced and reproduced by subjects. Subjects have interests, strategies, and competences when using language and often are quite familiar with the effects of their language use. This is true not only for subjects with high cultural capital (such as politicians, industrial spokespersons, academics, and medical doctors) but for also many others who use language and therefore engage in discourses. As a football supporter, I am supposed to engage in debates about the final day of play and as a professor I am supposed to use certain types of academic language. Thus, subject positions are related not only to what people say but also to how and when they speak and how they behave when they produce discourses. For the analysis of the potential of social change, we are interested not only in the typical discourse productions but also in the exceptions because they show enough liberty to not follow the hegemonic order of discourse.

Social actors can also influence discourses involuntarily. Their subject position that is external to a specific discourse can shape discourses and their infrastructure in a concrete field. An example from drug discourses would be the case of the USA in the late 1970s, when crack was primarily consumed by "stock brokers and investment bankers, rock stars, Hollywood types, and a few pro athletes [...]. Congress passed new laws to extend health insurance coverage to include drug treatment" (Reinarman and Levine 2004: 182). However, when crack use in the 1980s became primarily identified with African Americans and Latinos, "[c]ongress passed new laws to extend the length of criminal sentences for crack offenses" (ibid.). Here, the social status of the consumers (i.e., their racial and class identities) clearly shapes the discourse both about the drug as a substance and about drug-related behaviour.[2]

As we have said, subject positions are the result of positioning practices that are also social, that is, the result of powerful mechanisms that put people in their social place. In terms of discourse analysis, we could speak here of the discursive construction of subject positions. In other words, subject positions are the result of discourses. Social actors must "learn" about their identity. Sometimes the learning process is quite obviously forced upon an individual. In discourse-analytical terms, this means that both the non-discursive and the discursive infrastructure of discourses can create settings in which individuals must reproduce the dominant discourse on themselves.

Identities or subject positions created through discourses are not an "objective" reflection of reality; subject positions are offered by discourses and create realities. People often come to fit the categories offered to them by discourses. These categories are not value-neutral; instead, they are the expression of dominant discourses, which means that they are also the expression of dominant value systems. During the last century, the dominant communist discourse attempted to build the worker, proletarian, or member of the working class as a specific subject position. The neoliberal discourse participates in the building of "You Inc.", the rational, self-employed worker, responsible for his or her own economic success (see also on that point Fairclough 2004). The success of such discourses depends not only on the logical coherencies of discourses but also on a non-discursive infrastructure. Although the identities offered by a discourse are sometimes adopted because of an almost omnipotent discursive structure, they can also be merely strategically asserted.

Furthermore, similar to the case of practices and materialities, positions are excluded from certain discourses and positions that are not produced by discourses but that receive a specific content through discourses. One wonderful example of the exclusion of certain positions, here the position of female subjects from political and academic discourses, is described

---

[2] On that example, see also Herzog (2009, 2016b).

by Terry Eagleton (2011). This example also shows how exclusion processes have changed over time and we now find female subject positions and feminist positions as a highly relevant part of political and academic discourses:

> At a conference in Britain in the early 1970s, a discussion took place over whether there were certain universal features of human beings. One man stood up and announced 'Well, we've all got testicles.' A woman in the audience shouted out 'No, we haven't!' Feminism in Britain was still in its early days, and the remark was greeted by a good many men in the room as merely eccentric. Even some of the women looked embarrassed. Only a few years later, if a man had made such a fatuous statement in public, he might rapidly have become the only exception to his claim. (Eagleton 2011: 96)

Unlike materialities or practices, (at least the symbolic aspects of) subject positions are not directly observable. Therefore, we cannot divide our analysis into a discourse analysis and a social analysis. We must analyse the discursive production of symbolic subject production. However, as we have said, physical aspects and behaviour can be important hints of subject positions. Furthermore, we have discussed *practices* of subjectivation. This means that although subject positions are not directly observable through social analysis, they are indirectly observable beyond discourses. In other words, in the case of subject positions, we can also perform both an analysis of discourses surrounding subject positions and an analysis of non-discursive aspects of subject positions. Again, both types of analysis can take place in the common frame of discourse theory as a theory that includes both an analysis of discourses on subjects and an analysis of the conditions of discourse production.

We can even broaden the horizon of non-discursive materialities when talking not about subjects but about social actors in a more general sense. A social actor can also be an institution such as a ministry or a university. Although institutions cannot speak or act—only people can do so—we can analyse them as social actors not only by analysing the production of discourses of institutions but also by analysing their non-discursive reality.

We can analyse the number of people involved in an institution, their working practices, material infrastructures, hierarchies, budgets, and so on.

The reference to institutions as social actors is especially interesting in regard to the analysis of obstacles of social change. Remember that the aim of our analysis is on the one hand to analyse the normativity and normative potential of social actors and on the other hand to evaluate systemic obstacles. Institutions with rules, traditions, and bureaucratic structures (Graeber 2015) are often quite "unwilling" to change. There seems to be a certain inertia, at least in formal institutions.

However, institutions as social actors cannot only be an obstacle for social change, as Axel Honneth (2011a) shows. In his "normative reconstruction" of modern institutions, he argues that institutions can also have a normative surplus that points towards further development. So, for example, democratic institutions are not exclusively based on the norm of equality. For equality to become effective in democracy, people must be able to follow public debates and be free of coercive economic pressure. Historically, these insights have led to the creation of public education and the welfare state. In other words, democratic institutions historically had (and probably still have) a normative surplus that points towards further development.

The task of our discourse analysis as social critique now is not to reconstruct the normative implication of subjects, subject position, positioning practices, or social actors in general. Being a mother, a vegetarian, an expert on nuclear energy, and so on—all of these positions include affirmations of how these people *should* speak, act, evaluate situations, and so on. When looking closer at these positions, most of them will probably have some normative surplus that points to liberation from constraints. So, for example, an expert in nuclear energy should be free to analyse and speak about the results of its analysis without fearing economic losses. He or she should be independent, especially in economic and political terms. At the same time, we should also should analyse the structural or systemic obstacles of the surplus to become effective. Only with that simultaneous analysis can we decide whether the surplus points towards corrective or transcending critique.

2.3.4 Knowledge, Ideology, and Worldviews

When turning towards knowledge, ideology, and worldviews, we are almost completely leaving the field of the directly observable. We cannot see knowledge, and we have no further access to those elements other than through their perceivable, discursive, and non-discursive effects. Before turning to the question of which aspects of those elements of symbolic orders are the most interesting for our purposes, we should attempt to understand the particularities of these elements.

When turning our attention to the international academic literature about knowledge, we will find that in the Roman languages that make important contributions to post-structuralism and discourse analysis, the word knowledge has two common, but different, translations. For example, in France, we have the word "connaissance" such as in "Sociologie de la connaissance", which is translated into English as the sociology of knowledge. Conversely, we can find the word "savoir", as in Foucault's famous methodological work "L'archéologie du savoir", published in English as "Archaeology of knowledge" (Foucault 2002). The difference between these notions of knowledge is not very large; for our purposes, though, it is revealing nevertheless. Whereas "connaissance" refers to fixed knowledge, a stock of knowledge that can be passed on explicitly, "savoir" includes more implicit and practical aspects of knowledge. "Savoir faire" also means being able to do something. Although this type of knowledge is also passed on and learned in society, it is not theoretical, not explicit, and often not even conscious.

Although it is quite likely that explicit knowledge appears in discourses, implicit knowledge has to be reconstructed from what people say or do. However, as we noted at the beginning of this chapter, we are not talking about isolated, independent pieces of knowledge. Meaningful knowledge is embedded in structures that also include other knowledge. My knowledge about Leo Messi, the Argentinean football player working for Barcelona Football Club, is related to my knowledge about football, the "Primera División" (the Spanish football League), the Barcelona Football Club, and so on.

Discourse analysis has proposed several names for mental schemes that people can use to make sense out of diverse social phenomenon. There are interpretative schemes, frames, narrations, phenomenal structure, ideologies, cosmovisions, worldviews, and many more (see e.g., Keller 2005b; Lenk 1984; Zizek 2012). It is important not to confuse these schemes with discourses. Although mental schemes can be smaller parts of discourse, they can also be quite broader. A neoliberal ideology is not a discourse about neoliberalism. A neoliberal ideology can be the background for discourses both on the educational system and on individual responsibility or international relations without even mentioning neoliberalism. Conversely, a discourse can include several main narrations that compete or peacefully coexist within a discourse.

Here, I do not want to differentiate all possible schemes of symbolic organization of knowledge. I just want to note one insight from the notion of ideology as it is classically formulated by post-Marxist theories. I am not interested in the aspect of the falsity of ideas but on their *necessary character*. When Marxists say that some ideas are either necessary or necessarily false, they do not understand ideas as the conscious product of some ruling class that invents ideas to blindfold the subalterns. Although this type of conscious hoax may exist, the necessary character of ideology refers to something else. It refers to the fact that social order, that is, social reality itself, produces a specific type of knowledge about that reality.

One classical example from post-Marxist author György Lukács is that of individuals who, because of the social conditions of production and work-contract, must imagine themselves as isolated individuals even though, in reality, they share a situation in common with their fellows from the working class. Bourgeois individualism as described by Lukács is therefore a correct perception of an incorrect reality. The organization of the social produces imaginaries of given individuals who relate to each other as economically rational beings.

For our purpose of social critique, this insight from the critique of ideology means that every knowledge structure must be analysed in the discursive and non-discursive context of its formation, appearance, and consequences. Knowledge is itself a dynamic, social relation, and we must analyse this "social relation of knowledge", which is highly contested and can change over time. Here, we can also speak of the politics of knowledge to describe the struggle about what must be seen as uncontested truth or secure knowledge in a given society.

Analytically, we can differentiate four types of knowledge structures. The first type of knowledge structure produces discourses. Discourses are the most common method of passing on explicit knowledge. Knowledge can also be acquired through other simple methods than verbal communication, observation, trial and error by showing practically, and so on. However, explication via language use has a pre-eminent position in our societies. Some specific knowledge must be passed on through text and talk. So, for example, most academic knowledge must be passed on, that is, it requires discourse production. Michel Foucault, quoting Samuel Beckett, speaks of that "voice" in academia that says. "You must go on, I can't go on, you must go on, I'll go on, you must say words, as long as there are any, until they find me, until they say me, strange pain, strange sin, you must go on, perhaps it's already, perhaps they have said me already, perhaps they have carried me to the threshold of my story, before the door that opens on my story, that would surprise be, if it opens" (Foucault 1981: 51). In academia, this feeling is also described as "publish or perish". In other words, academic knowledge must produce discourses.

In the second (and very common) type of knowledge structure in discourse analysis, we can find knowledge produced by discourses. When we say that speech acts are a common way of passing on knowledge, we can state that knowledge is not only the origin but also the end point of the communication process. Again, we can think about almost everything that we formally learn in educational contexts as the result of discourses.

The third type of knowledge structure involves knowledge that is not part of a certain discourse. An example of this would be my knowledge about cooking that is not part of the discourse on German idealism. In the fourth type of knowledge structure, we can analytically differentiate knowledge that becomes part of discourses and therefore gets a specific "shape". Let us imagine that I have certain knowledge about football, the most important players and teams, rules, tactics, and styles. A discourse on national identity can include this knowledge as a typical "national" knowledge, about football as a "national" sport, including specific "national" styles and tactics.

2.3.4.1 The Practice of Analysing Knowledge Structures

When engaging in the discourse analysis of knowledge, we can rely on a specific approach developed by Reiner Keller (2005a, b) that takes several elements of the sociology of knowledge and combines it with discourse analysis. In his "Sociology of Knowledge Approach towards Discourses" (SKAD), Keller proposes four analytical units or concepts that originate in the sociology of knowledge but that can be used for discourse analysis: First, he mentions *interpretative schemes* or *frames*, which are "socially typified historically embedded interpretation devices for occurring events, urgencies of action etc." (Keller 2005a). With general or "master" frames, people turn to diverse objects of knowledge. Keller himself presents the example of "Risk" as a frame that can structure our knowledge of such diverse topics like nuclear waste or genetically modified plants.

Second, Keller presents *classifications* as an analytical unit for the discourse analysis of knowledge. Especially in discourse analysis on the knowledge of identities, the importance of categories has been widely explored. Ethnic, national, and gender categories structure our knowledge both about the world and—very important for our purpose of social critique—on how the world and the people in it *should* be.

Phenomenal structures are Keller's third analytical unit. This notion refers to the relation of several parts of the knowledge structure. The phenomenal structure of an object of knowledge includes "cognitive devices like the concepts used to name an object, the relations between those concepts, the introduction of causal schemes and normative settings, the dimensions, urgencies and legitimations for action, along with the kind of practices considered to be suitable to a particular phenomenon" (Keller 2005a). Finally, Keller mentions *narrative structures, story lines*, or *plots* as those elements of knowledge that convert a set of elements into a story that can be narrated to others.

We must not forget that for us, the aim of this discourse analysis of knowledge has the goal of analysing the normative content and normative surplus of knowledge while analysing knowledge as blocking the way of fundamental social change. Every piece of knowledge about an object includes normative statements that go far beyond the particular object. Knowledge about the desk upon which I am working includes statements of how all desks should be to permit good work. If this is true for a simple desk, then it is true *a fortiori* for a complex knowledge structure such as my knowledge of political systems, world markets, or solidarity.

Conversely, fixed, static knowledge about any object often includes the inability to change not only someone's knowledge but also someone's discourses, practices, identities, and so on. David Graeber (2011) mentions, for example, how simple, common knowledge that is seen as a universal truth by the World Bank, politicians, and citizens that "One has to pay one's debts" blocks discussion (or discourse) about other ways of interrelation. In other words, a simple moral statement considered universal truth at a given historic moment can impede the creation of alternative practices and alternative social structures. Again, if this is true of a simple statement on debts, then it is true *a fortiori* of more general truths or "secured knowledge" about democracy as the best way of governing, capitalism as the least bad economic system, or humans as having certain natural characteristics.

2.3.5 Power, Domination

When entering the analytical field of our next concepts, power and domination, we are moving deeper into the zone of the invisible. We can see the effects of power or domination, we can listen to people who have power, we can directly perceive the insignias and emblems of power, and we can see practices of power or—directly—of violence. Power and domination seem to be ubiquitous, and a quick glance at the literature shows that from its beginning, power and power relations have been important for discourse analysis (for an interesting overview of the topic, see van Dijk 1995). Can we not understand Foucault's famous "will not to be governed" as a critique of power and its perverse effects? However, power itself seems to be one of those elements that is difficult to grasp.

The classical definition comes again from Max Weber, who differentiates power from domination. For him, power is "the probability that one actor within a social relationship will be in a position to carry out his own will despite resistance, regardless of the basis on which this probability rests" (Weber 1978: 53). This definition, which has been the basis for several similar definitions of power in sociology, includes four important aspects. First, power is somehow "sociologically amorphous" as it appears in different social situations and can have very diverse qualities. Second, power is not deterministic; it is only a "probability" or "chance" of success. Third, for Weber, power is always bound to persons. Fourth, power requires a social relation, that is, it requires other social actors who (at least potentially) can resist power. Thus, power exists only where there is the possibility of resistance.

In contrast to this very broad definition, Weber proposes domination "as the probability that certain specific commands (or all commands) will be obeyed by a given group of persons" (Weber, ibid.: 212). This definition includes a somehow voluntary obedience, that is, some way of legitimating the power. Here, the relation of domination and legitimating knowledge or ideology becomes obvious. There are very diverse reasons that we consider certain power as legitimate and voluntarily obey. Weber himself pointed to charisma, tradition, and legality as typical sources of legitimating. The problem for social critique here is how to criticize domination that is considered legitimate by those who follow the rules. Would we not end up performing an external critique instead of an imminent one when arguing against the general sense of legitimacy?

We should not lose track of this important problem. Perhaps Foucault, with his—at first sight—very critical approach to power, can help in this regard. For Foucault, power is not personal. This does not mean that there are neither individual nor collective winners and losers in the game of power, nor does it mean that there are no subjects involved in the exercise of power. Instead, it means that power is not a characteristic that is bound to persons; instead, it is impersonal. Like Weber, Foucault understands power not as a thing that someone can possess but instead as a social relation. However, unlike Weber, the social relation is not a relation between a powerful and a powerless. For Foucault, power can be found at every level of the social structure, not just where governments, armed forces, and the like appear at the scene. Power can also be found at the micro levels of social relations. Indeed, these micro levels were often those cases in which Foucault himself was interested. For example, Foucault was interested in the power-knowledge relation, that is, in the question of how our knowledge is not neutral but instead has very important power effects. Because the power of knowledge operates not at an openly violent or conscious level, in Weberian terms we would speak here perhaps more of domination than of direct power. The most common definition of power given by Foucault is that of "the name that one attributes to a complex strategical situation in a particular society" (Foucault 1979: 93). In the very same definition, Foucault also states that power is not a structure (ibid.). However, as I understand Foucault here, power is not a structure itself; instead, it is inherent to social structures. Furthermore, with Foucault's refusal to identify power with structures, he is probably insisting on the contingency of power, its dynamics, and its even war-like, strategic shifts and games.

Martin Saar (2009) calls this notion of power immanent because it is present in all social relations. There is no point outside of it. Power as immanent to all social relations also means for Foucault that power is not only repressive, "overpowering" possible resistance through diverse strategic means but also power constructive. Only within a powerful social order can we produce those material goods, subject positions, or discourses that we produce every day. When power can be found in all social orders, a general critique of power is not possible. Power itself cannot be criticized in Foucauldian terms. However, what we can criticize is a specific type or outcome of power. Foucault does not say that he does not want to be governed at all; instead, he says that he does not want to be governed "like that, by that, in the name of those principles, with such and such an objective in mind and by means of such procedures, not like that, not for that, not by them."

Here we can close the circle of Foucault's critique of specific power and the Marxist notion of alienation. What Marxists criticize is not production *per se* but the lack of consciousness about the possibility of alternative forms of production (and thus of social relations) and the forgetting of the social sense of that production. In the same sense, Foucault's critique of a specific type of power is a critique of an unconscious acceptance of knowledge-power relations instead of a conscious use of the productive potential of power.

Luc Boltanski attempts to bridge the gap between power on the one hand and domination as a legitimate form of power that therefore is difficult to criticize on the other hand. For him, social domination "serves to identify and condemn manifestations of power deemed extreme and abusive" (Boltanski 2011: 16). Thus, domination is exactly the opposite of the unproblematic use of power. In other words, even if the use of power is widely accepted by the vast majority of a society, it still can be the object of immanent critique. Although this critique can also refer to the sources, the structure, and the legitimating of power, initially, critique usually refers to the *outcome* of power use and, based on these consequences of power, critique can shine back on power itself. Perhaps an example could clarify this process:

In the USA, the majority of the population would likely agree that, in general, police are needed to enforce laws and guarantee security. The same is true regarding an independent judicial system. However, it seems that despite the general desirability of the power of law enforcement, the practical result is widely criticized. The prison population has risen spectacularly in the USA, and the black male population suffers especially high levels of social stigmatization through criminalization. In some cities 80 % of black men have criminal records (Alexander 2010). Therefore, the result of the use of police power and (let us say) domination through the general ideology that policing is the best way of fighting undesired behaviour is justice that suffers from a clear racial bias. It is from that outcome, which is widely accepted as negative, that any social critique on power must begin, and not from the concrete use of the police force that is widely accepted as necessary. Similar to the normative surplus, the critique of the outcome of power and domination points towards the entire process, including practices of power, ideologies, and institutions.

Because of the invisibility of power itself, for power, it is more important than for the cases of the analysis of other elements presented here to embed the research on power in the social context. When we perform discourse analysis on power and domination, we therefore have to take into account practices, ideologies, institutions, material manifestations, and so on, of power and domination. However, we can continue to use our analytical division of four relations of power and discourses. There is power that produces discourses. In a democracy, political and military power must appear publicly to justify their use of power. Next, we have power produced by discourses. The discourse on the danger of drugs and discourses of law and order surely lead not only to special police forces and the expansion of police power but also to the creation of new law enforcement units. After that, we have external power that is excluded from certain discourses and power that is included in certain discourses. For example, consider the power structures of religious communities in the Western world. Whereas in the Middle Ages, these power structures were quite present in discourses of political power, with the ideal of the laical nation state, religious power structures were given the status of private and therefore apolitical phenomena. However, it seems as though during the last decade and with the growth of multiculturalism, the mediating power of religion for political processes has been rediscovered (e.g., Taylor 1994) and therefore, religious power has been re-included in the discourse on political power.

When, as Foucault says, power is everywhere and is not necessarily a form of domination but instead can be used consciously to create society, the direction of discourse analysis as social critique of power becomes clear. Discourse analysis must uncover the positive, normative potential of power and point towards its full realization. This means that we can also (probably) find a normative surplus in the power to create insofar as power points towards effective creation. Even the most repressive military power is based on the ideal that it enforces security and enables people to live together in peace. This means that especially through legitimizing, power points towards an end that often is not yet realized. It is here that the second aspect of discourse analysis of power comes into play: We must simultaneously analyse power as an obstacle for social change. In other words, the very form of power and domination can impede the full realization of the normativity inherent in legitimized power. We could ask, for example, the extent to which real peace based on military "peace enforcement" is possible compared to situations in which the military itself is an obstacle to peace. In this example of military power, we can also perceive the impossibility of analysing power without context. Power always means ideologies of justification, power practices, institutionalized forms of power, materialization, and the creation of some subject positions legitimated to use violence and others that can be the object of violence, and so on.

2.4 Analysing Discourses and Non-discursive Realities

In discourse analysis, these analytical concepts can be interesting tools to structure the procedure. Practices, materialities, subject positions, and so on are not a peripheral part of discourse analysis; instead, they are at its core. If research really should make a difference and if discourse analysis really should matter, then it must pursue extra-discursive reality. The aim of social change is a change of extra-discursive reality. The reason for social change is the existence of unreasonable material and practical conditions. Nonetheless, insistence on the importance of the non-discursive should not be taken as an argument against discourse analysis. Discourses give sense to practices, material realities, and so on. They give rise to subject positions; they create knowledge and they mediate between different aspects of social reality.

For social or sociological discourse analysts, it becomes clear that although discourse analysis continues, the focus cannot be language but instead extra-discursive aspects of discourses. The perhaps-surprising conclusion of what has been presented from a sociological perspective is that *discourse analysis means analysing extra-discursive reality. Discourse analysis means analysing non-discursive infrastructure, effects, and the content or meaning of this infrastructure.* This is Foucault's original approach, as presented in "The Order of Discourse" (Foucault 1981), as Hook (2001) rightly states:

> Rather than moving from discourse towards its interior, towards the 'hidden nucleus' at the 'heart of signification', discourse analysis should move forward on the basis of discourse itself, on the basis of those elements that give rise to it and fix its limits: its external conditions of possibility [...]. Foucault's methodological injunction here is that of exteriority. Critical readings, he claims, will prove inadequate: looking at what can be shown to be within the text is insufficient because alternative 'showings' will always be possible. This is the problem of textual relativism, where any reasonably supported textual interpretation will hold, within relative confines, as well as any other. Hence the results of our analyses will be of little significance beyond the scope of the analysed text. (p. 538)

Analysis of language and linguistic aspects is only one *means* for that type of discourse analysis. However, this does not mean that there is no longer a distinction between discourse analysis and other approaches in the social sciences. When I presented the different analytical parts of extra-discursive reality, I presented them under the common frame of discourse theory. All of these parts are held together by the epistemological approach of discourse theory. The *relation* between a practice, a language use, an identity, and a physical materiality is only understandable through discourse analysis. "Discourse facilitates and endorses the emergence of certain relations of material power, just as it justifies these effects after the fact. Similarly, material arrangements of power enable certain speaking rights and privileges, just as they lend material substantiation to what is spoken in discourse" (Hook 2001: 540). This relation, or the net that holds together the diverse parts, often is also called the dispositive (Bührmann and Schneider 2007, 2008; Foucault 1979; Keller 2005a, 2007), although the dispositive concept is not very clear in discourse analysis and sometimes also refers not only to the relation of the parts but also to the whole (Bührmann and Schneider 2008).

To return to the starting question about what exactly discourse is, we can now say that it is not very important what "discourse" is but what *discourse analysis* is for our purpose: the analysis of material, practical, knowledge, and so on, effects, conditions, and content of language use. In this relation, language is often the most visible part: it is often the most obvious part that proves the relation and thanks to the advances in the field of linguistic discourse analysis, it is often the most easiest or common way of starting the analysis. However, I showed the different forms of the relations of discourse and each of the analytical concepts.

The presentation of the interrelation between discursive and non-discursive reality could be understood as a more sociological, a more social approach to discourses. We can use the conceptual tools presented here for planning and carrying out sociological discourse analysis. However, the presentation of that more-sociological approach was not an aim in itself. Instead, it was only a tool for using discourse analysis as a means of social critique. Social critique was understood as immanent critique, that is, a normative critique of social structure that takes its criteria from society itself. As we have observed, the broader sociological discourse-analytical approach can help us better understand the normative content of discursive and non-discursive practices and struggles. More sociologically based approaches help us not only perform internal critiques on discourses but also use immanent critique to better understand discourses and material realities. We can now analyse the differences between (implicit) normative claims and realities. In most practices, materialities, knowledges, and so on, there are included and often crystallized social norms that point towards a more general application. This normative surplus often collides with an inert, institutionalized social reality.

Nonetheless, although we can evaluate the consequences of these differences, it does not necessarily follow that discourse analysis is the empirical research method for immanent critique. To combine both strands, it is important to note three aspects that are frequently omitted in contemporary immanent critique and discourse studies.

1. Contrary to the notion that immanent critique means revealing the contradiction between socially accepted claims and reality, these contradictions have always been *necessary* in Critical Theory (Browne 2008).

As seen previously, "necessary" here refers to those contradictions that inevitably arise from the social order. Thus, immanent critique is not a matter of merely holding a mirror up to the criticized individuals and showing them their contradictions so that they can deliberately change their behaviour. This type of critique would surely have a transformative effect, but its transcending character would be limited.

Immanent critique should demonstrate that it is not primarily concerned with the intentional acts of individuals, collectives, or institutional actors. There are structural and/or systemic conditions that impede the resolution of these contradictions. Therefore, discourse analysis that seeks to follow the insights of Critical Theory must not only compare claims with (symbolic and material) reality but also reveal the (symbolic and material) obstacles that prevent these claims from becoming reality. As it extends towards the analysis of material resources, sociological discourse analysis has prepared the ground for merging immanent critique (as found in Critical Theory) with discourse analysis. Immanent critique can find practical tools for analysis in the discourse-analysis toolbox. However, for discourse analysts, this merger will yield clear research questions, including the following: What are the differences between claims and reality, and are these differences necessary (i.e., structural or systemic) contradictions?

All of the elements presented as conceptual tools have been shown to be both structuring and structured tools. In other words, on the one hand, they reproduce social reality and on the other hand, they are also the result of permanent (re-)creation. This recreation either permits varieties and interpretations or simply is prone to errors so that the social reality created out of the process of social reproduction constitutively includes the possibility of change. In discourse-analytical terms, we could even say that all of the extra-discourse elements are discursively and non-discursively structured and structure the discursive and non-discursive reality.

As we have seen, there are given possibilities of social change. However, this does not mean that we can easily free ourselves from structures. Perhaps the analogy to the structure of language might be useful to explain the relation between structural obligation and liberty. On the one hand, as a unique social actor, I am supposed to combine words to sentences and paraphrases that have never been expressed. Merely reproducing the existing structure never is sufficient, we *always* must fill it with life and either apply or interpret the structures in a particular way—not as deviation of the norm, but as the norm itself. On the other hand, language use requires that I use the structure or grammar of a given language. I cannot escape this obligation if I want to communicate effectively. Analogously, when discussing social structures and structural contradictions, we are not referring to contradictions that can be directly influenced by individual, collective, or institutional acts of will. This does not mean the end of critique as aiming at change but instead at the beginning of *social* critique. When showing the difficulties of change caused by social obstacles both inside and outside of individuals, *immanent critique is always social critique.* Immanent critique is never limited to criticizing single social actors and always refers to systemic inadequacies.

2. Regarding the dialectics of the notion of immanent critique, we can clarify the problem of the transcending normative viewpoint. Foucault seems to take his critical stance from the outside by referring to the "art of not being governed like that" (Foucault 2007). However, Critical Theory currently seems to insist that the immanence of institutions is so overwhelming that a transcending position is no longer visible (see also Herzog 2014). Nonetheless, as Zamora affirms, dialectical immanent critique also means that the "the total immanence of the system – even through mediation – ultimately is external and forceful to the individual" (Zamora 2011). This clarification means that there can be spaces of exteriority even in a totally administered world. According to diverse representatives of Critical Theory (Adorno 1970; Honneth 1992), these spaces might be understood as suffering. Thus, individual and collective human-made sufferings are the engine for normative progress. *The fact that human beings can suffer from social relations indicates the existence of this ultimate normative point of reference for social critique.*

It is this movement away from suffering that is the central normative element of practices, materialities, subject positions, and so on. The principal aim of practices, materialities, and subject positions relevant for our analysis is the prevention and abolition of avoidable suffering. Here we must think not only of practices, materialities, and subjects involved in alleviating direct suffering, for example, in the field of health care. Instead, everyday practices of educating our children, relating to our neighbours, or working can have a component of providing recognition to prevent avoidable disrespect either now or in the future.

By merging immanent critique and discourse analysis, we can hypothesize that it is exactly this individual suffering that leads Foucault to his attitude of refusal. In other words, the reason that Foucault refuses "to be governed like that" is the social suffering described in Critical Theory, for example, the experiences of disrespect described by Honneth (1992). Foucault partly experienced this disrespect himself and was partially able to emphatically understand others who suffered disrespect. Therefore, the capacity to suffer as proof of the existence of a normative perspective that is alien to the system might precisely represent that socially immanent anchor, referring transcendingly to that position outside of a given society.

Therefore, theoretically informed discourse analysis must uncover social suffering and reveal the degree to which this suffering is humanmade. Individuals do not necessarily verbally express their suffering. Their affective reactions are frequently either silent or expressed non-verbally. Here, the methodological toolbox of sociological discourse analysis can be helpful given its capacity to analyse not only text and talk but also non-verbal practices and affects (see also Renout 2012; Gutiérrez-Rodríguez 2007). In addition, merging Critical Theory and discourse analysis would offer a methodological approach to a researcher interested in immanent critique and provide theoretically informed research questions for discourse analysts.

3. When performing immanent critique, we must be aware of yet another aspect that is not only alien to poststructuralist discourse analysis but also often openly suspect of it. As made clear by Gregor Sauerwald's (2008) description of the immanent critique of "context-bound uni-

versalism", the notion of normative transcendence refers to a type of universalism. However, it is precisely the notion of universal norms that is sharply criticized by Foucault and other post-structuralists. For example, Foucault demonstrates that apparently universal norms are historically contingent, extremely particular, and "rare" constellations (e.g., Foucault 1981). Here too, discourse analysis can help reveal the particularity of apparently universal norms.

My hypothesis is that ultimately there is only one universal social norm: (human-made, i.e., social) suffering should be avoided. This norm can be used as a superlative norm with which to measure all other norms. Considering the norm of avoidance of suffering as superior to all others, we might solve the conundrum of ideological norms: if a norm (e.g., the specific recognition of white identities) is not reconcilable with the superlative norm of avoiding human-made suffering, it must be rejected. Similarly, we can demonstrate that implicit or explicit norms of liberty, equality, solidarity, or autonomy are principally compatible with the superlative norm. In other words, although there is a driving force away from suffering, this force does not necessarily lead to a more emancipated society. It is the social researcher's task both to show the implications of the diverse possible forms of sublating existing disrespect and to help create consciousness about the possibility of universal and sustainable forms of abolishing social suffering.

Again, this merging would mean a methodologization of immanent critique and the possibility of theoretically informed research questions for discourse analysis. With this approach, researchers might ask which norms are immanent in a society and the extent to which these norms are reconcilable with the (superior, universal) norm of the avoidance of suffering.

2.5   Assembling the Parts

To perform practical discourse analysis as social critique, we must join the parts that we attempted to separate as analytical concepts in the previous pages. When social critique is not the critique of a single practice, material phenomenon, identity, or worldview, but instead the critique of fundamental social structures, then we must analyse more than one specific element. We must assemble several parts to identify them as fundamental, interrelated structures that do not allow a simple adjustment of a single aspect of social reality. Conversely, every practical research, regardless of how complex it might be, must necessarily find an appropriate way of delimiting the research. Therefore, we need tools or second-order concepts that combine several elements in a meaningful, coherent, and especially manageable way.

In what follows, I would like to propose two second-order concepts, both of which operate at the meso level: social structures on the one hand and the concept of discursive exclusion on the other hand (Herzog 2011, 2013b). When I say that the level of analysis is the meso level, this does not mean that the unit of observation must be from the same level. Moreover, the conceptual tools and the proposal of assembling the parts could mean taking data from diverse micro-sociological research and combining it to allow generalizations even on a macro level. This is mesosociology in its original sense as intermediating between the micro and the macro approaches, taking the analysis of a *specific* social phenomenon and turning it to a *general, social* critique. The first approach to social structure is quite general and may serve as a "roadmap" for a variety of research proposals. The second approach, that of discursive exclusion, is already narrowed down to specific research questions concerning processes of social exclusion.

2.5.1 Social Structure

Social structures can be seen as both analytical tools and units of analysis. As units of analysis, however, social structures are perhaps the most complex. At some point, we have even noted that social structures are the end of critique because the aim of transcending social critique is not to change a single practice or one specific material object but to prepare a change in social structure itself. Until now, we have not stopped by asking what exactly a social structure is. In social science and humanities, social structure seems like an often-used notion often used that is therefore perceived as self-evident. However, it is often unclear in everyday usage what exactly social structure is; moreover, the difference between a social structure and a social system or a society is unclear. When I present social structures as unit and not as elements of analysis, I mean that, strictly speaking, structures are an assembly of elements.

Perhaps we can best imagine the idea of social structure when turning first to other examples of structures. We all have seen at some moment the structure of a multi-storey building during its construction process. The structure is not the same as the building itself. The structure here could refer to walls, pillars, and ceilings, perhaps space for an elevator and floors for underground car parks. We do not know whether the walls will be painted in white, grey, or yellow or whether the people in the building will have blonde or brown hair. By observing the structure, however, we can predict some of the things that will happen in the building. We can appreciate whether there will be offices or flats in the building, that is, whether people will work or live in it. Furthermore, we can foresee by simply analysing the bedrooms in the housing units whether there will be more families or one-person households. On the one hand, therefore, a structure necessarily needs to be completed (here with paintings, people, furniture, etc.). On the other side a structure is characterized by the *relation* of its parts. Pillars relate the ground to the top and in some cases, stairs relate the first floor to the second; the characteristics of these elements (strength, width) must be consistent with the related elements.

Therefore, a structure in general is a relatively stable ensemble of *elements* (or nodal points) and *relations*. The elements can be walls or ceilings, as in the example of the building, or social actors, institutions, practices, and so on, in the event that we speak of social structures. The relations can be pillars, elevators, or power relations, hierarchies, practices, and so on. On the one hand, the existence of a social structure is a relatively stable social order that renders predictable which elements can appear within that structure. On the other hand, in the same way that the structure of a building does not determine whether the people living in the house prefer to listen to classical music or to jazz, the social structure leaves a certain degree of liberty to the social actors within the structure.

Moreover, actors are required to fill the structure, to bring it to life, and to interpret it in diverse manners. In that sense, structures present frames that limit behaviour but always must be completed.

Nonetheless, we should not forget that social structures themselves are human-made. They are not natural entities but the product of human behaviour. Although humans usually do not consciously create social structure, the structure itself is the (secondary) outcome of people's everyday behaviour. Pierre Bourdieu therefore speaks of structuring and structured structures. It is important to take this point into account when talking about the possibilities of change in structures. Principally, structures that are created by humans can also be changed by them. Moreover, even the maintenance of social structures requires the constant, at least tacit, approval of individuals. By accepting ways of interrelation, hierarchies, and power relations in everyday life, people reproduce basic elements of social structure.

With this approach to structures in mind, it becomes clear why I refused to talk about structures as elements of analysis. Structures are not isolated elements but an ensemble of such elements, primarily nodal points and relations. For social analysis, it becomes important to (at least provisionally) decide the nodal points and types of relations in which we are interested. Do we want to analyse institutional actors and their hierarchical power relations or are we interested in their everyday practices of collaboration? Are we interested in subjects with a class identity and their internal discourses or are we interested in the discursive relations between technical and political knowledge? Of course we can—and indeed, we should—use more than two elements for our analysis of social structure. However, in our research practice, we must place limits on the number of elements we are able to analyse. Every limitation and selection presents a reduction of complexity and excludes interesting aspects that probably are also worthy of analysis. Moreover, all of the concepts presented here have been described as structured elements, that is, as elements that are not isolated but that depend on other elements in which they are in contact. These multiple contacts present relatively stable patterns of relation. For that reason, every analysis of an element cross-refers to other elements.

It is up to us how far we want to follow this network of relations and nodal points and at which point we must terminate the analysis. In general, there are two methods of analysing structures. The first is by taking one or several elements and then, by analysing these elements, following them to other nodal points. The second procedure consists of selecting a number of elements and analysing their interrelation or structure. In both cases, we end up with structures that are an ensemble of elements. One problem of the analysis of social structure in general—but especially of following the second modus operandi—is that we tend to work with the very strong hypothesis that *there is social structure*. This hypothesis is strong insofar as we presuppose the existence of patterns and social order that can impede in our perception of contingencies, casualties, incidents, and events that also not only form part of our societies but also can play a very important role (Reichertz 2005). Post-structuralist authors insisted on the difficulty of social order and on the general openness of analysis. In other words, even when analysing social structure, we should also work with the alternative hypothesis that there is no such a thing as social structure. This (also very strong) hypothesis helps us to be open to alternative and surprising findings, not to presuppose what we wish to show.

Therefore, the discourse analysis of social structures can be understood as the consciously combined analysis of several already-described elements. This ensemble produces discourses, is produced by discourses, and is excluded from some discourses while being included in others. The aim of such a combined analysis is to understand not only a part of the ensemble but the specific way of assembling as a *normative order*. Therefore, we must extract the normativity in this ensemble and uncover whether there is a normative surplus that indicates a fundamental change in the social structure. That notwithstanding, we have seen that social structures have relative stability. The static of a specific ensemble can be an obstacle to social change. In other words, depending on the fixity of structures, the normative surplus points to either a slight reform of the elements of the structure or a fundamental change in it.

When performing discourse analysis as a social critique of social structures, therefore, we engage in something like a second-order analysis.

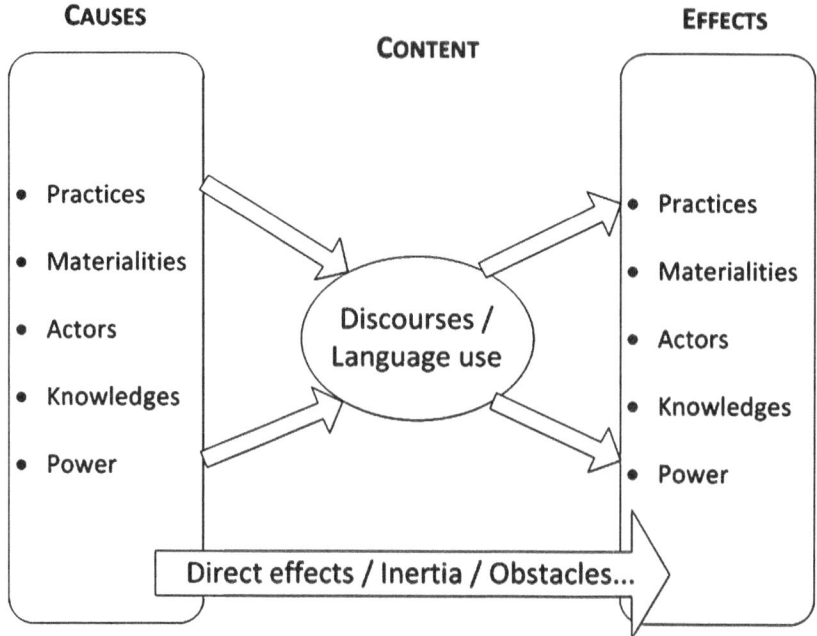

Fig. 2.2 The logics of structured sociological discourse analysis

In the first order, we have the analysis of the discourses and discursive and non-discursive conditions of the elements; in the second-order, we have the analysis of the social structure. When turning to the analysis of social structure, then, the first thing that we notice is the almost complete absence of discourses on social structure. Whereas discourses on subject positions, practices, and materialities can be found almost everywhere that people encounter these elements, discourses on social structures are expert discourses produced by sociologists, politicians, and the like. As ensembles, social structures are second-order concepts of (discourse) analysis. However, we should not forget the centrality of language use for this type of analysis. Language is almost always located at the centre of that analysis and in most cases, research on language is best situated to answer questions related to its content. Figure 2.2 shows this centrality of language in the proposed approach.

2.5.2 Discursive Exclusion

For those to whom "social structure" seems an overly second-order concept for combining diverse symbolic and material aspects within discourse analysis, there are other possibilities to normatively criticize society. We can adapt sociological concepts for our purpose, as I did in earlier works with the concept of social exclusion (Herzog 2009, 2011, 2013b).[3] We have seen that what is important for this type of sociological discourse analysis is to relate material, extra-discursive realities and language use under the umbrella of discourse analysis. Therefore, I have developed the concept of "discursive exclusion", which is the combination of three moments of exclusion[4]:

1. *Causes*: The exclusion from the production of discourses. In my research on diverse discourses on migration, I showed that migrants often do not participate in the discursive construction of what migrants (as social imaginary) are. In other words, migrants as physical beings are excluded from the production of migrants as bearers of social meaning. This exclusion can refer to several elements or concepts presented above. People cannot be given the subject position to be taken seriously in discourses, they cannot have the material or "cultural" capital that permits them to participate, and there can be specific practices—here, racist practices—that exclude some groups from partaking in discourses.
2. *Content and belonging*: Exclusion through or by discourses. Actual, dominant discourses create migrants as either not really part of society or as part of it in a subordinated way. Migration discourses create a specific social place for migrants as different—and inferior—as the rest of society. Here it is important to underline questions of belonging of certain parts of reality to the migration discourse. For example, discourses, practices, and materialities related to security, criminality,

---
[3] In a similar manner, Ruiz Ruiz (2014) speaks of "hidden or silenced discourses" (p. 180).
[4] As I point out in the cited works, I do not understand the pair inclusion/exclusion as binary and univocal but instead as gradual displacements.

or cultural identity are fundamental to understanding the hegemonic discourse on migration. This belonging of some topics to the migration discourse creates the hegemonic image of the typical migrant.
3. *Effects*: Extra-discursive or material exclusion. Migrants are often excluded both legally and socially. They are the objects of specific laws, practices of deportation, or racist practices. We can see, therefore, that exclusion is not only the cause of typical discourses: discourses can also have specific effects that go far beyond language. Material exclusion, understood as gradual discrimination, can be the direct or indirect result of a denigrating discourse. For discourse analysis, however, it can be especially interesting to study those cases in which a discourse does *not* produce the expected effect. This would mean that there are other, structural reasons that prevent a discourse from becoming effective.

Following the example of the social exclusion of migrants, we can see the threefoldness of sociological discourse analysis:

1. Exclusion from the production of discourse means doing research on the material or extra-discursive infrastructure. Knowledge, identities, practices, or physical materiality are part of that infrastructure as *causes* of specific contents. In the case of migration discourses in the media, this is, for example, the absence of migrant journalists writing about migration, the practice of contacting primarily migrant-free institutions instead of migrant associations when writing about migration, or the common "knowledge" that this is the valid way of conducting journalistic enquiries (Herzog 2009).
2. Exclusion through the discourse means analysing the *content* of the discourse. In this case, there is a question about how migrants are constituted by the discourse. Which characteristics were ascribed to them? What is the social meaning of being a migrant? And so on. In the case of (mainstream) migration discourses, it is possible to show that the migrants are created as ontologically different to natives. Furthermore, the discourse of migration is about these differences leading to problems because of the presence of migrants.

3. The material or extra-discursive exclusion as the *effect* of the discourse. Migration discourses legitimize specific behaviour towards migrants, the creation of laws, public institutions, police units, knowledge, and identities. One impressive example in my research involved the practice of calling the police to fight migrants' binge drinking, whereas the practice for fighting natives' binge drinking called for more free leisure alternatives (Herzog et al. 2008).

The purpose of this example is not to show three separate spheres of analysis but instead to underline that for a complete understanding, *all three spheres must be analysed* and in particular, they must be analysed *in relation to each other*. The relation is described here as the discourses' cause, content, and effect because the content is the central part of that relation. This points to the centrality of language or rhetoric analysis in discourse studies. However, the logic must be circular: extra-discursive aspects leading to discourses/language use, leading to the construction of extra-discursive reality, preparing the way for discourses, and so on. It is important to underline that extra-discursive effect is not a deterministic result of discourse, nor are discourses totally determined by extra-discursive infrastructure. As analysts, we must do research on the complex discursive constellations to understand the entry, exit, or failure of discourses.

With regard to anti-racist discourses in primary schools, Hernàndez and Herzog (2011b) have been able to show the systematic failure of discourses of equality. Although talk about equality was very present in teachers' activity, combined with visual stimuli, such as pictures of children of diverse colours playing, dancing, or holding hands, the antiracist discourse was unable to fundamentally transform the children's knowledge structure. The discourse of equality directly contradicted their knowledge, their observations of everyday practice, and material reality (and sometimes also the discourses in their homes). What these children saw and knew was not that all humans are equal. They saw different skin colour, they saw that children often played in separate ethnic groups on the playground (see also Tatum 1999), and they noticed that sometimes they spoke different languages. In other words: the discourse about abstract equality did not have the power—even if repeated devotedly by the children—to change behaviour and the knowledge structure because of the lack of an adequate discursive infrastructure (knowledge, practices, etc.). For educational purposes and the planning of teaching activities, an adequate analysis of the discursive infrastructure would have helped prepare appropriate teachings against racism, or, as Hook (2001) notes, "without reference to materiality [...] discourse analysis remains largely condemned to 'the markings of textuality', a play of semantics, a decontextualized set of hermeneutic interpretations that can all too easily be dismissed" (p. 542). The question that is broached here is the following: Under what conditions (discursive infrastructure) does a particular discourse become effective? Or, in other words, when and to what degree can an effect be related to a specific discourse?

Following our approach to social critique, we can state that the term "exclusion" is usually used in a normative way to denounce a situation that has been identified as unjust. To follow our line of argument of normative and immanent social critique, we must show that the situation of exclusion either contradicts the explicit will of the actors or strikes against that which is normatively implicit in the practices in a specific field. So only in those cases in which the exclusion of a group of persons clashes with an explicit or implicit accepted norm of equality can exclusion then be criticized. This is one of the reasons that social movements claiming the same rights for men and women, heterosexuals and homosexuals, whites and blacks have had such relative success since the French and American Revolutions. From then on, equality was accepted in general terms. All social movements had to do was to show that a given practice or social order contravened the official discourse of equality.[5]

Using discursive exclusion for the purpose of social critique means simultaneously analysing the existence of exclusion and the normative content of elements such as practices in the field of research. The advantage of such a procedure is that the very approach of sociological discourse analysis displaces attention from the excluded and the state of

---

[5] Of course, this is a gross simplification of a complex historic process. In a real analysis of these processes, other structural discursive and non-discursive factors would have to be taken into account.

exclusion in favour of the process of production of social exclusion, thus showing the active creation of a criticizable state. In other words, we can criticize the discursive construction of exclusion in all cases in which the effect of exclusion contravenes societies' implicit or explicit normative self-description.

2.6 Conclusions

So far, the problem of social critique has been that we have lacked a coherent connection between theoretical critique from social and political philosophy on the one hand and empirical findings from social research on the other hand. Without empirical research, critique remains distant, sterile, and detached from social reality, thus creating the danger of presenting not the critical position of society but that of the philosopher pronouncing the critique. Without a theoretical foundation, social research is like a group of building workers who lack an architectural plan. This type of social research cannot overlook its nearby field of analysis—it can provide only a critique of a specific social phenomenon, not of the social order as a whole.

Normative critique that takes its normative stance from the analysed material itself, aiming not at a mere correction of social order but instead towards a fundamental change, has been briefly referred to as immanent critique. The question that I attempted to answer in this second chapter was how to extract the normative criteria from social reality and how to oppose the normative claims to social reality. To avoid analysing either a casual claim or a social situation with little relevance, I turned to those phenomena that appeared structured: practices, subject positions, structured materialities, and so on. An approach that was especially promising in analysing explicit and implicit claims of structured realities could be found in sociological discourse analysis. I understood that to mean an analysis that focuses not only on language but also on the extra-discursive conditions and extra-discursive effects of discourses. When speaking of discourses, I consciously employed a narrow notion of discourse as an "institutionalized way of speaking" (Link 1986), not the broad, un-handy notion of Laclau and Mouffe (2014). That notion allowed me to differentiate a series of non-discursive elements that seemed especially interesting for the extraction of normative criteria while having the ability to be related to the overall frame of discourse analysis. Practices, materialities, actors, identities and subject positions, knowledge, power, and domination were the elements presented here. With this selection, I did not want to present a closed list of elements for discourse analysis as social critique. Instead, what I attempted to offer was a specific reading of those elements, a reading that permits adjustment of the discourse analysis towards a specific research objective: social critique. Finally, I attempted to provide tools for the practical limitation of discourse analysis as social critique and proposed both a broad (structures) and a narrow (exclusion) conceptual example of how one might relate some of the elements. I presented social structures and the concepts of discursive exclusion as possibilities for organizing the empirical research and researching a coherent set of elements. Again, the proposed linking tools were only intended as examples. Other methods of combined analysis are not only possible but also desirable because the analytical tools must always adapt to the specific research question and the field of investigation.

However, it is not always necessary to conduct discourse analysis as social critique from beginning to end. Because of both the prolific tradition of discourse analysis and other types of analysis of structured elements, we can stand on the shoulders of those who previously worked on particular questions. All we must do is either "read" those analyses in a specific way for social critique or re-examine the material in the light of our own research interest. This reading can be understood as a "normative reconstruction" (Honneth 2011a) of discourses and the social conditions and effects of discourses.

References

Adorno, T. W. (1970) *Negative Dialektik. Jargon der Eigentlichkeit*, (Frankfurt/Main: Suhrkamp).
Alexander, M. (2010) *The New Jim Crow: Mass Incarceration in the Age of Colorblindness*, (New York: The New Press).

Angermuller, J. (2007) *Nach dem Strukturalismus. Theoriediskurs und intellektuelles Feld in Frankreich,* (Bielefeld: Transcript).
Angermuller, J. (2014) *Poststructuralist Discourse Analysis: Subjectivity in Enunciative Pragmatics,* (Houndmills: Palgrave Macmillan).
Berger, P. L. & Luckmann, T. (1967) *The social construction of reality. A treatise in the sociology of knowledge,* New York: Anchor Books.
Boltanski, L. (2011) *On Critique – A Sociology of Emancipation*, (Cambridge: Polity Press).
Browne, C (2008) 'The End of Immanent Critique?', *European Journal of Social Theory* 11(1): 5–24.
Bührmann, A. & Schneider, W. (2007) 'More Than Just a Discursive Practice? Conceptual Principles and Methodological Aspects of Dispositif Analysis', *Forum: Qualitative Social Research*, 8(2).
Bührmann, A. & Schneider, W. (2008) *Vom Diskurs zum Dispositiv - Eine Einführung in die Dispositivanalyse,* (Bielefeld: transcript).
Davies, B. & Harre, R. (1990) 'Positioning: The discursive production of selves', *Journal for the Theory of Social Behavior* 20: 43–63.
Eagleton, T. (2011) *Why Marx was right,* (New Haven: Yale University Press).
Fairclough, N. (1992) *Discourse and social change,* (Cambridge: Polity Press).
Fairclough, N. (2004) 'Critical discourse analysis in researching language in the new capitalism: Overdetermination, transdisciplinarity and textual analysis', in: Harison, C. & Young, L. (eds.) *Systemic functional linguistics and critical discourse analysis*, (London: Continuum), pp. 103–122.
Foucault, M. (1975) *Discipline and Punish: the Birth of the Prison*, (New York: Random House).
Foucault, M. (1979) *The History of Sexuality Volume 1: An Introduction*, (London: Allen Lane).
Foucault, M. (1981) 'The order of discourse', in: R. Young *(ed.) Untying the text: A post-structural anthology,* (Boston, MA: Routledge & Kegan Paul), pp. 48–78.
Foucault, M. (2002) *The Archaeology of Knowledge*, (London and New York: Routledge).
Foucault, M. (2007) *The politics of truth*, (Los Angeles: Semiotext(e)).
Graeber, D. (2011) *Debt: The First 5000 Years,* (New York: Melville House).
Graeber, D. (2015) *The utopia of rules. On Technology, Stupidity, and the Secret Joys of Bureaucracy,* (London: Melville House).
Gutiérrez Rodrígucz, E. (2007) 'Reading Affect—On the Heterotopian Spaces of Care and Domestic Work in Private Households', *Forum: Qualitative Social Research,* 8(2). http://nbn-resolving.de/urn:nbn:de:0114-fqs0702118.

Hernàndez, F. & Herzog, B. (2011b) 'Expropriierte Identitäten. Diskursive Exklusionsmechanismen und deren Wirkungsweisen', Contribution at the conference *Neuer Strukturwandel der Öffentlichkeit*, Innsbruck, October 2011.
Herzog, B. (2009) *Exclusión discursiva – el imaginario social sobre inmigración y drogas*, (Valencia: PUV).
Herzog, B.(2011) 'Exclusión Discursiva - hacia un nuevo concepto de la exclusión social', *Revista Internacional de Sociología*, 69(3): 607–626.
Herzog, B. (2013b) 'Ausschluss im (?) Diskurs. Diskursive Exklusion und die neuere soziologische Diskursforschung', *Forum Qualitative Sozialforschung / Forum: Qualitative Social Research*, 14(2), http://nbn-resolving.de/urn:nbn:de:0114-fqs1302199.
Herzog, B. (2014) 'Was bedeutet immanente Kritik für die empirische Sozialforschung? Überlegungen zur Erschließung notwendiger Widersprüche', in: Romero, J. M. (ed.) *Immanente Kritik heute*, (Bielefeld: transcript), pp. 157–178.
Herzog, B. (2016b) O'Reilly & Jessica Lester (eds.) *The Palgrave Handbook of Adult Mental Health*, (Houndmills: Palgrave), pp. 101–116.
Herzog, B., Gómez-Guardeño, E., Agulló-Calatayud, V., Aleixandre-Benavent, R. & Valderrama-Zurián, J. C. (2008) 'Discourses on Drugs and Immigration: The Social Construction of a Problem', *Forum: Qualitative Social Research*, 10(1) http://nbn-resolving.de/urn:nbn:de:0114-fqs090172.
Herzog, B. & Hernàndez, F. (2012) 'La noción de «lucha» en la teoría de reconocimiento de Axel Honneth. Sobre la posibilidad de subsanar el «déficit sociológico» de la Teoría Crítica con la ayuda del Análisis del Discurso', *Política & Sociedad*, 49(3): 609–623.
Honneth, A. (1992) *Der Kampf um Anerkennung. Zur moralischen Grammatik sozialer Konflikte*, (Frankfurt: Suhrkamp). [English: Honneth, A (1995) *The Struggle for Recognition: The Moral Grammar of Social Conflicts*, (Cambridge: Polity Press).]
Honneth, A. (2004) 'Anerkennung als Ideologie', *WestEnd Neue Zeitschrift für Sozialforschung*, 1: 51–70.
Honneth, A. (2011a) *Das Recht der Freiheit*, (Berlin: Suhrkamp).
Honneth, A. (2013) 'Theorie der Anerkennung als kritische Theorie der Gesellschaft? – Ein Interview mit Axel Honneth', *Soziologiemagazin* http://soziologieblog.hypotheses.org/4000.
Hook, D. (2001) 'Discourse, knowledge, materiality, history - Foucault and discourse analysis', *Theory & Psychology*, 11(4): 521–549.
Jaeggi, R. (2014a) *Kritik von Lebensformen*, (Berlin: Suhrkamp).

Jaeggi, R. (2014b) 'Was (wenn überhaupt etwas) ist falsch am Kapitalismus? Drei Wege der Kapitalismuskritik', in: Jaeggi, R. & Loick, D. (eds.) *Nach Marx – Philosophie, Kritik, Praxis*, (Berlin: Suhrkamp), pp. 321–349.

Keller, R. (2005a) 'Analysing Discourse. An Approach From the Sociology of Knowledge', *Forum: Qualitative Social Research*, 6(3).

Keller, R. (2005b) *Wissenssoziologische Diskursanalyse – Grundlegung eines Forschungsprogrammes*, (Wiesbaden: Verlag für Sozialwissenschaften).

Keller, R., Hirseland, A., Schneider, W. & Viehöver, W. (Eds.) (2005) *Die diskursive Konstruktion von Wirklichkeit: Zum Verhältnis von Wissenssoziologie und Diskursforschung*, (Konstanz: UVK).

Laclau, E. & Mouffe, C. (2014) *Hegemony and Socialist Strategy, Towards a Radical Democratic Politics*, (London: Verso).

Link, J. (1986) 'Noch einmal: Diskurs. Interdiskurs. Macht', *kulturRevolution*, 11(4): 4–7.

Lenk, K. (1984) *Ideologie. Ideologiekritik und Wissenssoziologie*, (Frankfurt a.M.: Luchterhand).

Reichertz, J. (2005) 'Order at all Points. Lassen sich Diskursanalyse und Hermeneutik gewinnbringend miteinander verbinden?', in: Keller, R., Hirseland, A., Schneider, W. & Viehöver, W. (eds.) *Die discursive Konstruktion von Wirklichkeit*, (Konstanz: UVK), pp. 149–178.

Reinarman, C. & Levine, H. G. (2004) 'Crack in the Rearview Mirror: Deconstructing Drug War Mythology', *Social Justice*, 31(1/2): 182–199.

Renout, G. (2012) *Wissen in Arbeit und in Bewegung? Wissenssoziologische Diskursanalyse aktueller Strategien von LebenskünstlerInnen in Kreativarbeit und zeitgenössischem Tanz*, (Wiesbaden: VS).

Ruiz Ruiz, J. (2009) 'Análisis sociológico del discurso: Métodos y lógicas' *Forum: Qualitative Social Research*, 10(2).

Ruiz Ruiz, J. (2014) 'El discurso implícito: aportaciones para un análisis sociológico', *REIS - Revista Española de Investigaciones Sociológicas*, 146: 171–190.

Saar, M. (2009) 'Macht und Kritik', in: Forst, R., Hartmann, M., Jaeggi, R. & Saar, M. (eds.) *Sozialphilosophie und Kritik*, (Frankfurt/Main: Suhrkamp), pp. 567–587.

Sauerwald, G. (2008) *Reconocimiento y Liberación: Axel Honneth y el pensamiento latinoamericano. Por un diálogo entre el Sur y el Norte*, (Berlin: Lit Verlag).

Schütz, A. (1967) *Phenomenology of the social world*, (Evanston: Northwestern University Press).

Searle, J. R. (1995) *The Construction of Social Reality*, (New York: The Free Press).

Stahl, T (2013b) *Immanente Kritik. Elemente einer Theorie sozialer Praktiken,* (Frankfurt M./New York: Campus).
Tatum, B. D. (1999) *"Why Are All the Black Kids Sitting Together in the Cafeteria?" And Other Conversations About Race*, (New York: Basic Books).
Taylor, C. (1994) *Multiculturalism – Examining the politics of recognition,* (Princeton: University Press), pp. 149–163.
van Dijk, T. (1993) 'Principles of critical discourse analysis', *Discourse & Society*, 4: 249–283.
van Dijk, T. (1995) 'Discourse, Power and Access', in: M. Coulthard & Caldas-Coulthard, C. R. (eds.) *Critical Discourse Analysis,* (London: Routledge).
Weber, M. (1978) *Economy and Society – An outline of interpretive sociology*, (Berkeley: University of California Press).
Wodak, R. (1996) *Disorders of discourse,* (London: Longman).
Žižek, S. (ed.) (2012) *Mapping Ideology*, (London: Verso).
Zamora, J. A. (2011) 'Lässt sich der Kapitalismus immanent kritisieren? Reflexionen mit und über Theodor W. Adorno', Contribution at the international seminar: *Immanente Kritik. Grundlagen und Aktualität eines sozialphilosophischen Begriffs*, Frankfurt/M.

3

Practical Examples

3.1 The Empirical Application of Theoretical Concepts

How could this work's approach to "Discourse Analysis as Social Critique" be used in practical, empirical research? My proposal is that there are several ways of doing so. Every possibility has both strengths and weaknesses. One of the main problems with every study is to find a balance between a sufficient complete and complex analysis on the one hand and limited resources (along with the need to reduce complexity) on the other hand. In what follows, I will present several examples of approaching social reality from the discourse perspective to formulate a fundamental social critique. All of these examples aim to illuminate one or several aspects of the approach presented here. None of these examples is complete and all of them have good reasons to argue for further development of numerous aspects of the case presented.

Based on what was said in the previous chapters, it should be clear that the approach to discourses presented here is by no means an approach that inevitably begins with an analysis of linguistic communication. To understand discourses, we often must analyse the material and practical *conditions* of discourses, and we must consider either what *is not* said or what *cannot* be said. Furthermore, we have seen that we can also analyse non-verbal elements and verbal elements using similar techniques. Practices, materialities, and so on, are not only structured similar to language but also have an intersubjectively understandable (often normative) content.

The approach suggested in this book requires a holistic perspective on several elements of social reality at the same time. An in-depth study of every topic presented here as an example would surely exceed the scope of this book. However, the examples should clarify the complexity of such an analysis and the diverse methods of performing social critique. The first example of the discourse of the merit principle comes quite close in its procedure to more "traditional" discourse analysis. However, this first example aims, with the help of social philosophical reasoning, to understand the systemic impossibility of meeting certain discursive claims, thus transforming the analysis into social critique. Although the second example of practices surrounding migration is accompanied by elements of discourse analysis of language use, its primary focus is to understand the normative content of a series of *practices*. To transform this analysis into genuine social critique, the systemic difficulties of meeting the normative exigencies are revealed. The third example turns again to the classical analysis of discourse. The purpose of this example of the discourse of same-sex marriage shows the apparent *failure* of the critique of fundamental social structures. Nonetheless, insight into that failure can be quite useful and thus, it shows how the approach presented here can also be applied to *defend* society against unjustified critique: In the debate about same-sex marriage, it is sometimes—falsely, as I will note—claimed that these partnerships corrode society as a whole, thus formulating a fundamental, social critique through the critique of same-sex marriage.

With these three examples, we should be able to gain a clear view of the possibilities and limits of discourse analysis as social critique. In summary, the three examples will be followed by a series of general guidelines of how to perform Discourse Analysis as Social Critique. The purpose of these guidelines is to offer the researcher who is interested in using the approach some practical advice about how to structure the research process. However, in a final series of examples, I want to go a step further and show cases of silent and silenced suffering. To perceive this type of suffering, I use three examples from the field of aesthetics. To make this use of aesthetic products for social analysis, I first present to the reader the relationship between social analysis and aesthetics. The Frankfurt School has an especially long and outstanding tradition in this type of analysis, albeit one that likely is not well-known to the researcher coming from discourse studies. This approach to aesthetics can help us overcome some of our problems related to the empathic understanding of the suffering of others. As we will see, art provides us with a very sensitive source of acceding to social reality. In the fourth example, the case of the Ph.D. Comics, this relation between art and reality is quite obvious given that the art aims directly to show suffering in social reality. Here, we can quite easily understand the production of art as struggle for recognition. However, even in the fifth example of the *Sacrifice of Isaac* by Rembrandt, we will see how we can empathically understand elements that we can use for social critique. Even a totally fictitious story like *The Metamorphosis* by Franz Kafka can be used to elaborate social critique, as I will explain in the last example.

All of the examples are unfolded and discussed; they exemplify some of the conceptual tools presented in the second chapter.

Example 1: Meritocracy

The following example is perhaps the closest to classical discourse analysis because it starts by analysing discourse—or better, by sketching such analysis—that holds legitimate social status and distribution in our society. Here, it is not possible to realize a complete discourse analysis. Instead, I must rely on others' research findings. Therefore, the affirmations made below have the status of (I think, well-founded) hypothesis. However, this example shows the logical and practical impossibility of meeting a society's own criteria of legitimating social inequality, thus turning the discourse analysis into genuine social critique, that is, a normative critique of the mode of social reproduction. I will show how discourse analysis (step 1) requires theoretical reflections (step 2) and an analysis of material and symbolic infrastructure (step 3) to become a critique with the ability to contribute to social change (step 4).

Step 1. Discourses about inequality: the merit principle

What, we could ask, legitimates social inequality in our societies? In other words, there are differences in status and access to material goods that seem not problematic but justified. For what reason do we accept person A to possess more goods and to be of higher social status than person B? To answer these questions, a classical discourse analysis would perhaps analyse the arguments presented in public discourses, such as arguments from politicians, public intellectuals, newspapers, and so on. By doing so, we would probably find something like the hegemonic discourse on social inequality. However, all of the mentioned social actors themselves possess a relatively high social status and access to material goods and benefit from social inequality. To capture the perception of the "normal" population, we could also conduct interviews and ask about the legitimate and unjust social distribution of goods and status. Note that by proceeding in this classical way, we still make a certain type of selection. We only capture the more-or-less conscious positions of those able to speak about distribution, thus capturing only the explicated legitimating strategies and the explicit suffering. The silent suffering that was important for the theoretical approach is not covered in this methodological procedure. That said, we will return to the silent and silenced suffering.

Based on a classical discourse analysis, we would most probably find that all Western societies broadly accept the merit principle. As described in Sect. 1.4, merit is widely accepted as legitimating the distribution of wealth. If we analyse philosophical texts, we will find this merit principle in classical liberal authors such as John Locke, who says that the outcome of one's labour must belong to oneself (Locke 1960: 287f) and in socialist authors who claim that the whole "fruit of the labour" (Lasalle) must be for those who work, that is, the proletarians. We can find similar rhetoric by ultra-libertarians like Robert Nozick (1974) and well-accepted philosophers like Peter Sloterdijk and in principle, Axel Honneth (see e.g., Herzog and Hernàndez 2009).

However, the individualization of labour and of the "fruits of one's labour" is not as clear as it seems, as Marx remarks in his "Critique on the programme of Gotha". Marx criticizes this formulation because it remains unclear what is meant by "the fruit of one's labour" because parts of the labour outcome must be reused in the production process, as reserves for future misfortunes, or for social costs such as schools, streets, or health care (Marx 1972). He also adds "funds for those unable to work, etc., in short, for what is included under so-called official poor relief today" (ibid.: 14). A similar critique of ultra-liberals is formulated by Honoré (1987) or more recently, against Sloterdijk by Honneth (2009). However, these latter critics are particularly unlikely to question the merit principle as such; instead, they add the understanding that individual merit can only produce value when basic social conditions are guaranteed. Here, we can get a first glance of the idea that merit *is* not individual but social. However, most critics of ultra-liberalism defend the idea that merit *needs* the social, which is slightly different.

If we analyse political speech, we can see that from the right to the left of Western societies, the merit principle is widely accepted. Whether referring to the "hard working" family father who should be able to earn a decent living or so-called "top performers" who should not be unjustly taxed, in all cases, the argument is that people deserve what they have or even more because they perform well. They simply do a good job. The merit principle is even legally coded in several laws or legalistic texts. Employers, especially public ones, are obligated to choose the most competent candidate, and for the same work (read, the same merit) the same salary must be paid.

Even if we were to finally analyse the discourses of "ordinary" people, for example via interviews, we would probably find the conviction that those who work more or better deserve either a better income or a higher job position. So through classical discourse analysis, we could conclude that there is a broadly—and quite consciously—accepted norm that merit should pay. Nonetheless, we probably would find in such discourse analysis important disputes and differences related to the following two questions:

The first issue that probably will not result in a clear societal consensus is the extent to which individual contributions should be the basis for the distribution of social goods. This question includes on the one hand, the issue of which other mechanisms should exist to distribute these goods. Most people probably would admit that to some extent, measures, such as social welfare, on the basis of individual necessity should protect from misery even those who make little or no social contribution. However, the discussion about the extent of these welfare politics reveals important differences between social actors. On the other hand, the question of distribution of social goods would probably show that there are also differences related to *which* social goods should be distributed by the merit principle. Is it only material wealth—especially income—that must be distributed by the merit principle? Or does the merit principle also include the distribution of certain rights? In public debates, we sometimes can hear the argument that "as someone pays taxes", he or she should also have specific rights, for example, voting rights. Here, we see an argument that understands certain rights not as bound to one's status as a moral person but instead to one's contribution to society (here, via taxpaying).

The second question that probably will not result in a clear societal consensus is that about what should count as merit. How can we measure merit? On the one hand, we will identify issues about what is socially valuable and therefore should be included in the calculation of distribution of goods and benefits. Here, we confront the classical question of whether reproductive labour, bringing up children, cleaning one's own house, caring for the elderly, and so on should entitle a person to benefits. On the other hand, we confront the question in the field of paid labour of how to measure individual contributions. Is it valuable to spend a great deal of time at work, to do responsible tasks (and what does this mean?), to be creative in the job, or to perform highly skilled labour? Who decides the worth of various types of work?

Wages attempt to measure merit and often are interpreted as recognition of individual contributions. However, the fact that people often argue that certain income differences are unfair shows that we cannot take a monetary measurement as equal to a social/moral measurement of contribution. David Graeber (2013) even argues that often jobs that most people agree are highly necessary and valuable for social reproduction, such as kindergarten teaching, nursing, or cleaning hospitals, often are extremely poorly paid compared to jobs that people often think are dispensable, such as "private equity CEOs, lobbyists, PR researchers, actuaries, telemarketers, bailiffs or legal consultants" (ibid.).

However, despite this dispute about the extent and content of merit, there seems to be a clear consensus that merit should entitle a person to social goods. When we have discussed merit or contribution, we have withheld what perhaps was obvious but now requires deeper analysis. Specifically, we have not discussed that when people talk about deserving and contribution, they refer to *individual* merit. It is not because *our boss* works hard or *our neighbour* performs highly skilled labour that I deserve certain entitlements; instead, it is because my personal contribution is valuable.

Step 2: Questions from social and political philosophy

(a) Individual vs. social merit

At this point, however, we encounter some very interesting philosophical questions about identity, personhood, self-ownership, and property. The question here is as follows: What characteristics belong exclusively to my merit and entitle me to a certain share of the fruits of the use of my meritorious characteristics? Whereas there seems to be a broad societal consensus about the second part of this question, namely, that individual merit should entitle (to some extent) access of certain social goods, in practice the first two parts present a conundrum even for contemporary philosophers. If me being tall enables me to play better basketball or to better pick apples from a tree, does this mean that being tall is a merit that should entitle me to have more social goods than others? Can we blame someone for being small or physically disabled? Or are we confronted by an unequal distribution of natural characteristics? In that case, this distribution of individual characteristics cannot be understood in terms of justice. Natural distribution is neither just nor unjust. However, the social distribution of goods and entitlements based on these natural inequalities can be either just or unjust. Even if we accept that only those characteristics that are the fruits of our merit should entitle us to social goods, it is not at all clear which talents are natural and which are not. Initially, we would perhaps agree that a hard-working person should be better off than a lazy one. However, is diligence or laziness somehow different from being small, tall, able, or disabled? When we dig a little bit deeper, it is far from clear which characteristics or capacities represent our individual merits and which do not. So, for example, the very idea of talent means that there is a somehow innate capacity to perform better than others in a specific field, although talent must often be developed by an individual.

Here, we experience two more problems, both pointing towards the social character of individual capacities. First, "individual" development can only be understood in a *social* context. Individuals who live in a particular social context (read: societies or families) who are unable to discover or to foster specific capacities will be unable to obtain that particular, "individual" capacity. Second, what is considered a merit or a valuable capacity is strongly dependent on the society in which a person lives. In agrarian societies, physical skills are highly valued, whereas in "information societies", intellectual capacities seem more important. Additionally, capacities and skills are not generally valued; they are only valued in a certain amount. For example, it seems that our societies very highly value certain people with artistic skills. The best artists in a society are famous and usually can earn a great deal of money. On the contrary, the best primary teachers, nurses, and dustmen are usually unknown and do not receive significantly higher salaries than their workmates, although almost everybody agrees on the importance of their work. However, this example does not show that, in general, artistic capacities are socially higher ranked than other skills. We all have heard the complaint of poor artists living in very precarious situations.

Summing up the problem with individual capacities that should be moral grounds for entitlement to certain social goods, we can say that on the one hand, it seems we have a complex pattern of characteristics that are somehow *natural* and therefore morally neutral. On the other hand, we have *social* conditions that either enable us to develop certain skills or impede that development.

(b) Self-ownership

These problems lead us to the general question of self-ownership. The question of how far we own ourselves is directly linked to the question of property rights involving the fruit of one's labour and the individual or social character of property in general. What does it mean to have property in oneself? Do I own (my) body, (my) talents, (my) labour, (my) wage, and the objects bought by me? And if so, do I own them in the very same way or are there differences regarding the implications of the notion of property? Depending on the answer, there will be the possibility of justifying social retribution. If I do *not* own one of these categories mentioned above or if I have only "shared" ownership, than either these categories themselves or their outcome is reliable with respect to social redistribution. To answer these questions, Honoré (1987) could help. Honoré differentiates ten incidents of ownership. He defines the full liberal concept of ownership as a notion that enables these ten incidents to be united in a single person. The list contains mainly rights, such as the right to possess or the right to use; it also contains restrictions, such as the duty to prevent harm or liability for execution. As Honoré notes, we can also imagine a notion of property (and therefore of self-ownership) that includes only some of these incidents. We could call this the thin notion of property.

Christman (1991) brings us a step nearer to this thin notion by distinguishing control right from income right. Control rights "are aspects of the person's *independent* powers over the thing owned; that is, these rights are not conditional on the consent of others" (29). Conversely, there are income rights, which are the right to increased *benefit* from ownership (ibid.). Christman argues that control rights are linked to individuals' autonomy, liberty, and self-determination. Because these rights are independent from other members of society, they should not be liable to be redistributed. So, for example, the right to control one's body would be a control right. Nobody, we could argue, should have the right to take away some parts of our body without our consent, even if it benefits others to do so.

However, the possibility of obtaining a benefit from our ownership depends on social factors that are external to the individual. Christman names not only political and social structures but also the distribution of resources. Income rights are conditional, that is, they depend on others interchanging with me in given social structures and therefore, they "are *essentially* tied to the distribution of goods" (ibid.). Because they do not depend on the individual, they are not a manifestation of an individual's (invulnerable) autonomy or liberty. Moreover, because the benefit resulting from our ownership depends on social structures, it can be used to maintain or change these structures. One of the criteria that we can use to do so could be equality; however, other criteria are also imaginable—for example, individual need.

Accordingly, with these analytical tools at hand, we can understand, for example, the general rejection of forced labour and the (general) acceptance of taxation. Forced labour violates our right to control our bodies. This explains our intuitive reaction against any type of forced labour. Taxation, however, does not violate our control rights. Taxation usually refers to taxation of income, which stems from income rights. Therefore, society could use (parts of) the income to maintain or change social structures. Taxation does not violate our liberty or autonomy. The equalization of taxation and forced labour, similar to the formulation of, for example, by Nozick (1974), is inadmissible as the two terms refer to two different types of rights. Thus, we are underlining the importance of society instead of full self-ownership for autonomy. Autonomy includes the possibility of developing and choosing among a diversity of possibilities. "Since the 'existence of many options consists in part in the existence of certain social conditions', including the availability of collective goods such as educational and welfare institution, the provision of such goods must be assured for autonomy to prevail" (Cohen 1995: 236). Thus, we have seen that it is highly doubtful that there is one clear way that merit is used to justify inequality. This is one reason that several authors speak openly of the "myth" of merit (e.g., Jenkins 2013; McNamee and Miller 2009) or the "ideology" of merit (e.g., Elmgren 2015; Girardot 2011).[1]

Step 3: The materiality of discourse analysis and the transcendence of critique

Now we can summarize our provisional example of the merit principle by focusing on three aspects relevant to our approach on discourse

---

[1] Note that both authors use the term "ideology" slightly differently, as presented in this book (see Sect. 2.3.4). They use it in the tradition of Hannah Arendt as the "logic of an idea" that "has distorted our conception of reality and replaces the complexity of life with the simplicity of an idea. The conception of merit has become totalizing" (Elmgren 2015: 156).

analysis as social critique: the discursive aspects of the example, the material aspects, and the justification of why this example presented a *social* critique in the sense described in the first chapter.

1. Regarding the discursive aspects, we could say that we came up with the merit principle using a (hypothetical) classical discourse analysis. By analysing text and talking about what justifies (in the eyes of society) the unequal distribution of goods and benefits, we saw that at least in part, the merit principle holds. That is, there is a broad discourse stating that people who perform better because of specific individual characteristics should receive a bigger share of certain social goods.
2. However, we have argued that the point of discourse analysis is to analyse the "feared materiality" of discourse. We must analyse not only the material causes of certain discourses but also their material effects. In that sense, the merit principle serves directly as justification to (re-)distribute both material and immaterial wealth. As the main justification for the amount of a person's salary, the merit principle seems to be the most accepted reason for material wealth and social inequality. In that sense, we can draw a clear line from discourses about merit to the material *effect* of distribution through paycheques and other related means of distributing material goods, such as taxation systems, pension schemes, and the like.

Perhaps we could also find the material *causes* of these discourses of justification. Our entire socialization is influenced by learning the merit principle. As early as elementary school, we learn that only one part of the recognition that we receive is because of the joy or passion of learning new material or our progress compared to our previous knowledge. Very quickly, children aged 6–10 learn that what seems most important for the majority of the grownups are marks and that the marking system simultaneously equalizes and individualizes people. It equalizes because everybody is recognized by the same marking scheme, not by any other individual characteristics. Indeed it would cause indignation to mark male achievements differently from female achievements or upper-class achievements differently from lower-class achievements. At the same time, by giving everybody individual marks, we are creating individual, singular learning histories over time or, as Foucault (1975) rightly states, the individual subject is produced through these techniques of "surveillance and punishment" (as the literal translation of his work states). These assimilations of the merit principle through the material organization of our society could, according to my hypothesis, be understood as one main reason for the (re-)production of the merit principle, which is a discursive claim or justification.

Another source for that discourse lies in the material organization of labour in modern societies. In other times, for example, in Christian agrarian societies, it was understood that not individual labour or achievement but divine order was the reason to justify differences in material wealth. Additionally, natural (or divine) forces were seen as the most important factor in the economic outcome of an individual's work. Following the Christian worldview in pre-modern societies, "God wants human beings to work, but he does not want them to believe that it is work that maintains them" (Herzog 2008: 146). Thus, the capitalist organization of society that puts an individual price on the labour force that relates directly to individual capacities represents the same equalizing and individualizing tendencies as the marks used in the educational system.

The hypothesis is that it is not coincidence that the merit principle starts to become hegemonic when wage labour becomes dominant and school attendance becomes obligatory and accessible for the vast majority. Therefore, we could understand the social organization of labour and of education as material causes of the discourse on merit, individual achievement, and (re-)distribution related to individual capacities. Education and labour are part of the infrastructure of discourses on inequality and merit. In-depth research would probably have to trace other elements—whether material or symbolic—of the infrastructure of these discourses.

3. This type of discourse analysis pointing towards the materiality of discourses is social critique in the sense of immanent critique. It is *immanent* because it takes its standards—that is, its norms—to criticize society from society itself. The merit principle is a widely accepted social norm. And it is social because the critique aims at the very core

of the justification of social (re-)distribution. Additionally, in our society not only economic but also educational, cultural, and social capital is accumulated, directly contravening the accepted norm of merit and individual achievement. Inherited wealth, whether material or because of the heritage of cultural and social capital, is not wealth that is justified by individual merit. Taking the accepted norm of merit to its logical end would mean the death of the possibility of accumulating capital (or to use accumulated goods and knowledge as capital).[2] In other words, it would mean the end of the form of social reproduction known as *capital*ism. The justification of distributing wealth based on merit therefore is a logical impossibility. Systematically, it must fail.

In this example, we could also see the procedural character of critique mentioned above (see also Jaeggi 2015). We start with a norm accepted by society. However, by unfolding this norm and using it critically against social reality, the content of the norm itself changes. There is something like a "normative surplus" in the merit principle itself that pushes the norm beyond its actual realization in society.

Step 4: Critique and the logics of social change

Finally, we could argue that this critique is not only a passion of the head but the head of passion (Marx) that should and can lead to effective social change. The argument here is a logic based on four steps: suffering, disrespect, indignation, and change.

We start with real *suffering*. People suffer from a lack of income or low income. People suffer because they are paid less for their work than others doing the same work and people are suffering because they lack basic goods even in rich societies. We can understand suffering as a motor of change. Suffering points towards the abolition of suffering. However, this change does not point automatically towards social emancipation, towards a society in which nobody experiences this type of suffering.

---

[2] However, this distinction between the accumulation and use of capital is somehow artificial because the very logic of capital is that of a process, that is, the usage of something as capital. If it is not used, we should speak of stock instead of capital.

There are plenty of other possibilities in which an individual can attempt to stop that unsatisfying situation. One can rob a bank, play the lottery, commit suicide, resign, attempt to gain "compensatory respect" by blaming others (and especially lower social groups), and so on. In other words, many actions and psychological reactions point towards an individual, non-socially sustainable way of ending one's suffering.

To lead towards sustainable social change, suffering must be understood as social suffering, that is, as *disrespect*. Critique must show that suffering is not casual, natural, or immovable. It must explain that the suffering is caused by the feeling of not being recognized for one's merit and one's social value. The critic must show that even in cases in which individuals feel they deserve little because they contribute little to society, it is not only the valuation of their contribution that is socially created. In addition, the ability to contribute is not an individual moral merit but a socially created capacity, depending, for example, on a family background and educational system that permits a person to discover and develop his or her talents and abilities. In other words, the critic has to return his or her observation to the people.

Once individual suffering is understood as disrespect, that suffering can become *indignation*. Moral indignation here is the discovery that individual misery is related to the socially made process of social reproduction. Understanding that there is something fundamentally wrong with the socially accepted norm of recognition of merits, individual contributions, and achievements can lead to indignation, which becomes understood as a directed feeling, a moral reaction directed towards social change.

Change is possible because there is a broad moral complicity: norms related to the merit principle are accepted by the vast majority of society. However, there are systemic obstacles that are not to be underestimated. As we have seen, social reproduction is based on the possibility of accumulating capital (whether material or immaterial). Attempting to change the unfair merit principle or (what is the same) attempting to unfold it to its potential would mean challenging the current capitalist order. Discourse analysis as social critique cannot guarantee the success of social change, but it can show the direction of social change and its legitimacy; moreover, it can warn of systematic resistances.

Example 2: Migration Practices

The next example attempts to move a step away from classical discourse analysis. As we have seen because of its structured and ultimately communicative character, meaningful elements other than verbal language can be analysed with a discourse analytical approach. Therefore, our next example is less concerned about language use than about practices. Remember that we identified Stahl's (2013c) Marxist tradition of immanent critique as a *practice-based* one. In practice, an implicit knowledge or social sense is incorporated. We have also seen that the practices in which social scientists search for a normative surplus shifted from work practices in more classical Marxism to speech acts in Habermasian discourse theory and to practices of disrespect and struggle for recognition in Axel Honneth.

Below, I will show how an analysis of practices understood as meaningful structured events could contribute to social critique. I will develop my example using practices related to migration. We will see how various individual practices could be socially understood as struggles for recognition. By the term "different practices", I refer to various subjective or social senses, for example, various reasons to migrate. Although two persons who move from one country to another seem to perform the very same practice, by doing so for various reasons we can speak of various practices.

Migration is a topic around which a large number of discourses are produced. Therefore, it is unsurprising that migration discourses are one of the most popular fields of discourse analysis (for a good overview, see Reisigl and Wodak 2001). However, the public discourse is dominated by the non-migrant population. Here, we see a typical example of discursive exclusion. Migrants are even physically excluded from the (public and hegemonic) discourse production. Of course, it would be possible to analyse migrants' discourses, for example, by interviewing the migrant population.

However, what I want to propose here, to make the point about practices as elements of Discourse Analysis as Social Critique, is to analyse and to attempt to understand practices related to the migration process. As I said, I will interpret these practices as either struggles for recognition or struggles against misrecognition. The aim of this exercise is not only to understand practices but to normatively ground social critique. Therefore, we must understand not only the practices of struggles for recognition but also the corresponding forms of disrespect as structural, global social pathologies. In this sense, we can understand multiple practices, which are often perceived as individual decisions against unreasonable forms of disrespect, as forms of *social* critique.

Aiming at social critique in that sense means aiming at the critique of a (somehow necessary) recognition order that structurally produces disrespect. We therefore want to understand migrants' practices as related to that recognition order. However, here we face an initial problem: in the case of migration, we can identify several of those orders of recognition and disrespect. Migrants relate their practices to the host society and to the society of origin; they are also embedded in global migration regimes that can be understood as global normative orders. Therefore, we will divide the example into three parts related to these three different recognition orders. Again, these examples are not meant to be exhaustive analyses of practices performed by migrants. Their purpose is much more humble, aiming at exemplifying how practices could be understood according to the approach offered in this book.[3]

The Host Society: Creating Diaspora Communities

The migrant population does not find itself in the host society from one day to another in the same way that non-migrants do. They often create new structures, groups, communities or institutions that, among other things, also organize recognition. These diasporic communities can be ethnic, national, linguistic, religious, or cultural. They organize a portion of their members' lives following criteria different from those that dominate the host society. Indeed, there is frequently a dialectic relation between the recognition order of the host society and the need to create independent diasporic groups. Often, migrants find themselves in a more structural situation of disrespect than of recognition. They encounter multiple situations of open and latent racism, along with social exclusion.

---

[3] For an incomplete but far broader treatment of this example, see Herzog (2016c).

The creation of diasporic communities can be a valid strategy for countering this type of exclusion.

Thus, what we are interested in here is not practices of recognition and disrespect that are similar (although not equal) to those of natives. To develop my example, I only want to note one practice as a specific practice with recognitional content. Here, I am referring to the practice of creating and participating in these particular diasporic groups.[4] The practice of creating groups depends on several factors. However, some of these factors can be understood as related to the possibility of receiving recognition in the host society. Therefore, the creation of diasporic groups can be interpreted as a struggle for recognition by establishing alternative structures that allow individuals to find themselves recognized. The "otherness" of individuals in these groups, i.e., the fact that they seem to belong to a group outside the majority of society, is no longer seen as a defect. In these diasporic groups, outsiderness is seen as normal or even as a virtue. Therefore, we can understand these communities as a diasporic recognition order. In them, members often fulfil functions of emotional support and care. Knowing that the others find themselves in a similar situation, there is often a major sensitivity to other members' emotional needs. Furthermore, equality is often organized in these groups. Although the nation state of the host society often discriminates migrants as legally unequal, in their community they can feel equal. This fact also explains (in part) the creation of ethnic ghettos. In these areas, minority groups can live free from discrimination that they would encounter when living alongside the ethnic majority. Their particular characteristics, merits, and achievements, which often go unappreciated by the rest of the society, could be better judged as valuable contributions by their particular diasporic "community of values". Honneth (1995b) also speaks of these particular groups and their practices as "practical reactions to these daily experiences of injustice", resulting in the creation of "a counter culture of compensatory respect" (p. 218).

---

[4] Elsewhere, I have analysed struggles for group recognition as struggles for second-order recognition (Herzog 2015).

The Society of Origin

In her work on female domestic migrant workers in Europe, Maria Kontos (2014) makes an interesting observation. Apart from the complex constellation of the recognition of domestic migrant workers—their situation of being somehow embedded in a family (see also Gutiérrez-Rodríguez 2007), their uncertain legal status, and the social valuation of their work—they receive another, very important source of recognition/disrespect: recognition from their country of origin. Most migrants have family and friends in their countries of origin and most maintain contact with those countries through the multiple forms of communication offered by modern society. Even when there is no direct contact, there is often an "inner dialogue" with the society of origin. In the same way that we can have an inner dialogue, imagining how a friend or a relative would react to our practice or proposal, migrants can also remain in "imagined" contact or even "imagined communities" (Anderson) with their societies of origin.

Independent of whether the contact is imagined or real, migrants know themselves as embedded in a relation of recognition with their society of origin. In research about highly qualified young Spaniards and their plans to emigrate, we can find the motive of disrespect (Herzog et al. 2013). If these young Spaniards emigrated or planned to emigrate, they did so because of a feeling of disrespect, of structural failure by Spanish society. Spanish society does not offer them an acceptable way to proper. They cannot find work related to their studies and cannot form and maintain a family. Therefore, we can—simplifying a complex constellation—describe the relation with the society of origin as a relation of disrespect. The *practice of migration* presents the possibility of escaping from this disrespect and therefore could be understood as struggle for recognition.

Maria Kontos describes a relation of recognition from a distance for Filipina migrants. Emigrants from the Philippines often prosper and send money back home, thus making their families prosper. The society of origin considers these migrants "modern national heroes" (Chang and McAllister, cit. by Kontos 2014). The women interviewed by Kontos and her research team were fully aware of this relation of recognition. This relation helped them to endure the difficulties in the host society, thus reinforcing their decision to emigrate. This prolonged relation with the host society can also be found in the narratives of many migrants from Africa. For many migrants, the feeling of failure if their migration project does not succeed and the shame related to that failure hinder or obstruct their ability to return to the country of origin.

Whether the relation with society is "real" or "imagined", full of expectancies, a relation of disrespect or recognition, the recognition of migrants is not exclusively dependent on the normative order of the host society. Migrants find themselves in the midst of a constellation that also includes the society of origin, from which they know they are observed, and cultural and social expectations that they have internalized in a certain way. A social critique that stems from migrants' practices must analyse all of those situations of disrespect, not only those involving the relation to the host society. Here we can imagine the analysis of many practices with normative relevance because migrants know whether or not a practice would be approved by their home society.

Supranational Constellations

There are several grounds for starting a migration project. There are several reasons—both structural and individual—to leave one's country. Moreover, there are both structural and individual reasons to choose a specific host society. Some of these reasons and motivations are recognized by the so-called international community as acceptable, whereas others are not. So, for example, emigration on the ground of political persecution is recognized as an international right. Conversely, migrating for economic reasons is considered undesirable by most societies. Frontiers are reinforced to restrict the entrance of poor economic migrants. However, these regulations or migration regimes change over time. Ruth Cox (2013) interprets the acts (or better, the practices) of migrating and the struggles for legal changes in migration regimes as struggles for recognition. She understands the primary reasons to emigrate and the legal regulations of migration in the sense of the three spheres of recognition. In other words, although we can analyse the practice(s) of migration as social critique, we can also accompany this type of analysis with a classical discourse analysis of political and legal advocacy discourses (and their related practices, including organizing protest marches, etc.).

1. An important part of migration flows is prompted by family reasons. The migration project often foresees family migration in several steps. First, one family member migrates to find work, become established, and generate the ability to guarantee a basic level of well-being. Afterwards other members migrate, including partners, children, and even elder family members. It is possible, therefore, to understand this type of migration for the sake of family reunion as struggle for recognition in the first mode described by Honneth: the mode of love. To be able to provide and receive emotional support and to effectively guarantee the care of other, beloved family members, a certain amount of mobility and frontier crossing is required. Border crossing here can mean leaving the family behind to help them from a distance or joining the emigrated family member, thus guaranteeing the emotional and practical support by physical presence. In other words, here we have a practical form of struggle for conditions in which emotional support can become effective.

    There is a corresponding legal struggle parallel to this individualized migration practice. Most legislation contemplates the right of legally married partners and underage children to reunite their families. However, for elder parents or same-sex partners, this right seldom exists. Therefore, we can also understand the legal battles fought by NGOs and political groups to change the law as a struggle for recognition, a struggle aiming to facilitate foreigners' emotional dedication to their parents or same-sex partners.

2. It is slightly more complicated to also interpret migration as struggle for recognition in the second sphere, the sphere of the state. The notion of the State as it stands in Honneth's Hegel-inspired Theory of Recognition could hardly be used for transnational migration. Still, Cox's analysis uses the main mode of recognition in this sphere: *equality* in the form of *rights* for which people (sometimes) aim when they

create a migration project. Conversely, people often flee from political persecution, that is, from inequalities and legal injustices from their home countries. Migration here would be another struggle for recognition. Instead of struggling for legal protection in their home countries, these types of migrants are struggling individually by migrating to another State in the hope of being recognized there as person with basic human rights and legal protection against persecution on unjustified grounds.

Once more, there is an international struggle parallel to this individual strategy to identify certain conditions of legal recognition. There have been several attempts either to internationally abolish various forms of legal discrimination (i.e., forms of disrespect in the sphere of the State) or to recognize various forms of legal discrimination, thus receiving protection, for example, as an asylum seeker. One example from the ongoing debate in that sense would be the question of whether discrimination based on gender or sexual orientation should be recognized as a reason for political asylum. The struggle for a legal framework that allows everybody to be protected from legal misrecognition can also be understood as the struggle for recognition.

3. Finally, we can also often relate the practice of migration with the third sphere of recognition and its mode of recognition of one's specific contributions and merits. Here, we find the big group of all who migrate for labour reasons. The possibility of working in something related to one's own capacities and interests and to receive a corresponding salary could be understood as a form of recognition of these specific capacities. A person who does not perceive the possibility of being valued in his country according to her individual capacities and expectancies can easily feel disrespected. This person does not have the appropriate condition for developing what Honneth calls practical self-relation in the form of self-esteem. Therefore, migration for work reasons could also be interpreted as an individualized struggle for recognition. It is not a collective struggle for better salaries or work conditions in the country of origin. Instead, the struggle consists in

crossing a border to find one's own capacities recognized. We can find this motive both in those migrants who flee from poverty and misery and in the "elite" that attempts to improve its economic and social position with the help of a globalized labour market.

Again, there is a legal struggle attached to this practice. For example, take the various initiatives aiming to facilitate better international circulation of "human capital". Here, we find not only bilateral agreements (e.g., for temporary agricultural workers) but also international attempts to facilitate the recognition of titles and work experiences. An example for this last case would be the initiative for a Blue Card in the European Union that allows highly qualified workers from outside the EU to live and work in any country of the Union. This would improve the possibilities for migrants to have their merits recognized in the form of labour contracts.

(Discourse) Analysis of Practices as Social Critique

We have seen how we can read practices as structured actions that enclose social sense and moreover, contain normative content that we can understand. We have interpreted very diverse practices as struggles against disrespect or struggles for recognition in the three modes proposed by Honneth: emotional support, equality of rights, and social valuation. These practices were social in a double sense. On the one hand, although often individually motivated, here we are confronting practices shared by millions of people. On the other hand, these practices are social because they are related to a specific social context. The context can be that of the society of origin or the host society. It can be national or supranational; alternatively, a practice can refer to several contexts at the same time. These contexts can be understood as recognition orders, orders of disrespect, or simply normative orders. Individuals, independent of whether they are conscious, establish moral relationships to these normative orders.

This moral argument is important when using the analysis of practices as social critique. To use these practices for immanent critique, as I propose here in reference to the "practice-based" immanent critique in the Marxist tradition, we can draw on the normative content of these practices for critique. If we are aiming not only at corrective critique but also at real, transcending social critique, we furthermore must relate the critique to the fundamental social structure. I suggest that this structure here is not capitalism (as in the previous example) but migration regimes based on the organization of the world into nation States.[5] In other words, the social critique defended here does not aim at changing merely one or several laws but instead seeks a fundamental change in global migration regimes. However, the normative and social character of diverse practices is often not conscious for the migrants involved but can be understood empathically by others. It is this empathic understanding that moves thousands of professional workers and volunteers all around the globe, working in quite diverse NGOs and defending either the multiple reasons for migration or a large number of non-discrimination policies. It is this empathic understanding that is the basis for a structured analysis and for theoretical reasoning that can be used by the critic to question existing social structures.

A world in which liberty, equality, and solidarity are completely unfolded or, to continue to use the language of Recognition Theory, in which everybody receives emotional support and care, cognitive attention as a person with equal rights, and social esteem of their particular characteristics, without doubt would be a world with a reproduction mode fundamentally different from the one we know. The type of critique that can be developed beginning with migration practices does not present simple corrections but instead possesses the power to challenge (at least intellectually) the current migration regime. In that sense, all of the practices mentioned include what we have called a "normative surplus", a development potential, a potential of generalization or individualization. In other words, the social system that would recognize the total legal equality of everybody who is willing to change their residence would have a fundamentally different character from the existing system. This

---

[5] There is surely a relation between the rise of capitalism and the success of the nation state as a general form of organizing the political space (see, e.g., Balibar and Wallerstein 1991; Rodríguez de Liévana et al. 2013; Hirsch 2001; Wallerstein 1979). Although this relation is outside the scope of the example made here, it probably must be analysed when performing an in-depth social critique.

complete unfolding of the normative claims made implicitly through the mentioned practices would likely question the very *raison d'être* of the nation State and thus the very world order based on the principle of separate nations. This type of critique would clearly have a transcending character.

One final critical and transformative turn to that reflection can be identified with Rahel Jaeggi (2015). As we have seen, Jaeggi notes that immanent critique not only refers to existing, (even implicit) norms but also transforms the norms themselves in the process of critique: "The fact that a norm cannot be realized in the existing social formation […] reveals a deficit and a need for *transformation of the very norm*" (ibid.: 23). One example of this modification in the case of the norm of freedom would be that this norm is not only about claiming formal freedom, e.g., open borders for everybody. This "negative freedom" (Honneth) in the form of an absence of obstacles to the free movement of people must be transformed into "social freedom", that is, the freedom to create societies so that nobody feels obligated to migrate. In other words, the very same norm of freedom of circulation that is claimed at least implicitly by (often illegal) border crossing should be transformed during the process of social critique. The norm should be transformed into social and creative freedom, that is, in the power to participate in decisions about global social reproduction. With this final turn, the immanent norms that served in the first step as a model for critique have a dynamic character. They are transformed in the *practical process of critique*. Here, we will see an immanent critique that points towards a fundamental change in the order of social reproduction and, by doing, fosters a change in the very norms of transformation.

Example 3: The Usefulness of the Limits of the Approach: The Debate About Same-Sex Marriage

Let us turn our attention towards an example of discourse analysis that does *not* lead to social critique. Moreover, it is an example of how critique that aims at the very structure of modern societies goes wrong. Although this example shows that discourse analysis cannot always be used for the purpose of social critique, the approach presented here can simultaneously exemplify how it can be used as a defence against unjustified social critique. The example is that of the debate on homosexual marriage.

The legal and social recognition of same-sex partnerships in general and same-sex marriages in particular is becoming an important social and political issue beyond the Western world. When Denmark recognized same-sex partnerships in 1989, it started a wave of various forms of gay couples' rights worldwide. With the beginning of the new millennium, it was the Netherlands that first fully recognized the right to marriage for same-sex couples, followed by Belgium (2003), Canada (2005), and Spain (2005). As of the beginning of 2016, 14 countries recognize same-sex marriages as legally equal to heterosexual ones.[6] Several subnational jurisdictions allow same-sex couples to marry and in a variety of countries, public discussions and legal procedures related to recognizing same-sex relationships are ongoing. However, approximately 40 % of the world's population lives in one of the 76 countries in which same-sex sexual acts between consenting adults remain illegal (UN 2013).

Discussions about that issue are usually prepared and accompanied by demonstrations in favour and against equality of rights for gays, lesbians, and transsexuals. Recent disputes in France and in Eastern Europe had even shown the violent potential of those advocating *against* homosexual rights. Although the growing global movement in favour of same-sex marriages usually unites under the banner of human rights, arguing that the right to marriage should be extended to gay couples (Human Rights Watch 2009; UN 2013), their counterparts are mainly arguing about culture, tradition, religious values, and biological concerns (Chamie and Mirkin 2011).

In public debates, there are many arguments for and against same-sex marriage. Whereas the strongest arguments for the legality of same-sex marriages are based on the equality of civil and human rights, the arguments against the legal unions of same-sex couples comes from two almost incompatible views. On the one hand, there are the arguments

---

[6] These countries are Argentina, Belgium, Brazil, Canada, Denmark, Iceland, Netherlands, New Zealand, Norway, Portugal, Spain, South Africa, Sweden, and Uruguay.

of the often religiously motivated traditionalists that dominate the public campaigns against same-sex marriage. On the other hand, there are arguments stemming from feminist and often post-structuralist positions. These arguments, which often use a general criticism of matrimony and extend it to same-sex relationships, dominate the *academic* positions against same-sex marriage. In what follows, I will show the main discourses of these three important positions (one in favour and two against). Again, here I did not perform a complete discourse analysis on the diverse discourses. Instead, I sketch such an analysis. By asking whether the critique implicit in discourse can be used to transcend the existing social order, I will show that we are *not* confronted by Discourse Analysis as Social Critique; instead, we are confronted by a critique that is merely corrective. However, this insight can be helpful for social and political debates and changes.

Arguments for Same-Sex Marriage

Arguments for same-sex marriage that are made by LGBT groups (LGBT, Lesbian, Gay, Bisexual, and Transgender), human right advocates, and a broad range of left or "progressive" individuals are usually based on some idea of egalitarianism (Chamie & Mirkin 2011). These supporters often refer to article 16 of the United Nations Universal Declaration of Human Rights, which states as follows: "Men and women of full age, without any limitation due to race, nationality or religion, have the right to marry and to found a family. They are entitled to equal rights as to marriage, during marriage and at its dissolution." Although in 1948, when the declaration was adopted, it is unlikely that any of the implications included in the elaboration or ratification of the concept of marriage were intended to extend to same-sex couples, in this article and in the entire declaration, there is a spirit of equality. Equality in the sense of legal equality and equal rights is at the centre of this argumentation. Following this discourse, marriage is a human right and everybody should have the same rights independent of their race, religion, or sexual identity. Consequently, according to advocates for same-sex marriage, the right to marry and build a family should be extended to same-sex couples (Eskridge 2002; Kitzinger and Wilkinson 2004).

Full legal marriage includes a series of rights, such as prison or hospital visiting privileges for imprisoned or hospitalized partners, inheritance and financial rights, the right to make decisions for an incapacitated partner, and—probably the most controversial right—adoption rights. Some countries that do not allow same-sex couples to get legally married provide specific legal arrangements such as civil unions, civil partnerships, and registered partnerships that include some (but usually not all) of the above-mentioned rights.

The equality discussion about marriage and its corresponding rights builds the core of the public debate in favour of same-sex marriage. The arguments and claims for recognition refer to the State and the legal sphere's ability to grant or deny equality. Nevertheless, legal equality also radiates to the other spheres of recognition. Although other spheres have their own dynamics, logics, and forms of recognition, they are strongly linked to the legal sphere. Therefore, the legal framework has a strong influence on the possibility of institutionalizing love and affective care. As we have seen, in the sphere of the family, recognition is provided to organize emotional support between the members of the family or primary relation group. Recognition is given on the basis of the members' needs and the emotional bonds (i.e., commitments based on love or friendship) between them. However, it seems that emotional commitment is inadequate to provide full care, as we know from bourgeois, heterosexual families. The State's legal arrangements provide a framework for not only the possibilities but also the limits of care. In the debate with Fraser (Fraser and Honneth 2003) and the public discussion with Sloterdijk (see also Herzog and Hernàndez 2009), Honneth leaves no doubt about the importance of legal (and economic) conditions for love as recognition to become effective. In that sense, we can say that for love to become the commitment that we positively value in heterosexual families, certain legal conditions are sometimes indispensable.

Additionally, because marriage is a "complex social institution" (Zurn 2013)—that is, it intersects with diverse legal, sexual, social, or economic dimensions—legal recognition can also lead to broader social acceptance. The social valuation of homosexual couples as a valid form of social organization does not depend solely on—but is strongly related to—their legal recognition. In civil society, we said with Honneth that social esteem is distributed on the basis of individual traits and capacities. The legal recognition of the capacity to affectively care for another person independent of her sexual orientation is already part of the social recognition of these types of capacities.

Arguments Against Same Sex-Marriage

The arguments against equal rights for same-sex partnerships are twofold. On the one hand, there are the arguments of traditionalist, religious, and right-wing groups. This discourse makes an argument based on nature, stigmatizing non-heterosexual sexuality as not natural or even as anti-natural. We can also find worries about procreation and therefore, social reproduction. In addition, we can find the religious argument for the holiness of marriage. We can also see a motif that appears in the non-religious context: the fear that homosexual marriage may have a negative effect on traditional marriages. More generally, we can see the fear that the public recognition of homosexuality may negatively influence the rest of society. This is what Harding (2008) refers to when she states that the "heterosexism of the 'traditional' family serves to displace lesbians and gay men from both the public and the private spheres" (p. 2). The arguments against same-sex marriage either aim to avoid recognizing non-heterosexual lifestyles or have the effect of doing so. What is important is that this type of argument not only pretends to advocate against certain rights but also, at its very core, is intended to be a fundamental social critique. The recognition of same-sex marriage and the public acceptance of homosexuality, as we can summarize the argument, ultimately corrode both social reproduction and the overall social order.

The arguments presented here against same-sex marriage are only the most visible arguments in the *public* discourse on same-sex marriage. By performing a classical discourse analysis, we could probably quite easily identify the structure of this discourse. Conversely, there is a progressive academic debate, which is also present in radical left, feminist, queer, and LGBT groups, that criticizes same-sex marriages. However, that debate's criticism is based on a very different argument. The primary argument is based on the previously described "complex social institution" of marriage. Whereas some argue that the state should not interfere in private commitments, others aim at "decomplexifying" the institution of marriage and open it to commitments independent of the number of persons involved and their relation to one another (see e.g., Zurn 2013). This would open marriage to friends, brothers, a group of several persons, and so on, who could decide in a type of "civil solidarity pact" which type of commitments they want to give each other.

Until now, we have only sketched a discourse analysis that could trace the various discourses (public, academic, in favour, against) surrounding same-sex marriage. To turn this discourse analysis into a social critique, we must first show a normative surplus in the discourses that points towards social change; second, we must show a systematic failure to meet the normative claims because of a system of social reproduction that is fundamentally dependent on not fulfilling those claims. The first point is relatively easy to make. For example, in the discourse in favour of same-sex marriage, we have seen an underlying motif of equality. History has shown that equality is not an abstract ideal but must materialize and become concrete. Furthermore, we can see that there remains a potential of universalization in this ideal. Thus, just as in the past, when people of colour in the USA claimed the same legal rights as the white population or voting rights were extended to women, the generalization of equality would now mean that, for example, people would enjoy equal rights independent of their nationality or, to stay with the case that concerns us here, people in same-sex partnerships would enjoy equal rights.

Nonetheless, we will fail to find the systemic reason for failing to accept the claim for equality. When we analyse, for example, societies that have granted equal rights to same-sex couples for more than a decade, we find that this broadening of equality did not "corrode" society, as feared by some opponents of recognition of same-sex marriage. Same-sex partnerships have not negatively influenced either traditional marriages or "the youth"; instead, it has led to a more tolerant, less homophobic society. Now there are no, and have never been, systemic reasons to exclude same-sex couples from the institution of matrimony. From Hegel to Honneth and throughout contemporary sociology, we can find arguments for the universality of family as a stable institution for love and care, for socialization, and bringing up children. However, the concrete form of this institution, whether a nuclear family or an extended one, whether formed by same-sex couples, or by couples of different sexes, and so on, is not crucial for the institution itself. It can fulfil its function perfectly in quite diverse ways.

To summarize the argument, although some discourses embody the perception that same-sex marriage would lead to a fundamental social change and that the unique position of heterosexual matrimony is fundamental for the social order, social reproduction, and stability, we have seen that this is not the case. Conversely, the discourse (analysis) of arguments in favour of same-sex marriage can lead to what we have called a "corrective critique" but not a fundamental "transcending critique" given that same-sex partnerships do not call into question the fundamental functioning of society. This "failure" to transcend society does not mean that we should not perform this type of critique. It simply shows us how far reaching the critique can be—and how realistic the fears are that oppose this critique. In other words, here we are not speaking of Discourse Analysis as Social Critique as presented in this book. Nevertheless, testing the hypothesis of fundamental social critique could bring us good insights into the character of the discourse, even if the hypothesis does not hold.

3.2 General Guidelines and Questions for Discourse Analysis as Social Critique

The rupture of the world passes through the objects of discourse analysis, too.
At the beginning of the discourse analytical approach described here, there is a decision to attempt to develop a critique that points towards the very core of social reproduction. This decision is usually based on the assumption, suspicion, or hypothesis that there is something pathological in our society that is not a surface phenomenon; instead, social pathologies have underlying structural or systematic reasons. However, as seen in the case of the critique of homosexual marriages, this approach can be used to show that change does not always point towards underlying structures but instead can be treated as a surface phenomenon.

Generally, researchers should be acutely aware of these assumptions along with their other prejudices or biases. Researchers do have political positions, they are citizens embedded in ethical and moral disputes, and they have feelings about what is right or wrong and about what ought to be done. There is nothing wrong with taking these beliefs as the starting point for social research. However, awareness of this individual starting point shall allow one to eventually distance oneself from the ideas being defended. Under no circumstances should the starting point determine the results of the research.

Indeed, the approach of Discourse Analysis as Social Critique explicitly states that it should not be the investigator's norms that lead to social critique but the norms of the criticized society itself. Thus, it is the researcher's task to uncover these socially accepted norms and bring them to light by unfolding them and showing a (perhaps systemic) difference between socially accepted normative claims and reality. In general, we can distinguish eight steps for elaborating such a discourse analytical approach[7]:

1. Finding appropriate research objects and research questions

At the beginning of our research, we must find an object of discourse that seems to fulfil two conditions. First, it must be related to human suffering. In that sense, discourse analysis as social critique is always problem oriented and never a mere contemplative research aiming "simply" to broaden our knowledge. We always point towards forcing back human suffering, attempting to make a difference with our research. However, as we have seen, human suffering can occur silently and sometimes must be "read" empathically. Second, our object must enable us to see "the rupture of the world" (Adorno) through it. As we have seen in the example of homosexual partnerships, the hypothesis does not always hold that there is a structure that causes suffering and that is indispensable for social reproduction. However, a phenomenon by which it is beyond doubt that there is only a surface problem seems inadequate for this type of discourse analysis.

Research questions must be asked about the relation of human suffering and the structure of social reproduction. Furthermore, they must ask for the norms that are at stake here and whether these norms can be

---

[7] I do not want to hide that the resemblance of these steps and the steps proposed by Diaz-Bone (2005) is not coincidental. However, I have adapted his excellent seven steps formulated in general terms to create eight steps that point specifically to the purpose of social critique.

unfolded or come to light completely within the given society. Remember that our aim is to show social rupture through the object of discourse analysis, meaning that we must find the objects that show that rupture. A fundamental part of this first step is to review the literature about possible objects of research.

2. Exploring the object

In this exploratory phase, we must gather the most relevant information about our object of analysis. Which discourses seem to exist around the object? Who is involved in the (hegemonic) discourse production and who is excluded? How does the discourse seem to be expressed? Are there popular discourses, media discourses, and expert discourses and what seems to be the relation between them? Of course, at that stage we are not engaged in a discourse analysis, but we should have a sense of the discourses and dynamics involved.

Furthermore, we should gather information about the non-discursive realities that surround social suffering. Is there economic need or a lack of access to basic goods? Are there power inequalities, denigrating identities, or some type of exclusion that is legal, material, or ideal? Can we name practices that at first seem inappropriate or exclusive? At that stage, we must also ask for the significant silences. Who does not speak? Which affects or "psychological gaps" (Honneth) seem to have been produced? Silences may be related to non-discursive aspects of the phenomenon of research, but not all non-discursive aspects must remain silent.

3. Elaborating a corpus and a method

Next, we must create a provisional corpus and define our research methods. Because we do not yet know the results of the concrete analysis, we must be open to the possibility of broadening or changing our initial corpus or to adapting our procedure during research. What material do we need to collect? Do we want to analyse institutional or private documents, conduct interviews with experts or with those suffering the most? These techniques of gathering data are very close to traditional discourse studies. As we have seen, however, it is also possible to use empathic communication for discourse analysis. Are there practices, pictures, spatial arrangements, emotions, body languages, and so on, to read and analyse? These aspects can also form part of the corpus.

Furthermore, we must ask questions about the relation that we think might exist between discursive and non-discursive realities. Remember that our aim is to find the norms explicitly expressed in discourses or implicitly contained both in discursive and in non-discursive realities. While collecting the material, we must make our first ideas about how to analyse the material explicit. There is a great deal of literature on how to perform discourse analysis (see, e.g., Keller 2012; Wood and Kroger 2000) or even analysis of non-discursive material (e.g., Ruiz Ruiz 2009 or the special issue of *Forum Qualitative Social Research* 8(2) 2007). We must be aware that our corpus and our data-mix together with our research question are absolutely unique. Therefore, as in almost every interpretative study, we cannot just use a standardized method. Instead, we must adapt the existing methodological toolbox to our specific object and research questions.

4. Descriptive analysis

The analysis can be logically divided into two parts, although in research practice, both are often executed in parallel: a descriptive analysis and an interpretive one. During the descriptive analysis, we work closely with the material. It is important to be able to show outsiders at every point of that analysis the relation between what we do and the empiric material included in the corpus. The close relation is important not only for the sake of transparency and comprehensibility for outsiders but also to guarantee the intersubjective validity of our analysis. It is also important to control our own biases. All too often, researchers are too eager to confirm their hypothesis or prejudices. A clear, well-planned descriptive analysis helps us ground our later findings firmly in the empirical material.

For this type of analysis, we can use the whole range of social sciences and humanities research techniques. Quantitative data analysis can bring us a step closer, especially when treating huge amounts of data (see e.g., Bubenhofer and Scharloth 2013). Often, data for this type of analysis must be coded in a manner similar to that used for qualitative analysis.

Again, there is a great deal of literature regarding qualitative analysis (e.g., Strauss and Corbin 1998; Keller 2012). Most of this literature uses categorizations, coding, or heuristic questions to become acquainted with the material. Researchers usually go a step further to reduce the complexity of the material by synthesizing or grouping the information by means of meta-categories, meta-codes, or the like. The descriptive analysis gets us into the material and simultaneously is the ground upon which we then develop the interpretative analysis.

It is important to underline that although in most cases we will use the toolbox of sociological discourse analysis, it could be possible for our material to result from observation, aesthetic material, or material documents. In these cases, we can proceed logically in a similar way, using coding, categorization, or heuristic questions that are equally adapted to the empiric material.

5. Interpretative analysis

Independent of whether we started with quantitative or qualitative data analysis or a mixture of the two, at this stage we must begin to interpret the data. This means that Discourse Analysis as Social Critique ultimately follows a critical interpretative paradigm even though quantitative analysis can play an auxiliary part in this type of research. Initially, the interpretative task must be closely connected to the descriptive analysis to conduct a step-by-step reconstruction, in the sense of a second-order hermeneutics, of the social sense or signification enclosed in the data. Typical questions involve the relation of the categories. Are there logical connections, oppositions, or contradictions? Can we find regularities or patterns? Is there a difference in the interpretation of the norms regarding different social actors or different empiric material? Is it possible to sum up the findings in general schemes such as narrative structures or plots (Viehöver 2001), interpretative schemes or frames (Oevermann 2001; Lüders and Meuser 1997), or phenomenal structures (Keller 2005b: 243f)?

The aim of this part is to reconstruct the symbolic order and to find the implicitly or explicitly accepted norms, implications, relations, and degree of accomplishment in society's practices and material organization. Taking into account that we might have worked with non-linguistic data, we must be prepared to broaden our notion of symbolic order towards an order of meaning contained in material dispositions, iconography, practices, or silent affective reactions. An important indicator of quality is whether the findings at the general symbolic level can be sufficiently substantiated using the empirical material. Eventually we must return to step three and broaden our corpus.

6. Reflection upon social macro-analysis

We then must elaborate general statements about fundamental social structures. Here, we can draw on our literature review from the first step. Realistically, this part will involve theoretical research in which we combine reflections from social and political philosophy with the findings of macro-sociological analysis. The ideal here would be to develop our own, theoretically sound macro-analysis of social structure. In the practice of research with limited resources, however, we usually must rely on others' research findings.

This more theoretical analysis must focus on three classical sociological questions about statics, dynamics, and praxis. Perhaps the question of stasis—or integration or social reproduction—is the most fundamental. This is the question of how society reproduces its fundamental structure. In other words, we must elaborate the theoretical elements of social order, integration, or social reproduction. The question of dynamics asks how this order changes and whether these changes are fundamental or instead, whether they are only changes in the expression of the same order in the same manner in which there is often a visible change at the surface that leaves the fundamental, underlying order untouched. Finally, and with regard to the last step of our discourse analysis *as social critique*, we encounter the question of practice. How can humans collectively intervene in the processes of social reproduction and social change to transform social development into a deliberate and intentioned process?

Although the whole process of Discourse Analysis as Social Critique aims to avoid using our ideals of a good society as the normative guiding principles of critique, here it becomes clear that even this procedure does not present a norm-free technique. It is based upon the minimal consensus shared by structuralists (at least implicitly in Foucault 2007 and more explicitly in Butler 2001) and critical theorists (e.g., Honneth 2015; Jaeggi 2014a) that social progress must broaden our possibilities, not limit them. Independent of what one wishes for the future, irreversible, automatic, and coercive processes are seen as inferior to those processes that open possibilities for future changes, adaptation, and wilful interventions. Therefore, the purpose of the approach presented here is to empower society to create actual and future changes in social structures consistent with their own, often implicit, convictions.

7. The relation of norms and social structure

In this step, we must relate the results of the sociological discourse analysis in the broad sense, including the analysis of silent and silenced suffering, practices, material dispositions, and so on, to general insight about societal reproduction. What is the role of norms in guaranteeing social integration and stability? Is there a potential development of the norms—that is, are they already completely unfolded or are they realized incompletely in our society? What exactly is the relation between the norms, the material organization of society, and the suffering detected in the first step of the proceeding?

It is now the moment to test our initial hypothesis and decide whether our discourse analysis truly leads to social critique, understood as a critique of the fundamental social structure. In other words, we must now ask about the degree to which differences between normative claims and the social realization of norms are necessary contradictions and the degree to which they are mere surface phenomenon. Which logical and material obstacles are encountered by the unfolding of norms and would overcoming these obstacles require a fundamental social change or only a slight adjustment? Finally, how have the norms themselves changed in the process of analysis and unfolding and how must they change in the future?

8. Contribution to social change

Depending on the reader's academic tradition, the final step may seem outside the scope of academic research. As Marx says, however, the point is not to merely interpret the world, "the point is to change it". At this point, all of the important authors used to develop the described approach, including Marx, Adorno and Horkheimer, Habermas and Honneth for Critical Theory along with Foucault, Butler, van Dijk, and the rest of the critical discourse analysts, agree that social research is about making a practical difference. Social critique therefore must give its research results back to society. Academic publishing can be one part of this process; however, it is clearly insufficient because it reaches only a very specific minority. The social critic must become a public intellectual. She has to engage in debates and social struggles and most importantly, her interventions must contribute to the empowerment of those suffering under current social conditions. The enormous advantage of the critical approach presented here is that the critic can depend on norms already shared by the vast majority. Therefore, in the worst case—that is, in the case in which norms are only implicitly shared—she must show that the participants in a social interaction share some basic, normative assumption. She need not convince anybody of the validity of a particular norm that is not shared by others.

Finally, the critic must explain to those suffering how their suffering is socially produced and related to a specific social order. By showing the relation among suffering, the incomplete unfolding of accepted social norms, and a particular social order, the critic shows that the suffering is an objective moral wrong that must be abolished. Once suffering is understood as structural disrespect, indignation can take place as a first step towards social change. Or, in the words of Pierre Bourdieu, "As sceptical as one may be about the social efficacy of the sociological message, one has to acknowledge the effect it can have in allowing those who suffer to find out that their suffering can be imputed to social causes and thus to feel exonerated; and in making generally known the social origin, collectively hidden, of unhappiness in all its forms, including the most intimate, the most secret" (Bourdieu 2000: 629).

3.3 Going a Step Further: Empathic Analysis and the Aesthetics of Recognition

From what this book has said until now, there are two problems with discourse analysis that required a broadening of the methodological approach to social injustices. On the one hand, we experienced difficulty in that not all feelings of injustice that are perceived by social actors (and therefore that could theoretically be used for the purpose of social critique) are expressed in discourses. Moreover, "language theft" (Honneth) is often part of the problem of suffering. Suffering frequently has the capacity both to impede discursive expressions and to produce silent or muted subjects (see also Renault 2009).

Therefore, we had to broaden our approach to discourse analysis to include non-discursive realities, materialities, practices, and so on. However, this broader discursive approach—or this more sociological approach to discourses—is based on the anthropological assumption that human beings have the ability to empathically understand the suffering of others. When seeing others suffering, when perceiving the struggle against social suffering—that is, the struggle against the disrespect of others—then we have the ability to empathically engage in this struggle. In other words, the struggle against disrespect becomes part of the often-silent movement for social emancipation. However, it is here that the second problem comes into play: there are a whole lot of social mechanisms that disguise the suffering of others, that is, social mechanisms that impede the perception of the other as a suffering human being similar to oneself. When impeding empathically social relations, suffering can be inflicted upon others without becoming apparently social.

For several of the authors used to elaborate the approach presented here (so, e.g., for Adorno), one of the anchor points for the possibility to resist, to change society, lies in a process related to the psychology of development, in the fact that humans learn through imitation.[8] Following this Freudian anthropology, humans must have the innate capacity for empathy. However, this "original" capacity can be destroyed by "instrumental reason". In his perception of Freud, Adorno states (and Honneth 2005, seems to follow this argument) that people suffer when their innate capacity for reason is destroyed or limited. This includes also the capacity for empathic reason. Therefore, this type of suffering points towards the abolition of obstacles to developing empathy.

---

[8] On the physiological level, the capacity to imitate is related to the existence of so-called mirror neurons.

Additionally, all types of suffering, even types of suffering that are not verbalized, represent a type of "inner reflection" that can be understood as language. This language is not private—private languages do not exist—but can be understood by others. Thus, independently of whether we perceive others' suffering directly, in an empathic way, or whether we suffer under the limitation of empathic reasoning through either invisibilization or reification, there is always both the possibility of suffering and the possibility of intersubjectively understanding that suffering. For social researchers, this means that we can also empathically suffer and understand suffering, whether that suffering is caused by disrespect or the destruction of empathic reasoning. At the beginning, moreover, it seems even easier to analyse suffering or disrespect as negative events instead of as direct claims of recognition. Negative events are usually clearer and more easily comprehensible than are positive manifestations (see also: Honneth 2011b: 88).

However, the existence of the theoretical possibility of suffering—whether direct suffering or suffering caused by the destruction of empathic reasoning and the ability to empathically understand the suffering of others *in principle*—does not guarantee the social researcher's empathic perceptions. In other words, it is often quite difficult to empathically understand the socially silenced suffering of others. Social pathologies that produce structural feelings of disrespect are often difficult to perceive. One of the reasons for these difficulties lies in the limitations of established techniques of social research. "However, only very seldom do we encounter symptoms of this type [of social pathologies, B.H.] in the form of results of empirical research: the instruments of analysis of sociological research, although used qualitatively, generally speaking are not subtle enough to draw light on diffuse states of mind or on these type of collective mental states" (Honneth 2011a: 158).

One proposal to penetrate the veil of obfuscation of social suffering is to turn towards expressions of highly sensitive social actors. Here, I am referring to artists and the analysis of aesthetic products. Aesthetic products are often able to better express social processes. They aim at another, non-linguistic form of understanding social reality. The hypothesis that I want to defend therefore is that some aesthetic products can help us understand both the suffering of others and the processes of obfuscation that impede the perception of that suffering. This is also the proposal that Honneth's critique has in mind, and it follows that "the best way of diagnosing these pathologies still is as in the time of Hegel or of the young Lukács, the analysis of aesthetic testimonies in which these symptoms are presented indirectly: the novels, the movies or the artworks still contain that material from which we can obtain primarily knowledge about whether in our time there could be detected tendencies of a reflexive deformation of a superior level of the social behaviour and how widespread they are" (ibid.). In that sense, we can understand art as moral mimesis. Art imitates human actions. In one form or another, these actions are morally shaped. Therefore, art can help us decipher social normativity. However, art usually is not a simple doubling of reality, as Adorno underlines in a dialectical turn. Instead, art is *at the same time* a "constellation", a necessarily incomplete approximation that also points towards what is *not* the case (Adorno 2009).

As said before, in his analysis Honneth often uses specific aesthetic products such as novels or movies to ground his argument. However, in the tradition of the Frankfurt School, the analysis need not focus on a specific product such as a work of art. It can also analyse a style or a historic trend or tendency expressed in aesthetic ways. In that sense, for Siegfried Kracauer, first-generation Frankfurt School author, these expressions are even more valuable and revealing because of their unconscious character:

"The position that an epoch occupies in the historical process can be determined more strikingly from an analysis of its inconspicuous surface-level expressions than from that epoch's judgments about itself. Since these judgments are expressions of the tendencies of a particular era, they do not offer conclusive testimony about its overall constitution. The surface-level expressions, however, by virtue of their unconscious nature, provide unmediated access to the fundamental substance of the state of things. Conversely, knowledge of this state of things depends on the interpretation of these surface-level expressions. The fundamental substance of an epoch and its unheeded impulses illuminate each other reciprocally" (Kracauer 1995: 75). Another reason for dedicating us to physical expressions generally is the conviction shared not only by Adorno and Honneth but also by the Foucauldian tradition in that intellectual activity is also expressed in human bodies, practices, behaviour, and aesthetic products or, in short, in "the physical forms of life".

Bourdieu's (1984) famous work aims in a similar direction. In his very impressive line of research, Bourdieu analyses the consumption of cultural products and people's taste as an element of the reproduction of social inequality. However, he does not analyse the (aesthetic) products consumed, focusing more on the symbolic value of the practice of consumption. For our purposes, this would point towards an analysis of the normative and communicative content of practices similar to the second example described in this chapter, whereas the analysis of the contents of art products understands these practices more directly, as part of discourses.

Below, I want to take a closer look at the content (and in the first example, at the genre) of three aesthetic products, leaving the question of consumption outside the scope of the examples. The examples are not the result of social research in a broad sense. They are not photojournalism that aims at reporting situations of injustice and they are not art related to a clear political programme. However, the first example—the case of the *Ph.D. Comics*—presents a form of social critique more directly, whereas in the second case, Rembrandt's *Sacrifice of Isaac*, we take the scene as fictional. Nevertheless, even in the case of the analysis of fiction painted several hundred years ago, we will see how we can understand elements of disrespect that are still meaningful in contemporary society. The possibility of performing social research on fiction becomes even clearer in the final example: Franz Kafka's completely fictional story of *The Metamorphosis*.

Example 4: Discursive Inclusion—Ph.D. Comics

In the first example of aesthetic analysis, I want to point towards some thoughts on the opposite of discursive exclusion (see Sect. 2.5.2): the struggle for discursive inclusion. Remember that we understood discursive exclusion as exclusion, in the sense of displacement or marginalization, *from* the discourse production, *in* the discourse, and *through* the discourse. In other words, we understood exclusion as the cause, content, and effect of discourses. Inversely, the struggle for inclusion is a struggle to participate *as a producer* of discourses, thus both influencing the *content* of discourses and being positively *affected by* the discourse. In the struggle for inclusion that I will describe in this example, we can perceive the normative critique of the existing social order, although that critique is not explicitly formulated. In an emphatic way, we can identify and sympathize with the other, which means accepting his or her normative claims as justified.

The example that I want to give is the discourse on academic research. There are many ways of performing discourse on academic research or higher education (for an almost complete overview of that topic, see the two volumes of Angermuller et al. 2014). The vast majority of these discourse analyses are based on discourses of very specific social groups. Although it is beyond doubt that the analysis of these discourses can lead to very fascinating insights, we are primarily concerned with the material infrastructure of these discourses. We can say that there are groups both inside and outside of academia that produce the "bulk" of public discourse. Outside of academia, it is primarily specific politicians, journalists, and sometimes pressure groups that participate in the discourse. Inside academia, not all participants produce public discourse; that task is limited to specific social groups that occupy dominant positions in that discourse—for example, vice-chancellors, deans, tenured professors, and specialized humanities and social-sciences researchers who focus on the topic of higher education. This means that early-stage or non-tenured researchers, especially in the natural sciences, are seldom heard in public discourses on academic excellence. This obviously affects the content of the discourse on academia, such as the debate on academic excellence (see, e.g., Herzog et al. 2015), which again leads to specific distribution of material resources within the research context.

As an example for that struggle of discursive inclusion, we identify the online Ph.D. Comics—Piled Higher and Deeper. The comic is about the life of several Ph.D. students and post-doctoral researchers. It was created in 1997 by Jorge Cham, then a Ph.D. student in robotics at Stanford University, that is, a person usually excluded from the public discourse of higher education. The comic could be understood as a struggle for recognition in the third sphere described by Honneth and here in particular, in the sphere of labour relations. The underlying topic is the structural misrecognition that Ph.D. students and early-stage researchers receive in academia. It counters the ideal of academia as a structure that fosters the creation of intrepid, intelligent, and committed intellectuals. Because the method of participating in the claim of better research conditions is pre-structured by a very powerful order of discourse, Cham found the Web comic was a tool to reach the research community. His comics receive 69 million visits each year (6.5 million unique visitors), he has edited 5 books, and 2 movies have been launched based on his comics about the lives of young researchers. Although Cham finished his thesis, he now earns his living from the Ph.D. comics.

The comic is a struggle for inclusion in the described triple sense. A struggle:

- In the discourse: As a young, natural-science researcher, Cham is largely excluded from the production of the discourse on higher education and research. Through the comic, he finds a way both to enter the discourse and to reach a large community. We could even go further and say that Cham is a spokesperson for other young scientists. The comments on his website, along with the fact that several of the comic ideas come from fellow researchers, indicate Cham's representative role.
- Through the discourse: With irony and humour Cham shows the "other side of excellence"—boring laboratory sessions, long office hours, exploitation, alienated work, and so on. He is therefore reshaping the image of science with the knowledge of those at the bottom of academia. This means that Cham also treats questions of belonging, that is, of what belongs to academia. Aspects of personal aspirations in contrast to academic expectations are included in the discourse of the comic. What could seem irrelevant for research is shown to be extremely relevant for those involved in research and therefore for research itself. For example, Cham has drawn comics about the complicated situation (that has a special impact on women) in which researchers must conceal their wish for a family life because academic careers seem to require enormous flexibility.
- Effects of the discourse: There are many initiatives to improve the material conditions (working hours, salaries, job stability, etc.) of young researchers. Surely it would be presumptuous to think that a single comic is responsible for these initiatives or improvements for young scientists. However, it is this struggle for material inclusion that is present in Cham's accusations presented as humour.

We can perceive the materiality of a comic, the practice of drawing, reading, and commenting on it, the language used, the subject positions of those reading the comic or described in it, and so on, as objects of sociological discourse analysis. The task of such an analysis would be to understand the normative claims immanent to those practices, subject positions, and so on. By so proceeding, we can generate criteria for our immanent critique. Thus, let us take a closer look at two of the comic strips and how they relate to the theoretical approach formulated above.

This first comic strip, "Brain on a stick" (http://www.phdcomics.com/comics/archive.php?comicid=1126), shows in the first picture one of the protagonists, Tajel, a Ph.D. student, and describes how she sees herself: as a complex human being with hopes, dreams, and aspirations. The next pictures reads "How professors see you". The picture simply shows a brain on a stick. This comic strip drastically speaks of the reification that takes place in the highly competitive, but crowded, world of modern academia. The reader can immediately understand the normative claim made here: a (complex) human being should not be treated as a brain on a stick and that this situation causes people to suffer in academia. Using Freudian anthropology, we can understand that empathy between professor and research student is quite limited, thus producing suffering.

The second comic strip, "The Origin of the Theses" (http://www.phdcomics.com/comics/archive.php?comicid=1139), starring the nameless protagonist (who bears an astonishing resemblance to his creator), can perhaps provide an explanation that is better than a long philosophical article of what Adorno meant when he said that suffering becomes physical. It shows the nameless protagonist in different moments of his life: First as an erect and proud graduate, then with a stoop working in the laboratory, next sitting at a computer, now with a pronounced stoop, and finally kneeled down obsequiously in front of his supervisor handing him in his dissertation. Here, we can see the embodiment of suffering, imposition, and subjugation that takes place. Remember that Foucault described critique as a practice of de-subjugation. The proud and freshly graduated research student learns through busy and stressful work to subjugate himself to the authority of academia, here presented in an almost totalitarian manner, by kneeling in front of his professor.

We can also understand the struggle for discursive inclusion of the comic as a struggle for recognition. First, as struggle for personal recognition of the author, Jorge Cham. He did not necessarily start to draw the comics to become famous. However, it is no coincidence that Cham started to draw his comic when he entered grad school. For him, drawing was a practice of confronting the often stressful and alienated situation that he found in academia. We can even say that in academia, young researchers often face a situation of constant misrecognition: low salaries or unpaid labour, temporal and precarious contracts, heavy work load, a high degree of dependency on supervisors, insecure results in their own research, and so on. For Cham, aesthetic production and laughter had a therapeutic effect to help him endure his doctoral studies.

Additionally, we can identify another moment of struggle for recognition: the recognition of comics as an "adult" art form. We call artification the process by which society recognizes an object or a genre as art (Shapiro and Heinich 2012). The recognition of a genre is usually a very slow process. It is not only because of a growing and increasingly adult audience but also because of the work of certain stakeholder institutions that the comic is becoming a valid art form and can now, for example, be studied at least as part of the curriculum in several universities.

Humour can be an especially effective weapon in the struggle for recognition. On the one hand, humour is able to reach a broader public that is usually uninterested in long political philosophical arguments. Here, for example, *The Great Dictator* by Charlie Chaplin or *To Be or Not to Be* by Ernst Lubitsch made important contributions to the struggle against fascism. On the other hand, humour often escapes the logics of both argumentation and rational critique. So, for example, it is impossible to "explain" a joke. Because a joke is "only" humour, the critic always confronts the general suspicion that he has no sense of humour. Humour has the ability to inform people about situations of disrespect precisely through joking and exaggeration. This denouncement can be understood intersubjectively. So, for example people from outside of academia can understand the need for a decent salary, stable labour, and fair treatment in the workplace. Moreover, the broader public can understand that it is precisely academia in which the highest expectations are created because of the high formal qualifications of the people working there.

However, with what has been analysed thus far, we are not in a position to evaluate either whether implicit claims of recognition can be met in reality or which structural obstacles exist. We would have to perform a sociological analysis of the field to which the critique refers, in this case, academia. Therefore, the purpose of that example was not to show the entire process of Discourse Analysis as Social Critique but to explain how the inherent normativity of aesthetic products could be understood similarly to the inherent normativity of verbal discourses.

Example 5: The Sacrifice of Isaac

Whereas the example of the Ph.D. comics still describes, although in an exaggerated manner, actual social reality, we can also use the aesthetic analysis of fiction for our purpose. Let us consider a series of paintings (all called *The sacrifice of Isaac*) of the biblical scene of the sacrifice of Isaac by his father Abraham.[9] All three paintings show the moment at which Abraham is about to cut his son's throat when the divine voice (in the form of an angel) prevents him from doing so. The first two paintings are from Caravaggio. The first one was painted approximately in 1598 and the second one was painted approximately five years later. The last painting is from Rembrandt and dates to 1635. However, there are similar paintings by both Rembrandt and his pupils. However, for our argument, all the important elements are quite similar. Although all three paintings depict the same scene, there are important differences for our purposes: the analysis of social suffering and the processes of obfuscation.

The iconography of this famous scene was created during centuries that were determined by a theocratic worldview. During the Middle Ages, the representations of the sacrifice are all—in principle—similar to that of the first Caravaggio. No pain, no suffering, no inner struggle could be perceived either by Isaac (who is represented in a faithful, quite relaxed position) or his father. It could not be different. Following the Christian doctrine the Absolute One commissioned Abraham to perform

---

[9] I am grateful to Francesc Hernàndez for this example. A first attempt on that topic can be found in Ferrer et al. (2011).

a task and there can be no resistance, not even inner resistance, to that divine order.

However, this perception was about to change following the religious and philosophical debates of the beginning of the seventeenth century, which occurred primarily in the Netherlands (see above all Spinoza 1988: 332ff, 336). Are humans free? If they are free, then they are able not only to obey but also to disobey the divine voice. They must engage in some form of inner dialog to decide what to do. However, this freedom also means that God is not omniscient. That is why God must test people to determine the extent of their faith. Conversely, if humans are not free, then it makes no sense at all to probe Abraham's faith. The Omniscient God would know in advance how this test would end. The episode of Abraham would then be only a macabre, sadistic game. Therefore, with the beginning of the seventeenth century, the ecclesiastical doctrine admits human freedom.

This newly won freedom also must find its way into the aesthetic expressions of the mentioned scene. Where there is freedom, there is inner struggle and suffering. Remember that we said that suffering can be empathically understood by others. Therefore, where there is deliberate infliction of suffering, there must be mechanisms that prevent the creation or the perception of suffering. In Caravaggio's second painting, we can perceive the suffering of Isaac. Caravaggio paints Isaac with eyes and mouth wide open and forehead wrinkled to show his fear or even panic. The Italian painter used this facial expression in 1599 when painting *Judith Beheading Holofernes*. Similar to Judith, Abraham must use force to fulfil his task. While waiting for the angel, Isaac uses his left hand to press upon his son, holding him in an uncomfortable and forced position.

Rembrandt paints the *Sacrifice of Isaac* some 30 years later, and we have to presume his awareness of both the ecclesiastic debates in the Netherlands about human freedom and the paintings of Caravaggio. He knows quite well the effect that Holofernes' wide-open eyes and mouth had upon the audience—and upon the person committing the act of violence. To be able to kill one's own son, therefore, a free person must use mechanisms to inhibit the perception of suffering. Similar to the second Caravaggio painting, the Rembrandt painting depicts Abraham using his left hand to inflict force upon his son, whose body tension reveals some of the suffering that is about to be inflicted upon him. Unlike the Abraham painted by Caravaggio, the Abraham painted by Rembrandt is tapping Isaac's face with his left hand. The position of Abraham's hand is not strictly necessary for the physical fulfilment of the infanticide. However, it protects Abraham from perceiving the suffering of the other. The elimination of the perception of the human face is one very potent technique to terminate empathic relations between humans. Today, this technique of eliminating the human faces of those who suffer is a very common social process. Suffering can be better inflicted upon people upon whose faces we do not have to look. It is much easier to undertake actions that negatively affect an anonymous mass than those than affect a single, known individual. The process of dehumanization by veiling the individual human face is a technique used not only by Abraham but also in our reality.

That said, there is a second noteworthy aspect of the paintings of Abraham. By covering the eyes of his son, Abraham not only is impeding his perception of his son as a suffering human being but is also preventing his son from recognizing him as child murderer. Taking Ikäheimo's (2002) definition of recognition as "a case of A taking B as C in the dimension of D, and B taking A as a relevant judge" (p. 450), we can see the intersubjective and therefore social impact of Abraham being recognized as a child murderer. Several aspects of this definition can be underlined:

1. Recognition as a term referring to persons, that is, human beings with specific characteristics that can be either granted (recognized) or not. In this sense, when we recognize, for example, someone's right to express his opinion, we recognize the human being as a person with that right. More generally, when we recognize someone as a person, we recognize him as a human being gifted with specific moral capacities and reasoning capacities. To return to the example, when recognizing someone as father, we recognize him as a person able and willing to care for his child.
2. Recognition is a notion of social interaction in a double sense:

    (a) A person cannot be recognized only by him- or herself. Instead, there must be at least one person or institution that recognizes the other. In the case of Abraham, the eye contact would result in the recognition of Abraham both as father and as child murderer. Simultaneously, this eye contact would demand that the father recognize Isaac as his son.

(b) The recognizing institution/person must be in a certain sense recognized by the other as able to provide true recognition. Here, we can understand why it is so important for Abraham to terminate the emphatic relation produced by the mutual eye contact. In a father-child relation, we can presuppose that for both, the other is a "significant other", someone who is already accepted as a relevant judge in some way, someone who has already been recognized.

Next, the eye contact would force the full "moral power" of recognition upon Abraham. He would be confronted with double recognition as a father with a certain moral obligation, which he does not fulfil as an infanticide. He would be forced to recognize Isaac as his suffering son and it would be remembered that he gave his son moral power over him, recognizing Isaac as the "relevant judge".

We can find examples in contemporary society of this practice of impeding eye contact. For example, the practice of blindfolding those being executed is not about preventing those about to die from unnecessary suffering. Instead, it protects the members of the firing-squad from being recognized. Here, "recognized" means the recognition that the firing-squad members are (or should be) rational, empathic, moral human beings but instead are behaving as immoral murderers. Similar but more common is the example of policemen wearing dark sunglasses. When seeing such policemen, we intuitively know that we are not seeing the nice, local police officer who helps children and the elderly to cross the street. The impossibility of eye contact creates social and moral distance. We cannot suppose that we have been recognized (in other words, that we have been identified as human beings who will receive maximum respect and peaceful treatment) by those whose eyes we cannot meet.

Consequently, the political tasks of NGOs and other groups working for social emancipation and peace often attempt to give suffering a human face. For example, publicity campaigns force people in the first world to look into the eyes of people starving on other continents, fleeing from war and terror, and suffering (in our societies) from social exclusion. In these cases, it is not (only) the verbal argument but also the aesthetics that move people to solidarity and action. Aesthetics are linked to the moral fundamental consensus of our society: that human suffering should not be. In the same sense, aesthetic products such as the paintings of Rembrandt and Caravaggio can produce affective moral reactions by spectators. Such reactions usually cannot be expressed verbally in theoretical terms such as the recognition-theory terms presented here. Nonetheless, such reactions can be understood as moral reactions that are part of a struggle for recognition, a struggle that is always. It is both a struggle for recognition of those who suffer and a struggle against processes of obfuscating the perception of human suffering.

At this point, we must respond to three objections. The first objection is that we have analysed an aesthetic product that tells a fictional story. The paintings and the Biblical episode of the sacrifice of Isaac are not representations of social reality. The hypothesis that I wish to defend here, however, is that if a fictional story or a painting finds such enormous success, it must necessarily appeal to fundamental human experiences, fears, or hopes. The struggle between authority and humane behaviour is a struggle that almost every human being has experienced at some point. Moreover, we have seen that it is entirely possible to take some elements of the representation and translate them to diverse, daily situations. Fiction is often meaningful for individuals because it refers to general human experiences.

The second objection that might be raised by linguistic purists is that we left the field of discourse analysis by performing an interpretative analysis of aesthetic products. This type of analysis, as we formulate the objection, is neither better nor worse than the analysis of discourses, and perhaps it is more appropriate in this case. However, it is not discourse analysis. Nonetheless, the point that I attempted to make in the first two parts of this book is that discourse analysis *as social critique* must be something more than an analysis of verbal communication. Broadening the notion of discourse, this type of analysis includes also non-verbal and even empathic communication. Additionally, following Foucault's original approach, such a discourse analysis must analyse the possibility—or, as we have also seen in this example, the impossibility—of both verbal and non-verbal, empathic communication. The notion of discourse here refers not to simple speech acts, but to the possibility of normative and therefore socially relevant communication in general.

This explanation leads us to the third objection. To what extent, we could ask, is this type of analysis social critique, that is, a critique of a broader social order? Even when broadened to other social situations, such as that of policemen wearing black sunglasses or blindfolding the condemned during executions, are we not discussing specific social situations and not the social order in its fundamental structure? I think the relation between the paintings and the analysis becomes clear when returning to the second painting of Caravaggio, in which Isaac is represented with eyes and the mouth wide open in fear and panic. We can understand the strong reaction of the spectators of that time only partially by explaining it as empathy towards Isaac and his suffering. Conversely, every spectator of that time knows that this suffering is ultimately provoked by God, who is putting Abraham to that sadistic test. Therefore, we see not only empathy with those who suffer but also indignation about the social order that produces suffering, and indignation, we might think, against the theocratic social order.[10] Here, we can see how the theocratic social order limits what we have called the capacity of "empathic reasoning", thus producing suffering for those who are prevented from using their full capacity of (empathic) reasoning.

My hypothesis is that what is explained here using language and complex theoretical explication of the paintings was empathically, intuitively, and therefore pre-discursively understood by the spectators of the seventeenth century (and the end of the sixteenth century). It was the great artist Rembrandt who intuitively understood the struggle between obeying absolute authority and the moral obligation to protect his son from harm. It was Rembrandt who understood the need to eliminate the perception of suffering by covering Isaac's face. The strong moral force stemming from suffering must be covert to inflict harm.

---

[10] In this example, however, it is perhaps a bit early to speak of social critique because in the sixteenth and seventeenth centuries the idea that the social order was "social"—that is, made by human beings and therefore changeable—had not yet been developed.

Example 6: *The Metamorphosis* by Franz Kafka

A completely different example from modern times and a different artistic genre is that of Franz Kafka's *The Metamorphosis*.[11] However, the basic idea remains similar to that presented with respect to the paintings of Caravaggio and Rembrandt. Similar to the scene of the sacrifice of Isaac, *The Metamorphosis* ultimately also tells the history of a son being killed at the hands of his father (who throws an apple on his son and finally provokes his death). However, in contrast to the biblical scene, in Kafka's text, the empathic understanding of the son is complicated from the very first moment because he has no anthropomorphic features that could favour empathy.

We can argue that the title of the text is not about the physical metamorphosis of Gregor Samsa, the son, who has already been transformed by the very first sentence of the story "One morning, when Gregor Samsa woke from troubled dreams, he found himself transformed in his bed into a horrible vermin" (Kafka 2002). Below, I will argue that Gregor's family is transforming. Nonetheless, with the transformation of the family the relation towards Gregor changes. Ultimately, this change leads to a change in Gregor's social position. In other words, Gregor changes in a fundamental social way during the story. It is this social transformation that finally allows the family to kill one of its members. Again, the aim of this example is to show how aesthetic products can help us understand suffering and mechanisms that prevent the perception of suffering. In this case, we also address textual elements in a manner that does not involve a discourse analysis in the classical sense because we are not very interested in what is written in the text. Instead, we are interested here in the arguments that denounce the infliction of suffering towards others. These arguments are not presented explicitly but are communicated to the reader in another, aesthetic way. We are confronted by a discourse analysis of communication and arguments presented in an aesthetic form.

My argument is that to inflict harm, we can identify (and the reader does so intuitively) three moments of the family's metamorphosis. What

---

[11] This example was first presented with a different theoretical framing in Herzog and Hernàndez (2013).

transforms this analysis into a social analysis is that all three moments also exist in social reality. Moreover, my hypothesis is that Kafka's success both during his own time and now is grounded on the fact that the feelings of mechanism that enable the creation of suffering remain operative and present in our everyday life. The three mechanisms that impede the perception of the pain of the other are substitution, distortion, and generalization.

Substitution here means that what Gregor Samsa thinks is substituted by what his family says he thinks. For example, Gregor's mother says, "I'm sure he isn't well, he said this morning that he is, but he isn't" (ibid.). On the one hand, we can say that if communication is interrupted, there is a tendency to substitute the enunciations of the other by one's own enunciations. On the other hand, this type of substituting the speech of the other by one's own words is also a possibility of not having to engage in communication with the other. We know this mechanism from our own everyday experience: both when a person is declared incapacitated (such as persons with dementia or mental illness) and in political life, we often observe spokespersons, politicians, party leaders, and so on, speaking about what people "really" want. Instead of engaging in discourses *with* the people, those elites speak *about* the people. When thinking about Kafka, we surely should also mention the bureaucratic system that substitutes our words with words that are understandable and treatable by bureaucratic logics. It is these complaints about a lack of empathy that are most often directed at big bureaucracies.

The second mechanism used to emotionally distance oneself from the other is distortion of a person's intended meaning without the possibility of clarifying misunderstandings. As we have seen, communication is always ontologically distorted because two social actors never have the same "stream of consciousness" (Schütz). Thus, they never mean and understand in a manner that is exactly the same. However, the basic assumption of similarity permits one to continue communicating or explaining further what was meant in case one of the participants feels that there has been a misunderstanding. In *The Metamorphosis*, we can find several of these distortions. For example, the family repeatedly complains that Gregor did not understand them:

'If he could just understand us', said his father almost as a question; his sister shook her hand vigorously through her tears as a sign that of that there was no question.

'If he could just understand us', repeated Gregor's father, closing his eyes in acceptance of his sister's certainty that that was quite impossible, 'then perhaps we could come to some kind of arrangement with him. But as it is ...'

'It's got to go', shouted his sister, 'that's the only way, Father. You've got to get rid of the idea that that's Gregor. We've only harmed ourselves by believing it for so long. How can that be Gregor?' (ibid.)

The tragedy of this situation is immediately comprehended by the reader, who knows that Gregor is able to understand every single word spoken by his family. With Schütz, we now can understand that this is not a simple communication problem. Even with a person speaking a completely different language, we are able to communicate in a very basic manner. What is denied when refusing the principal possibility of understanding is that there is no similar "stream of consciousness" or what is the same, that the other person is either not human in the same way as we are or not human at all. This basic supposition that the other is a similar human being is blocked in the answer of the sister who denies that Gregor is himself, a human being, principally able to understand.

In our mass society, we know some of these mechanisms that impede participation. Newspapers and television are usually not open to interventions from those who feel misunderstood. Communication is unidirectional. There is no possibility of engaging in meta-discourses on "validity pretensions" as demanded by Habermas so that free discourses can lead to communicative understanding. Several groups, primarily those with little social power, have the ability to make themselves heard in mass media. This can lead, as in the case of Gregor Samsa, to the "othering" of people who do not belong to one's own group. "Othering" here does not only mean that others are constitutive for their own identity but that we make them distinct to us by distorting the communication between "them" and "us".

Generalization of naming is the third mechanism of creating an emotional distance that enables us to inflict harm on others. This process or metamorphosis of creating emotional distance by changing from the use of an individual name to a general and distant name is very clear in Kafka's text. Although in the first part, Gregor continues to be identified as the son Gregor, by the end the "person" has completely transformed into "object" and we can hear the cleaner saying "Well then, that thing in there, you needn't worry about how you're going to get rid of it. That's all been sorted out" (ibid.). The metamorphosis of naming from the son to "that thing" corresponds to an emotional and social transformation. Gregor is no longer the main supporter of the family but a disturbance to the others.

These mechanisms of the creation of distance through the use of general names is a well-researched field in the social sciences. For example, in research on migration (e.g., Herzog 2009) we can find that the more general and common the term used (such as "migrants" or "them" instead of "migrant" in singular, "neighbours", or the first name of a particular person), the more social distance is created and the more that speakers tend to engage in negative stigmatization of "the others".

What we can see in this example of a fictional story is the functioning of mechanisms of "discursive exclusion" (Herzog 2011), that is, mechanisms that exclude the other *from* discourses, *in* discourses, and materially, *through* discourses. Gregor is excluded from participating in the discourse that interprets the situation. Additionally, he is excluded through the discourse that is taking place in his family. He experiences a social change from Gregor, the son, to "that thing", and he is materially excluded, physically separated from his family, and finally killed. In other words, the analysis of the text leads not only to the analysis of what is said but also to what is done with words. This includes both the effects of the words and the practices of physical harm that would be impossible without the discursive mechanisms of exclusion. It is this feeling of exclusion in the modern, impersonal society that readers all over the world shared and that made Kafka's story a global bestseller.

What we took from Kafka was his extreme sensibility to the processes of de-personalization and the suffering created by these processes. The main critique of the use of such an approach as social critique would perhaps be that the translation of a societal critique was made by analogy and was *not* developed from an empirical analysis of the social world itself. However, by analogy and interpretation of the story of a very particular family as a modern-day tale about society, the social system could be criticized. It is exactly this analogy to social processes that converts the analysis of a fictional tale into *social* critique. This critique could be understood as immanent social critique: the norms stem from the family/society itself but are impossible to meet in the actual order.

In *The Metamorphosis*, the claim family members should love and care for each other is not fulfilled. The stability of the family system was only achieved by excluding Gregor. In modern, anonymous societies the claim that everybody is treated as an individual human being with specific needs is not fulfilled. The success of modern social systems is achieved through the use of enormous impersonal bureaucratic structures. The critique here is that society is not the *Gemeinschaft*, the community of close peers; instead, it is the *Gesellschaft*, the abstract society that refrains from recognizing a particular human being. As sociologists we know this complaint too well, not only from Tönnies's famous distinction between *Gemeinschaft* and *Gesellschaft* but also from other early sociologists who worried about the negative aspects of modern societies (e.g., Simmel 1957). Indeed, this remains a problem for sociologists and social philosophers, whether modern society can be organized to offer the cosy warmth of a family or whether those attempts would inevitably lead to totalitarian ideologies of strong communities. In this case, the only way out would be to favour psychologically strong individuals who can address "Civilization and Its Discontents" (Freud 2002) or the *Uneasiness in Culture*, which is the literal translation of Freud's classical work. In other words, *The Metamorphosis* points to a fundamental, structural problem of modern societies and thus, social critique based on that work would necessarily have a fundamental and probably transcendent character.

These final reflections from a sociological perspective should have made clear that artists are not the better social scientists. They are often better able to express and access pre-linguistic knowledge about social processes. However, we still need the sociologically informed critic for two reasons. First, we must express the implicit social critique of art with words that have the ability to relate to ongoing social discussions. Even more important, we must analyse the structural and practical possibilities of overcoming the criticized situation. Like the fact that suffering can be ideological (someone can suffer from having to share public transport with people of other races), suffering expressed through art should not be uncritically used for social change. Instead, we must consider not only the possibilities but also the consequences of certain social changes. However, if we are unsure about the epistemological status of aesthetic products or if we do not want to rely on others' empathic perception, we can also perform a more traditional—but inevitably sociological—discourse analysis to formulate social critique.

References

Adorno, T. W. (2009) *Ästhetik (1958/59). Nachgelassene Schriften, Abteilung IV: Vorlesungen, Vol 3,* (Frankfurt/Main: Suhrkamp).

Angermuller, J., Nonhoff, M., Herschinger, E., Macgilchrist, F., Reisigl, M., Wedl, J., Wrana, D. & Ziem, A. (eds.) (2014) *Diskursforschung. Ein interdisziplinäres Handbuch*, 2 vols. (Bielefeld: transcript).

Balibar, E., & Wallerstein, I. (1991) *Raza, nación y clase*, (Madrid: IEPLA).

Bourdieu, P. (2000) The Weight of the World: Social Suffering in Contemporary Societies, (Stanford: University Press).

Bourdieu, P. (1984) *Distinction – A Social Critique of the Judgement of Taste*, (New York: Routledge).

Bubenhofer, N. & Scharloth, J. (2013) 'Korpuslinguistische Diskursanalyse: Der Nutzen empirisch-quantitativer Verfahren', in: Warnke, I., Meinhoff, U. & Reisigl, M. (eds.) *Diskurslinguistik im Spannungsfeld von Deskription und Kritik,* (Berlin: Akademie-Verlag), p. 147–168

Butler, J. (2001) 'What is Critique? An Essay on Foucault's Virtue', in: *eipcp – european institute on progressive cultural policies*, online resource available at http://eipcp.net/transversal/0806/butler/en.

Chamie & Mirkin (2011) 'Same-Sex Marriage: A New Social Phenomenon', *Population and Development Review* 37(3): 529–551.

Christman, J. (1991). 'Self-ownership, equality, and the structure of property rights', *Political Theory*, 19(1): 28-46.

Cohen, G. A. (1995) *Self-ownership, Freedom and Equality,* (Cambridge: Cambridge University Press).

Cox, R. (2013) 'Recognition and Immigration', in: O'Neill, S. & Smith, N. H. (eds). *Recognition Theory as social research. Investigating the Dynamics of Social Conflict* (Houndmills: Palgrave Macmillan), pp. 192–212.

Diaz-Bone, R. (2005) 'Zur Methodologisierung der Foucaultschen Diskursanalyse', *Forum: Qualitative Social Research* 7(1).
Elmgren, H. (2015) 'Recognition and the ideology of merit', *Studies in Social & Political Thought*, 25.
Eskridge, W. N. (2002) *Equality Practice: Civil Unions and the Future of Gay Rights* (New York: Routledge).
Ferrer, A., Hernàndez, F. & Herzog, B. (2011) 'Hacia una estética del reconocimiento. La culminación den Rembrandt y el enigma de Goya', *Archivo del Arte Valenciano*, 02: 143–154.
Foucault, M. (1975) *Discipline and Punish: the Birth of the Prison*, (New York: Random House).
Foucault, M. (2007) *The politics of truth*, (Los Angeles: Semiotext(e)).
Freud, S. (2002) *Civilization and Its Discontents*, (London: Penguin).
Fraser, N. & Honneth, A. (2003) *Redistribution or Recognition? A Political-Philosophical Exchange*, (London: Verso).
Girardot, D. (2011) *La société du mérite – Ideologie méritocratique & violence néoliberale*, (Lormont: Bord de l'Eau).
Graeber, D. (2013) 'On the Phenomenon of Bullshit Jobs', *Strike Magazin*, August 17.
Gutiérrez-Rodríguez, E. (2007) 'Reading Affect—On the Heterotopian Spaces of Care and Domestic Work in Private Households', *Forum: Qualitative Social Research*, 8(2). http://nbn-resolving.de/urn:nbn:de:0114-fqs0702118.
Harding, R. (2008) *Regulating Sexuality: Legal Consciousness in Lesbian and Gay Lives*, (New York: Routledge).
Heinich, N. & Shapiro, R. (2012) *De l'artification. Enquêtes sur le passage à l'art*, (Paris: Éditions de l'EHSS).
Herzog, B. (2008). 'Arbeit, work, trabajo... - Kulturelle, politisch und ökonomische Aspekte des Arbeitsbegriffes in *Europa' UTOPIEkreativ*, 2, 144-156.
Herzog, B. (2009) *Exclusión discursiva – el imaginario social sobre inmigración y drogas*, (Valencia: PUV).
Herzog, B.(2011) 'Exclusión Discursiva - hacia un nuevo concepto de la exclusión social', *Revista Internacional de Sociología*, 69(3): 607–626.
Herzog, B. (2015) 'Recognition in Multicultural Societies. Intergroup relations as second-order recognition', *Revista Internacional de Sociología*, 73(2).
Herzog, B. (2016c) 'Los desprecios del régimen migratorio - Hacia una Teoría Crítica de las migraciones', in: unpublished manuscript
Herzog, B., Bernad, J. C., Hernàndez, F., Obiol, S. & Villar, A. (2013) 'Should I Stay or Should I Go? Analysis of Biographic Strategies of University Students

in Spain', presentation at the congress of the European Sociological Association: *Crisis, critique and change*, Torino, September 2013.

Herzog, B. & Hernàndez, F. (2009) 'Honneth vs. Sloterdijk – Duelo sobre el futuro del mundo', *Posdata, supplement of the newspaper Levante-EMV*, 6 November.

Herzog, B. & Hernàndez, F. (2013), 'Un ejemplo de Sociología del Desprecio y Exclusión Discursiva: La Metamorfosis de la Familia según Kafka', *International and Multidisciplinary Journal of Social Sciences*, 2 (2): 198–217.

Herzog, B., Pecourt, J. & Hernàndez, F. (2015) 'La dialéctica de la excelencia académica. De la evaluación a la medición de la actividad científica', *Arxius de Ciències Socials*, 33: 69–82.

Hirsch, J. (2001) *El Estado nacional de competencia. Estado, democracia y política en el capitalismo global*, (México: Universidad Autónoma Metropolitana).

Honneth, A. (1995b) *The fragmented world of the social: Essays in social and political philosophy*, (New York: New York Press).

Honneth, A. (2005) 'Eine Physiognomie der kapitalistischen Lebensform. Skizze der Gesellschaftstheorie Adornos', in: Axel Honneth (ed.) *Dialektik der Freiheit. Frankfurter Adorno-Konferenz 2003*, (Frankfurt a. M.: Suhrkamp).

Honneth, A. (2009) 'Fataler Tiefsinn aus Karlsruhe. Zum neuesten Schrifttum des Peter Sloterdijk', *Die Zeit*, 24. September.

Honneth, A. (2011a) *Das Recht der Freiheit*, (Berlin: Suhrkamp).

Honneth, A. (2011b) 'Conversación con Axel Honneth', in: ibid. *La sociedad del desprecio*, (Madrid: Trotta).

Honneth, A. (2015). *Die Idee des Sozialismus*, (Berlin: Suhrkamp).

Honoré, A. (1987) *Making Law Bind*, (Oxford: Clarendon Press).

Human Rights Watch (2009) *Together, Apart - Organizing around Sexual Orientation and Gender Identity Worldwide*, online resource available at http://www.hrw.org/sites/default/files/reports/lgbt0509webwcover.pdf.

Ikäheimo, H. (2002) 'On the Genus and Species of Recognition', *Inquiry*, 45: 447–462.

Jaeggi, R. (2014a) *Kritik von Lebensformen*, (Berlin: Suhrkamp).

Jaeggi, R. (2015) 'Objektive Kritik und Krise. Überlegungen zu einer materialistischen Grundlegung von Sozialkritik', in: Martin, D., Martin, S. & Wissel, J. (eds.) *Perspektiven und Konstellationen kritischer Theorie*, (Münster: Westfälisches Dampfboot), pp. 14–28.

Jenkins, F. (2013) 'Singing the Post-Discrimination Blues: Notes for a Critique of Academic Meritocracy', in: Hutchinson, K. & Jenkins, F. (eds.) *Women in philosophy – What needs to change?*, (Oxford & New York: Oxford University Press).

Kafka, F. (2002) *The Metamorphosis*, available at: https://www.gutenberg.org/files/5200/5200-h/5200-h.htm

Keller, R. (2005b) 'Analysing Discourse. An Approach From the Sociology of Knowledge', *Forum: Qualitative Social Research*, 6(3).

Keller, R. (2005b) *Wissenssoziologische Diskursanalyse – Grundlegung eines Forschungsprogrammes*, (Wiesbaden: Verlag für Sozialwissenschaften).

Keller, R. (2012) *Doing Discourse Research: An Introduction for Social Scientists*, (London: SAGE).

Kitzinger, C. & Wilkinson, S. (2004) 'The re-branding of marriage: Why we got married instead of registering a civil partnership', *Feminism & psychology*, 14(1): 127–150.

Kontos, M. (2014) 'Recognition dynamics in a misrecognised job. Domestic and Care Work of Migrant Women in Europe' *IfS Working Paper*, 4.

Kracauer, S (1995) 'The Mass Ornament', in: (ibid.) *The Mass Ornament: Weimar Essays*, (Cambridge/London: Harvard University Press), pp. 75–88.

Locke, J. (1960) *Two Treatises of Government,* (Cambridge: University Press).

Lüders, C. & Meuser, M. (1997) 'Deutungsmusteranalyse' in: Hitzler, R. & Honer, A. (eds.) *Sozialwissenschaftliche Hermeneutik. Eine Einführung*, (Opladen: Leske + Budrich, UTB).

McNamee, S. & Miller, R. (2009) *The meritocracy myth*, (Plymouth: Rowman and Littlefield Publishers).

Marx, K. (1972) *Critique of the Gotha Programme,* (Peking: Foreign Language Press).

Nozick, R. (1974) *Anarchy, State and Utopia*, (Oxford: Blackwell).

Oevermann, U. (2001) 'Die Struktur sozialer Deutungsmuster –Versuch einer Aktualisierung', *Sozialer Sinn*, 1: 35–81.

Reisigl, M. & Wodak, R. (2001) *Discourse and Discrimination. Rhetorics of Racism and Antisemitism,* (London: Routledge).

Renault, E. (2009) 'The political philosophy of social suffering', in de Bruin, B & Zurn, C. (eds.), *New Waves in Political Philosophy*, (Houndsmill: Palgrave Macmillan).

Rodriguez de Liévana, G. M., Saint Rodríguez, P., Romero García, E., Celis Sánches, R. & Lasa Fernàndez, L. (2013) *¿Qué hacemos con las fronteras?*, (Madrid: Akal).

Ruiz Ruiz, J. (2009) 'Análisis sociológico del discurso: Métodos y lógicas' *Forum: Qualitative Social Research*, 10(2).

Simmel, G. (1957) 'Die Großstädt und das Geistesleben' in: Landmann, M. & Susman, M. (eds.) *Brücke und Tür. Essays des Philosophen zur Geschichte, Religion, Kunst und Gesellschaft,* (Stuttgart: K.F. Köhler).

Spinoza, B. (1988) *Correspondencia*, (Madrid: Alianza).
Stahl, T (2013b) *Immanente Kritik. Elemente einer Theorie sozialer Praktiken*, (Frankfurt M./New York: Campus).
Strauss, A. & Corbin, J. (1998) *Basics of Qualitative Research: Techniques and Procedures for Developing Grounded Theory*, (Thousand Oaks: SAGE).
UN (2013) 'Countries must repeal laws that discriminate against LGBT individuals', *UN News Centre* – Online Resource available at http://www.un.org/apps/news/story.asp?NewsID=44931&Cr=discrimination&Cr1=#.UaSOWNiXlpw 17 May.
Viehöver, W (2001) 'Diskurse als Narration', in: Keller, R., Hirseland, A., Schneider, W. & Viehöver, W. (Eds.) (2001) *Handbuch Sozialwissenschaftliche Diskursanlyse Bd. 1: Theorien und Methoden, (Opladen: VS-Verlag)*.
Wallerstein, I. (1979) *The capitalist world economy*, (London: USW).
Wood, L. & Kroger, R. (2000) *Doing Discourse Analysis Methods for Studying Action in Talk and Text*, (Thousand Oaks: SAGE).
Zurn, C. (2013) 'Misrecognition, Marriage and Derecognition', in: O'Neill, S. & Smith, N., (eds.) *Recognition Theory as Social Research: Investigating the Dynamics of Social Conflict*, (Houndmills: Palgrave Macmillan), pp. 63–86.

4

Conclusions

There is no easy way to perform social critique. Although we often experience a general feeling of social and political apathy, it is quite common to feel outraged (Hessel 2011). Although moral indignation about injustice can be a good starting point, it can never be an end in itself, nor can it replace analysis. For many students and scholars, indignation is indeed a reason to conduct social research. However, there remains important intellectual and practical work to be performed to elaborate social critique, to ground it in society via empirical social research, and to consider the possibilities of its realization via theoretical reflections.

Critique is not a task that can be done once and then be considered as forever accomplished. Critique is a process of social learning. As in every real learning process, the learner changes substantially during the critique process. In contrast to a simple accumulation of knowledge, a real learning process changes the learner's mental structures and makes her a different person. In the same way, social learning changes society's structure and therefore its form of social reproduction. However, the norms and values, claims and expectancies, and the very understanding of the same norms change together with society. What society once thought was good must be reconsidered in light of both its own success and new social developments. For example, the growing consciousness of the finitude of natural resources and the possibility and reality of human-made ecologic disasters force societies to rethink their development ideals.

If society changes both with and without critique, it would be presumptuous to attempt to offer an elaborated end point of critique because it will be impossible to foresee all of the social and technical developments that will continue to confront humanity with new challenges. Offering a clear vision of a socially emancipated society would also be failing to seriously consider the need to anchor social critique in the (at least implicit) normative claims of society itself. Once more, only the vision of a particular critic or group of critics would be represented. However, anchoring critique in real, existing society is not the same thing as attempting to coincide critique with society's self-description. Societies and its individuals can be racist, sexist, despotic, cruel, and so on. The critic is not replaceable with the apparently expressed desire of society. The existing discourse is already a result of a process of powerful structuring—that is, it is an ordered discourse that plays its own role in the social reproduction of society as it exists. Moreover, that discourse has a deformed relation with social reality. On the one hand, the public discourse can deny the existence of alternatives to existing social reproduction, thus limiting the thought and expression of normative claims. On the other hand, the new populist discourses are often especially likely to confound the will to change with the actual possibilities of change, thus failing to consider systemic resistance.

This is where the social critic comes into play. Her work is to uncover the normative content both in discourses and in non-discursive reality. As we have seen, even practices and materialities can be analysed discursively as structured, meaningful entities. Therefore, on the one hand, we must explicitly formulate implicit normative claims and assumptions. On the other hand, we must show the structural or systemic reasons for claims not being fulfilled. Therefore, the critic makes clear that this (sometimes) does not require a simple act of will but a real fundamental or transcending change. By giving back this insight, moral indignation can become more directed and lead to the situation being overcome. Thus, the circle of suffering, indignation, and change can be eventually completed.

I am speaking of circle here not in the sense of a never-ending story but in the sense of the learning process. A new situation will make people see other types of socially produced suffering, requiring additional social critique. Perhaps, although the line from suffering to indignation to critique repeats itself, we could better speak of a spiral which underlines that although there is a circular moment, we can perceive a certain type of development. As Jaeggi (2014a) notes, what can be said about development is that it should not close the door to future changes/learning processes/developments. Instead, every change should enable an experimental learning process. Social progress should broaden, not limit our possibilities (on that point, see also Graeber 2015).

The reason for the need for social critique is the existence of human suffering. Suffering is not only about domination among humans that produces suffering; instead, it is about domination *over* humans in general. This includes all types of structural or impersonal domination by a systemic logic (Jaeggi 2015) that produces suffering. At the very core of social suffering, there are often mechanisms of silencing or "language theft" (Honneth). Suffering "often implies destruction of communities rather than solidarity" (Renault 2009: 168). Discourse Analysis as Social Critique therefore makes it possible for the silent voice of suffering to be heard.

Social critique, therefore, is not a passion of the head—it is the head of compassion for all those who suffer in this society. It is a compassion that not only is accompanied by profound theoretical knowledge about society's reproduction logics but also enables us to understand suffering as part of that process of social reproduction. We also need complex instruments to analyse rapidly changing societies, including their needs, claims, and implicit normativity. Discourse analysis offers us a very useful toolbox for a structured and joint analysis of discourses and other structured, meaningful elements of the social. Discourse theory can provide important insights into the relation of these elements. Finally, Critical Theory can help us understand the need to advance the analysis further so that it becomes real, transcending immanent critique. Alone, neither of these parts is sufficient. Since the beginning, Critical Theory has been acutely aware of the needs of empirical studies, although it always experienced problems in systematically integrating those needs into its work. Discourse studies, although partly understanding itself as critical, seemed to have problems in socially grounding and therefore in systematically justifying its normative claims. The aim of this book was to offer both practical and theoretical tools to bridge the gap between discourse analysis and social critique. The task of social change, however, is both theoretical and substantially practical.

References

Graeber, D. (2015) *The utopia of rules. On Technology, Stupidity, and the Secret Joys of Bureaucracy,* (London: Melville House).
Hessel, S. (2011) *Time for outrage!,* (London: Charles Glass).
Jaeggi, R. (2014a) *Kritik von Lebensformen*, (Berlin: Suhrkamp).
Jaeggi, R. (2015) 'Objektive Kritik und Krise. Überlegungen zu einer materialistischen Grundlegung von Sozialkritik', in: Martin, D., Martin, S. & Wissel, J. (eds.) *Perspektiven und Konstellationen kritischer Theorie*, (Münster: Westfälisches Dampfboot), pp. 14–28.
Renault, E. (2009) 'The political philosophy of social suffering', in de Bruin, B & Zurn, C. (eds.), *New Waves in Political Philosophy*, (Houndsmill: Palgrave Macmillan).

Index

A

Abraham (and Isaac), 178–81, 183
Action (social), 49, 68, 76
Actors (social), 38, 49, 53, 72, 74, 82, 84, 88, 95–101, 107, 115, 119, 136, 138, 166, 170, 171, 185
Adorno, Theodor W., 12, 15, 39–43, 46, 60, 115, 163, 168–9, 170, 172, 176
Aesthetics, 135, 169–73, 182
Arendt, Hannah, 42, 142n1
Alienation, 15, 42, 109
Angermuller, Johannes, 52, 90, 174
Art, 1–2, 10, 16, 23, 43, 54, 76, 115, 135, 172, 173, 177, 188
Autonomy, 2, 3, 46, 48, 55, 56, 117, 141, 142

B

Bauer, Bruno, 14–15, 23
Berger, Peter L., 54, 68
Boltanski, Luc, 45, 50, 86, 109
Bourdieu, Pierre, 36n5, 120, 169, 173
Bührmann, Andrea, 52, 54, 90, 112
Butler, Judith, 12, 20, 57, 58, 167, 169

C

Capital
 cultural capital, 35, 51, 98, 123
 economic capital, 36, 145, 154
Capitalism, 2, 13, 16, 29, 30, 36, 48, 94, 106, 145, 155
Change, 4–7, 11, 14, 19, 21, 22, 26, 28, 32, 33, 35, 38, 39, 41,

Note: Page numbers followed by "n" denote notes.

Change (*cont.*)
43, 44, 48, 49, 56, 59, 87, 89, 90, 92, 94, 95, 98, 100, 101, 104, 106, 110–11, 114, 115, 118, 120, 121, 125–7, 136, 142, 145–6, 151, 152, 155, 156, 161, 162, 167–70, 179, 184, 187, 195–8

Comunitarism, 25, 26

Contradictions, 9, 28, 49, 114, 115, 166, 168

Critical Theory, 1, 7, 9, 32, 43, 46, 67, 76, 113–16, 169, 197

Critique
  critique as social practice, 1–12
  external critique, 23, 24, 57, 107
  functional critique, 11, 29, 31
  Immanent critique
    hermeneutic immanent critique, 34, 37
    practice-based immanent critique, 38, 44, 76, 147, 154–5
  internal critique, 28, 113
  procedural approach to critique, 24, 29, 31
  social critique, 4, 5, 8, 12–28, 42, 44, 45, 50–3, 58–60, 67, 73–6, 80, 85–91, 101, 103, 105, 107, 109, 110, 113–19, 121, 126–8, 133–5, 142–3, 145, 147, 148, 151–2, 154–8, 160, 161, 162–70, 173, 178, 182, 183n10, 187, 188, 195–7

D

Democracy, 34, 35, 54, 101, 106, 110

Discourse
  critical discourse analysis, 1, 53–8
  discourse analysis, 1, 28, 38, 51–8, 67–75, 80–1, 85, 88–91, 94, 95, 99–102, 105, 106, 110–17, 121–8, 133–7, 143–7, 152, 154, 158, 160–9, 176, 178, 182, 184, 189, 197
  discourse-historical approach, 56
  discourse theory, 54n9, 60, 68, 72, 81, 82, 84, 91, 93, 100, 112, 147, 197

Dispositive, 112
  dispositive analysis, 112

Disrespect, 19, 46–53, 60, 76, 86, 87, 116, 117, 145–51, 153, 154, 169–71, 173, 177

Domination, 10, 16, 42, 106–11, 128, 197

Drugs, 110

E

Empirical deficit. *See* Sociological deficit

Exclusion, 3, 57–8, 83, 85, 93, 99, 100, 118, 123–7, 147, 149, 164, 173, 182, 187

F

Fairclough, Norman, 53–5, 70, 74, 99

Feuerbach, Ludwig, 5, 9, 12, 14–17

Foucault, Michel, 1–3, 9, 10, 12, 16, 17, 26, 27, 32, 44, 45, 49–52, 54, 56–9, 67–9, 81, 88, 90, 92, 96, 102, 104, 107–12, 115–17, 144, 167, 169, 176, 182
Frankfurt, Harry, 4, 5
Frankfurt School, 32, 37–53, 54n9, 60, 135, 172
Freud, Sigmund, 10n2, 170, 188

G

Graeber, David, 101, 106, 138, 197
Guidelines for discourse analysis as social critique, 134, 162–9

H

Habermas, Jürgen, 26, 27, 39, 43–6, 54, 59n10, 60, 86, 169, 186
Hegel, Georg W. F., 8, 9, 14, 15, 39, 40, 43, 46, 152, 161, 172
Honneth, Axel, 25, 31, 33–5, 39, 45–51, 60, 85–7, 101, 115, 116, 128, 136, 137, 147, 149, 152–4, 156, 159, 161, 164, 167, 169–72, 174, 197
Horkheimer, Max, 7–9, 11, 39–43, 46, 60, 169
Human rights, 23, 56, 57, 59, 153, 157, 158

I

Identity, 96–9, 105, 112, 118, 120, 124, 139, 158, 186

Ideology, 17, 18, 41, 50, 72, 74, 87, 102–7, 109, 142, 142n1
Inclusion, 83, 85, 93, 123n4, 173–8
Indignation. *See* outrage

J

Jaeggi, Rahel, 29, 30, 59, 80, 94, 145, 156, 167, 197

K

Kafka, Franz, 135, 173, 184–9
Keller, Reiner, 52, 54, 60, 67, 69, 81, 90, 103, 105, 112, 165, 166
Knowledge, 9, 20, 38–43, 52, 54, 58, 68, 70–5, 84, 91, 102–9, 111, 113, 120, 124, 125, 126, 128, 143, 145, 147, 163, 172, 175, 188, 195, 197
Kracauer, Siegfried, 39, 172

L

Labour, 19, 35, 76, 136–9, 141, 142, 144, 153, 154, 174, 177
Laclau, Ernesto, 70–2, 74, 80, 91, 96, 128
Left Hegelianism, 32
Legitimation, 105
Locke, John, 136
Luckmann, Thomas, 54, 68
Luhmann, Niklas, 44
Lukács, György, 18, 19, 41, 103, 172

M

Marx, Karl, 5–8, 12, 14–18, 20, 32, 33, 36, 40, 41, 60, 137, 145, 168, 169
Materiality, 17, 71, 91–5, 112, 124, 126, 142–5, 176
Meaning, 10, 15, 27, 37, 68, 70, 72–82, 84, 87, 89, 91, 93, 97, 111, 123, 124, 164, 167, 185
Merit, 35–8, 136–40, 142n1, 143–6, 149, 153, 154
Metamorphosis, 135, 173, 184–8
Migration, 123–5, 134, 147–55, 187
Misrecognition. *See* disrespect
Mouffe, Chantal, 70–4, 80, 96, 128

N

Non-discursive realities, 69–75, 80, 91, 111–17, 164, 165, 170
Norms
    normative order, 26
    normative reconstruction, 50
    normative surplus, 34, 36, 97, 113, 145
    normativity, 76, 86, 101, 111, 121, 172, 178, 197

O

Outrage, 195

P

Post-structuralism, 44, 54, 75, 102
Power, 2, 3, 6, 10, 12, 15, 16, 19, 20, 32, 40–2, 45, 52–6, 71, 72, 74, 81, 84, 91, 92, 97, 106–12, 119, 120, 125, 128, 155, 156, 164, 181, 186
Practices, 3, 6, 7, 10–12, 20, 23, 29, 33, 36–39, 41–44, 46, 48, 50, 52, 53, 56, 58–60, 70–101, 105–106, 109–13, 116, 117, 118–20, 122-8, 134, 139, 147–56, 165–168, 170, 172, 173, 176, 177, 181, 187, 196
practice of critique, 7. *see also* Critique, critique as social practice

R

Racism, 21, 29, 89, 126, 148
Rawls, John, 25
Recognition, 14, 35, 39, 40, 46–53, 59, 76, 86, 87, 116, 117, 135, 138, 143, 146–57, 159–61, 169–89
Religion, 6, 14–17, 19, 23, 25, 110, 158
Rembrandt, 135, 173, 178, 179, 180, 182–184
Rosa, Hartmut, 28

S

Same-sex partnerships, 157, 160–2
Schneider, Werner, 52, 54, 90, 112
Schütz, Alfred, 67, 68, 77, 185, 186
Searle, John, 69
Self-ownership, 139, 140–2
Self-relation, 47, 48, 153
Social pathology, 48, 148, 162, 171
Social reproduction, 114, 135, 138, 145–6, 156, 160–3, 167, 195–7

Social structure, 2, 5, 7, 8, 748,
  52, 60, 67, 71, 72, 74,
  75, 80, 89, 95, 96, 106,
  108, 113, 115, 118–22,
  128, 134, 141, 142, 155,
  167, 168
Sociological deficit
  of first generation of critical
    theory, 39
  of Habermas, 39, 43–5, 48, 51–3
  of immanent critique, 39, 50, 89
  of recognition Theory, 50–3
Sociology of Critique, 50
Sociology of Knowledge
  sociology of knowledge approach
    on discourse, 52, 68, 102,
    105
Spinoza, Baruch, 179
Stahl, Titus, 22, 28, 32–4, 37, 38,
  49, 76, 147
Stirner, Max, 14, 16–18
Structuralism, 44, 52, 54, 75, 102
Structure. *See* Social structure
Struggle, 39–41, 47, 53, 88, 90, 104,
  113, 135, 147–54, 169, 170,
  173–5, 177–9, 182, 183
Subjectivation, 58, 96, 100
Subjectivities, 95–101
Suffering, 11, 21, 48–52, 60, 86,
  115–17, 135, 136, 145, 146,
  163, 164, 168–72, 176,
  178–85, 187–9, 196, 197
Symbolic order, 52, 95, 102, 166

Taylor, Charles, 26, 32, 110
Theory of Communicative Action,
  26, 43–5, 49, 51. *See also*
  Habermas, Jürgen

Utopia, 24

Van Dijk, Teun, 53, 56, 57, 70, 107,
  168

Wallerstein, Immanuel, 155n5
Walzer, Michael, 26
Weber, Max, 76–78, 107, 108
Wodak, Ruth, 28, 53, 54, 56, 70,
  147
Work. *See* Labour
Working class, 26, 36, 39, 41–3, 99,
  103

Young Hegelians, 14–17

Žižek, Slavoj, 103

The manufacturer's authorised representative in the EU is Springer Nature Customer Service Centre GmbH, Europaplatz 3, 69115 Heidelberg, Germany. If you have any concerns regarding our products, please contact ProductSafety@springernature.com

Printed and bound by CPI Group (UK) Ltd, Croydon, CR0 4YY

23/03/2026

02076682-0001